T0330429

Managing Food Safety and Hygiene

To Esther

Managing Food Safety and Hygiene

Governance and Regulation as Risk Management

Bridget M. Hutter

Professor of Risk Regulation, Department of Sociology, London School of Economics and Political Science, UK

with Research Assistance from Clive Jones

Edward Elgar
Cheltenham, UK • Northampton, MA, USA

© Bridget M. Hutter 2011

All rights reserved. No part of this publication may be reproduced, stored in a retrieval system or transmitted in any form or by any means, electronic, mechanical or photocopying, recording, or otherwise without the prior permission of the publisher.

Published by
Edward Elgar Publishing Limited
The Lypiatts
15 Lansdown Road
Cheltenham
Glos GL50 2JA
UK

Edward Elgar Publishing, Inc.
William Pratt House
9 Dewey Court
Northampton
Massachusetts 01060
USA

A catalogue record for this book
is available from the British Library

Library of Congress Control Number: 2011926847

ISBN 978 0 85793 570 0 (cased)

Typeset by Cambrian Typesetters, Camberley, Surrey
Printed and bound by MPG Books Group, UK

Contents

Figures and tables

FIGURES

TABLES

Abbreviations

BHA: British Hospitality and Restaurant Association
BRC: British Retail Consortium
BSE: Bovine Spongiform Encephalopathy
CIEH: Chartered Institute for Environmental Health
CIEHO: Chartered Institute for Environmental Health Officers
DEFRA: Department for Environment, Food and Rural Affairs
DTI: Department of Trade and Industry
EFSA: European Food Safety Authority
EHO: Environmental Health Officer
FAO: Food and Agriculture Organization of the United Nations
FSA: Food Standards Agency
FSB: Federation of Small Businesses
GMO: Genetically Modified Organism
GVA: Gross Value Added
HACCP: Hazard Analysis Critical Control Point
HAZOP: Hazard and Operability Studies
HPA: Health Protection Agency
IFD: Indigenous Foodborne Disease
IGD: Institute of Grocery Distribution
IIDS: Infectious Intestinal Diseases
IoD: Institute of Directors
LACORS: Local Authorities Coordinators of Regulatory Services
LACOTS: Local Authorities Coordinators of Trading Standards
LGA: Local Government Association
MAFF: Ministry of Agriculture, Fisheries and Food
MHS: Meat Hygiene Service
NAO: National Audit Office
NCC: National Consumer Council
NFU: National Farmers Union
NGO: Non-Governmental Organization
SME: Small and Medium-sized Enterprise
TSO: Trading Standards Officer
UN: United Nations

vCJD: Creutzfeldt-Jakob Disease
WHO: World Health Organization
WTO: World Trade Organization

Preface

I have been researching various aspects of risk governance since the late 1970s, first examining views from the perspective of regulatory inspectors and then researching business responses to state regulation. The research presented in this book extends the focus to encompass non-state sources of regulation. It considers the relative importance of state regulation alongside other influences on business risk management. This further develops our sociological and socio-legal understandings of the social control of economic life in contemporary society. There are many gaps in our knowledge of how risk regulation works in practice. This book goes some way towards filling these gaps but as I have developed this research it has become clear that some areas of non-state regulation demand much closer empirical scrutiny. This is important for the development of theory and also to inform policy making and business decision making.

The particular area selected for this research is one that affects each and every one of us, namely, the regulation of food safety and food hygiene risks. This connects back with my earliest research to the extent that it once again considers part of the governance system implemented by local authority environmental health officers in the UK (Hutter 1988). But it does this by following a series of food crises in the late 1980s/1990s which radically changed part of the UK risk regulation regime for food safety and hygiene yet left local authority enforcement largely untouched. Many of the policy lessons emerging from this book are very similar to those arising from my earlier work.

There are also lessons which may be useful to other regulatory regimes, in the UK, the European Union (EU) and beyond. Food safety and hygiene are global issues and the regulatory problems encountered within the UK are replicated across numerous regimes. This has been underlined by the responses to presentations I have given on this research in many different countries, which in turn have helped to shape this book. My hope is that this research will contribute to broader understandings of how to manage the risks generated within contemporary societies. I hope to contribute to an improved understanding of the place of regulation in managing these risks, and also of the role and limits of state activities such as regulatory law. Important here is an appreciation of how varying social, economic and political situations may influence the governance of risk. In particular, researchers need to examine those features of risk regulation which seem to cross boundaries and also scrutinize the limits of transferability and generalization across domains, regions and cultures.

Research such as this is always a product of the broader intellectual environments we work in and the support of key people. This research would not have been possible without the very generous funding of the Michael Peacock Charitable Trust which supported my chair at the London School of Economics (LSE) and this research for five years. Michael Peacock also provided unstinting intellectual and moral support to the Centre for Analysis of Risk and Regulation (CARR) at the LSE and this was invaluable in setting up CARR and sustaining it in its early years. This research was undertaken while I was Director of CARR and colleagues there provided a vibrant intellectual environment within which to work. I am grateful to them and especially to Mike Power. The Economic and Social Research Council (ESRC) should also be mentioned for facilitating this environment by providing crucial centre funding for a decade, funding which helped to establish risk regulation studies in the UK and abroad.

Clive Jones should be singled out as a co-researcher at the data collection phase. Clive took much of the responsibility for managing the data collection and its analysis. Without his efficiency and persistence the participation of practitioners in the study would not have been as high as it was. His management skills are excellent and this study is a true testimony to this. Attila Szanto has assisted with this project throughout, helping with data queries, bibliographic and literature searches and the preparation of the manuscript for publication. As always his meticulous attention to detail has been invaluable. Sally Lloyd-Bostock and Clive Briault gave up precious time to read drafts of the manuscript, and their useful comments were very much appreciated.

This study could not have been undertaken without the involvement of the many individuals and businesses from the food sector who participated. Time in the food retail and hospitality sectors is precious and I am very grateful to those who found the time to talk to us and complete the survey. There are many people in the industry who are dedicated to high-risk management standards and many of them expressed the wish that research such as this could help to promote and sustain high standards. I sincerely hope that this research does indeed help to achieve this.

As always my family offered enormous support. Food is dear to them all and I sincerely hope that studies such as these can help promote high standards of risk management in food safety and food hygiene both in the UK and abroad. Each of my children has been promised a dedicated book and this one is for Esther.

Bridget M. Hutter
January 2011

Introduction: setting the scene

This book discusses a topic that touches us all, namely, food safety and food hygiene. We all have to eat and we are all to some extent dependent on others to ensure that the food we eat does not harm us. Modern food chains are complex. Food is big business and it is a truly global business. The food we buy in our supermarkets, corner shops, restaurants and cafes may have travelled thousands of miles before it reaches us. It may also have been handled by a chain of people upon whom we rely to ensure that the produce we receive is safe. Food is not only a significant part of our economy and our social lives, it also has profound significance for our wellbeing (see Chapter 2). In this book we focus on two major sectors of the food chain, food retailing and food hospitality, and we examine one food governance regime, namely, that pertaining to food safety and food hygiene.

RISK

This book is about risk, in particular the prevention of the risks associated with food safety/hygiene. There have been a number of very high profile food risk disasters in the lifetime of readers of this book, for example, the bovine spongiform encephalopathy (BSE) crisis and cases of *E. coli* fatalities (see Chapter 4). But the most common manifestations of food safety/hygiene risks are low level and undramatic episodes, typically upset stomachs leading to a day or two off work. These are events which may not even be traced back to food, while the effects may occur within hours or take days to appear and thus there may be uncertainty about the cause of the illness. The ill-effects also depend upon our general state of health, with some vulnerable groups being at high risk and generally healthy people left relatively unaffected (see Chapter 3). Overall, however, the cumulative effects of these episodes may be very costly to our health systems and most particularly to economic productivity and happiness.

The causes of these episodes are often routine and mundane in their origin. These are not high-tech failures. They can often be traced back to low key failures such as food handlers not washing their hands before touching food, or failing to separate cooked and uncooked meats, or not checking food storage temperatures and sell by dates. Our concern in this book is on the governance systems in place to protect us from the risks to which we are involuntarily exposed by others who handle the food they sell to us in the retail and catering sectors in the UK. In particular, we focus on the understandings of risk and risk governance held by those within the industry and governance regime rather than impose formal definitions of risk on respondents.

RISK REGULATION/GOVERNANCE

Business organizations in the food retail and catering sectors are subject to a food governance system which comprises the state and a variety of non-state influences. How the state intervenes to manage food safety/hygiene risks is one focus of this book. Food is a topic which attracted early state intervention through regulation. Food laws and institutions to implement these laws can be traced back to the nineteenth century (see Chapter 4). We know from the existing socio-legal literature on regulation that state regulation is 'necessary but not sufficient' as an influence on business risk management practices. We also know that a broader food governance system has emerged, embracing organizations and groups beyond the state (see Chapter 5). What is not clear is the relative importance of these other groups, in relation to each other and in relation to state regulation.

Risk regulation since the late twentieth century has increasingly been understood to include sources of regulation beyond the state. State regulation has gradually co-opted more non-state bodies into its regulatory activities. It has also experimented with new ways of managing risks which fall outside traditional public policy approaches, a prime example being the adoption of private sector risk management tools and perspectives. So we have seen relatively mundane food risks become subject to technical risk-based regimes (see Chapter 4). How able food businesses are to comprehend and implement these systems is a question posed by the findings presented in this study (see Chapter 6).

THE RESEARCH

The evidence in this book is a snapshot of one sector in one country at one moment in time. In order to make sense of these data and their implications it is necessary to compare them to other studies in the research literature. Indeed, the research design sought to develop previous research in a number of respects. For example, the last research project I undertook considered the impact of state regulation on one large nationalized business, British Railways (Hutter 2001; see also Chapter 2). The project forming the basis of this book examines the impact of a broader governance regime on a sector comprising very different business organizations – so the focus is more on inter-organizational than intra-organizational variation.

This research uses the empirical data we collected to connect theories about the governance of risk to the routine and often mundane food hygiene/safety practices of those on the shop floor. It considers the understandings of those in the industry about the role of the state and its influence on the risk management practices of business organizations and their employees. This necessarily involves exploration of the tensions between control, empowerment and responsibility. How far does the state endeavour to control business risk management practices? And how is this balanced against empowering businesses with responsibility for managing the risks they generate? The research looks beyond state regulation to consider broader governance regimes. These cover economic actors such as insurance companies and trade associations, and civil society actors such as non-governmental organizations and citizens. An important objective of the book is to explore how these risk governance regimes shape organizational risk management practices and the responses and routines of those employed within them.

Chapter 1 will consider the academic context of the research and its theoretical setting. In Part I, Chapter 2 considers the food retail and hospitality sectors in the UK, and the research approach used in collecting the empirical data for this study. Chapter 3 focuses on the food hygiene/safety risks associated with the food retail and hospitality sectors. It considers the official data and also findings from the empirical analysis, in this case examining the understandings of risk held by those working in the industry. Part II considers the risk regulation regime in place to govern food safety/hygiene in the UK. Chapter 4 considers the state regulatory regime, Chapter 5 the governance regime that exists beyond the state and Chapter 6 the risk regulation regimes put in place within organizations. In all of these chapters the empirical evidence of this research will be considered alongside the existing literature. Part III draws out the theoretical and policy implications of the research, considering in particular what prompts businesses to manage risk and the implications of these findings for contemporary food governance and regulatory policy making.

1. Risk regulation and business organizations

The majority of businesses in the modern world are subject to what many experience as a bewildering array of regulatory and risk management pressures. Each of these pressures may be decisive to the running of a business, and most will be competing for organizational resources and for attention. The objective is to reduce the risks generated by contemporary business organizations, risks which may expose those within their confines, and also beyond, to harm. How well businesses cope with these various risk management pressures is not well understood but is the subject of increased public scrutiny. This is especially so following a series of spectacular failures in the financial sector which have emphasized the very real importance of organizational risk management systems and reminded us all of their vulnerability to failure.

The objectives of this book are twofold. First, it investigates how business risk management practices may influence and be influenced by various sources of regulation. This includes those external to the business such as state regulators, trade associations, consultants, civil society organizations, insurance companies and consumers; and those internal to the business, for example, senior management, risk officers, colleagues and professional groups. Second, it examines the understandings of risk and risk regulation held by those in business organizations. This includes consideration of the tools and techniques, knowledge and expertise employed to manage risk within the organization. It also involves consideration of the pressures of compliance and non-compliance on managers and owners and how these relate to understandings of risk and uncertainty.

These issues are discussed with reference to an in-depth case study of the food retail and catering industries in the UK. The research specifically focused on the management of food safety and food hygiene risks by grocery and hospitality businesses in the UK, including large national companies, medium-sized businesses and small and micro businesses. Data were collected from 49 experts related to the food industry; 204 survey responses from 28 businesses; and 25 in-depth interviews with representatives of five of the large businesses included in the survey (see Chapter 2).

This chapter outlines the orienting concepts upon which the book is based, most particularly the notions of risk regulation and governance. It explores and extends the notion of risk regulation regimes to encompass sources of influence beyond the state. In particular it considers the inter-relationships between the economic, political and civil sectors and how they work together with inter- and intra-organizational business pressures to manage the risks associated with contemporary economic life.

RISK AND MODERN SOCIETIES

Modern businesses are embedded in a multi-layered web of risks. At a macro level social theorists talk of us living in a 'risk society'. This is consequential upon transformations in modern societies, so risk is related to substantive changes in the worlds we inhabit and to re-conceptualizations of the dangers surrounding us (Beck 1992; Giddens 1990). Beck's work *Risk Society*, which has been especially influential, argues that contemporary western societies are characterized by risks which are distinctive in a number of respects. First, they are manufactured as opposed to natural. Second, they transcend social and national barriers and may be global in their effects. Third, these risks are closely but ambivalently associated with science which is seen as responsible for the creation and definition of modern risks but is also seen to have failed to control these risks.

The notion of anticipation is central to these theories of risk (Hutter 2010). Beck (1992) argues that we are 'increasingly occupied with debating, preventing and managing risks' and have a growing preoccupation with the future. Giddens (1999) agrees that there is no longer a belief in fate but an 'aspiration to control' the future. This is partly attributed to the growth of science. Beck (2006) believes that a growing belief in science, rationality and calculability is significant. We live, he argues, in a world where we know much more about risks through science. But this greater appreciation of the risks serves to heighten feelings of insecurity and is rarely matched by a greater ability to control or manage risk.

These theories have been criticized for their exclusive focus on technological risks (Tierney 1999; Turner 2001). It has also been claimed that they are too abstract to be useful for empirically oriented research (Tierney 1999, p. 216). The concentration on technological risk has been a continuing difficulty but these theories have, contrary to their critics, spawned numerous grounded studies of risk. And certainly at an organizational level these theories do have resonance. We have witnessed the growth of risk ideas and perspectives which in many respects have become a new lens through which to view the world. There has been an apparent growth in the belief that we can anticipate and control the risks we generate (Clarke 1999; Hutter 2010). So organizations in the private and public sectors are experiencing the spread of risk management ideas and risk-based organizing templates. Risk does appear to have emerged as a major organizing category in some areas of modern societies (Ericson et al. 2003).

BUSINESS RISK MANAGEMENT

The use of formal risk tools and perspectives in the effort to avoid the repetition of previous risk events, and to help to identify and manage new risks, is premised on a realist view of risk which has spawned a whole industry of tools, techniques and consultancies for their promotion. Risk management approaches typically seek to define the risk; analyse its probability of occurrence and likely outcomes; determine acceptable levels of risk; and then act to reduce the risk. This is explained in the Royal Society's Report *Risk: Analysis, Perception and Management.*

> Risk management
>
> (i) Concept
> The overall subject concerned with hazard identification, risk analysis, risk criteria and risk acceptability, is generally known as risk management ... or loss prevention ... . This includes the various techniques that have been developed for the assessment and control of risk ... .
>
> (ii) Term
> Risk management: The process whereby decisions are made to accept a known or assessed risk and/or the implementation of actions to reduce the consequences or probability of occurrence.
>
> Note that a compromise is made considering increased cost, schedule requirements and effectiveness of redesign or retraining, installation of warning and safety devices and procedural changes ... . (Royal Society 1992, p. 5)

There are a number of important features exemplified in this definition. First is a reliance on formal techniques for analysing risk. Second is the separation of an unquestioned 'objective' determination of risk assessment, comprising risk identification and risk estimation, from the much more evaluative decisions about its acceptability and management. And third is the reference to cost-effectiveness. These are all features of modern regulation and the subject of critical social science scrutiny.

Risk Analysis

Risk analysis, which embraces both the assessment and management of risk, emerged as a defined area early in the 1970s.[1] The literature distinguishes between two components of risk analysis, namely, risk assessment and risk management. The former refers to the scientific, calculable component of risk regulation whereas the latter refers to the policy component (Pollak 1995). Early conceptions of risk assessment focused on identifying, measuring and evaluating outcomes from both natural and technological hazards. The concern was to estimate the probability of these events happening and to esti-mate their likely effects (Tierney 1999). The assumptions were essentially realist, so it was assumed that there is an objective world of risks which is discoverable, measurable, quantifiable and controllable by science (Gabe 1995). Policy makers saw risk assessment as a way of systematizing their approach to risk, prioritizing actions, and thereby hopefully diminishing expo-sure to risks and optimizing the balance between risks and benefits (Rimmington 1992).

The 1970s and early 1980s witnessed a growing recognition that risk management, which involves the choice of policy options, necessarily requires the assignment of values and politicized decision making. There was also increasing public awareness of scientific disagreements. Douglas and Wildavsky (1982) commented 'substantial disagreement remains over what is risky, how risky it is and what to do about it'. They pointed to scientific disputes over how to interpret data and how to then decide what is acceptable and pointed to a paradox, 'better measurement opens more possibilities, more research brings more ignorance to the light of day' (1982, p. 64). Commentators noted that values differed between countries, between succes-sive administrations, within countries and within the research community (Otway 1985). Moreover the tools of technical risk analysis came under much criticism for being too simplistic, making too many assumptions and for not recognizing the values which may surround them (Renn 1992).

A fundamental divide emerged in the mid 1970s as a gap between expert and lay opinions became increasingly apparent (Plough and Krimsky 1987). The term 'risk perception' emerged and psychological risk analyses aimed to explain why public reactions to risks are not always in proportion to 'objec-tive risks' (Krimksy 1992; Otway 1985). As some observers have commented these studies share similarities with technical risk assessments to the extent that their aims are purportedly scientific, objective and quantitative (Gabe 1995, p. 4). Indeed the notion of risk communication was introduced in an attempt to bridge the gap between expert views and lay perceptions. As some authors indicate, this communication typically means 'information transmis-sion' and 'persuasion' as the underlying assumption is that the expert view is indeed the correct one to follow.

There were variable consequences of these developments. One was an exacerbation of the challenge to expert opinion and an accompanying growth of mistrust in science and technology which were increasingly seen as the cause of many of the risks in the everyday modern world. There were some attempts to combine social science and scientific approaches to risk analysis. These were referred to by some authors as the 'hard' and 'soft' approaches to risk analysis, the former referring to technical approaches to risk analysis and the latter to social science approaches which take into account the human factors influencing risk (Blockley 1996). Some risk management practices incorporated both approaches, for example, Hazard and Operability Studies (HAZOP) (Hood and Jones 1996, p. 86). Indeed the influential Royal Society Report on risk (1992), first published in 1983, differentiates between 'technical risk estimation' and 'political risk decision', arguing that interaction between the two is necessary.

Risk Management and Risk Regulation

Risk management approaches have become professionalized over the course of the past 30 years and have become the preserve of specialist risk management personnel (Power 2005). Many governments and business organizations have created dedicated departments which are responsible for risk across the organization including risk identification, assessment and management. The objective of these departments is to anticipate and manage risks better (Hutter 2010). In some cases risk management ideas have also become part of the ways in which organizations are governed and constituted and risk has become an organizing category and a matter of internal control and governance (Power 2007).

These ideas have also spread into the public sector where a broad governmental call to 'modernize' government partly included running the administration as a business and the 'virtues' of private business, transparency and accountability were extolled (Hood and Jones 1996; Power 1997). There has been an emphasis upon adopting private sector styles of management and an almost unthinking acceptance that private sector practices were the benchmark against which to assess public sector activities. In Britain the adoption of risk management approaches in government is clearly related in a National Audit Office report on risk in government (2000, p. 40) to the influence of corporate governance codes, notably the Cadbury Report (1992), the Hampel Report (1998) and the Turnbull Report (1999). The Turnbull Report is identified as especially significant as a voluntary code which adopts a risk-based approach to designing, operating and maintaining a sound system of control in business financial management. In particular, it supports a top-down, integrated corporate risk management policy. The ideal is that risk is analysed, controlled, communicated and monitored. In other areas risk-based models were adopted from industries such as the chemicals industry, many years before the corporate governance codes which informed the modernization initiatives (Hutter 2004).

In the UK a large-scale modernization programme has encompassed the 1999 White Paper *Modernizing Government* (Minister for the Cabinet Office 1999), which emphasized the importance of improving the way in which risk is managed in government, through to the 2005 recommendations of the Hampton Report *Reducing Administrative Burdens*, which advocated risk-based regulation as a key recommendation. These approaches have a number of attractions for public and private sector organizations. For example, risk-based tools are regarded as particularly helpful in resolving conflict between competing interests and groups over appropriate levels of risk management. Their apparent objectivity and transparency may enable justification of the allocation of resources in a way which is well tested and trusted by the business community. The whole approach resonates with moves to minimize the so-called regulatory burden on business through cost justifications. This emphasis upon the scarcity of resources carries with it the message that some risks will not receive very much, if any, attention, especially if they are regarded as low probability and low impact. This approach may also be seen as defensive risk management to the extent that it serves as a transparent and seemingly objective account of agency decisions, thus implicitly at least it signals that there is not a zero-tolerance approach to risk management (see Black 2005; Hutter 2004, 2010; Lloyd-Bostock and Hutter 2008).

The risk-based approaches employed by some businesses have thus become popular and have been adopted by the public sector, including regulatory agencies. In turn these agencies have come to use these templates for directing their own activities and their expectation is that business organizations will similarly be using risk-based approaches to manage their own risks. But the research evidence is cautionary in warning of the difficulties which may be generated by too high expectations that risk can be anticipated and controlled. Perrow (1999), for example, argues that complex, tightly coupled systems will inevitably fail, thus he coins the term 'normal accidents' to emphasize the inevitability of something going wrong. Referring specifically to high-risk technologies, he focuses on complex systems where the interaction of unexpected multiple failures can lead to catastrophe, this being most likely where the system is tightly coupled and has no slack to cope with such eventualities. Other authors observe that attempts to anticipate risks are frustrated by a series of fundamental dilemmas – how to balance anticipation and resilience; how much to rely on past events and how much on foreseeing novel risks; how to balance learning with prediction; and how to balance high expectations of manageability with pragmatic realities (see Hutter 2010).

RISK REGULATION AND GOVERNANCE

Risk and regulation are inextricably related. Even the most traditional accounts of regulation regard regulation as a means of controlling harm in the public interest. More specifically regulation is seen to act on behalf of consumers, citizens and the environment and protect them from the risks to which they may involuntarily be exposed by organizational activities. Traditional accounts of regulation defined it very much in terms of state intervention in the economy. But there is growing recognition that regulation is not the exclusive domain of the state. The regulatory capacities of non-governmental actors are increasingly recognized and on occasions formally co-opted by the state.

Throughout much of the nineteenth and twentieth centuries regulation was regarded as the state's attempts to control economic activities. Indeed, for some authors, state regulation is a defining characteristic of modernization (Hancher and Moran 1989). But the growth in the use of the law to influence economic activities has been uneven and its use as a tool of government subject to changing political fashion. In the 1970s and early 1980s, Europe and the United States witnessed a proliferation of laws designed to regulate economic activities across a broad economic spectrum.[2] Sunstein (1990), writing of the experience in the United States, refers to this as a 'rights revolution', in which there was a proliferation of social regulation concerned with quality of life issues (see also Rose-Ackerman 1992; Sigler and Murphy 1988). This is in stark contrast to the late 1980s, which witnessed a growing disillusionment with state regulation and calls for a dismantling or 'rolling back' of the regulatory state (Rose-Ackerman 1992; Sigler and Murphy 1988). In the United States and Europe there was a strong deregulatory rhetoric, centring on claims of overregulation, legalism, inflexibility and an alleged absence of attention being paid to the costs of regulation (Froud 1998; Majone 1990). This 'regulatory crisis' was followed in the mid 1990s by a period of re-regulation and regulatory reform. So marked was the trend to regulate that the mid 1990s onwards has witnessed what some commentators refer to as the rise of the regulatory state, a prominent characteristic of which is the decentring of the state. This entails a move from public ownership and centralized control to privatized institutions and the encouragement of market competition. It also involves a move to a state reliance on new forms of fragmented regulation, involving not only the existing specialist regulatory agencies of state but also self-regulating organizations (Braithwaite 2000) and American style independent regulatory agencies.[3]

These moves to decentralization have been variously written about in terms of contracting out; the multiple occupation of regulatory space (Hancher and Moran 1989); and more broadly in terms of a move from government to governance, where the state attempts to 'steer' or 'regulate' economic activities through co-opting non-governmental actors (Osborne and Gaebler 1992). These changes are not simply related to disillusionment with command and control strategies to regulation, they are inextricably related to more general moves in public governance which veer to outsourcing and privatization of public management functions. They also parallel changes in broader patterns of social control which emerged in 'the mid twentieth century' (Cohen 1985; Hutter 2001). The patterns are characterized by increasing ideological attacks on the state apparatus running alongside an actual strengthening of control systems. So the state apparatus stays in place and new, diverse forms of control are added to the repertoire. The focus of control becomes more dispersed and diffused yet the methods of control stress inclusion and integration. Moreover the boundaries between different forms of control blur.

REGULATORY HYBRIDS: BLURRING THE BOUNDARIES

Debates in the late 1980s and early 1990s resulted in a consensus that state influence through law is a necessary but not sufficient influence upon effecting business risk management. It is perhaps for this reason that a regulatory mix which harnesses sources of regulation beyond the state is seen as one of the hallmarks of so-called 'smart regulation'. Ayres and Braithwaite (1992), for example, advocate tripartism in regulation, involving regulators, businesses and public interest groups. Similar themes are reiterated by Gunningham and Grabosky (1998) who suggest a variety of regulatory arrangements which range beyond the state to include business, third parties, non-governmental organizations (NGOs), insurers and consumers. All regard these arrangements as 'smart' regulation and also as a means of empowering different participants in the regulatory process in order to maximize the promotion and achievement of risk management. The arrangements which arose from these discussions blurred a number of boundaries – those between the state and beyond the state and also those between the various players in risk regulation regimes. Some authors believe that the boundaries are so blurred that we can no longer talk of the 'regulatory state' but of 'regulatory capitalism', a term which they believe better captures the web of regulation that has evolved over the past 20 years (Braithwaite 2008; Jordana and Levi-Faur 2004).

The boundaries between the inside and outside of business organizations have also become blurred as regulation increasingly focused on the technical features of internal control systems. So the inside of the organization has been increasingly recognized as a 'regulatory space' in which the various facets of compliance are determined. One aim of many modern regulatory regimes is to influence constitutively the risk management practices of organizations. The objective is for organizations to prioritize risk management practices high relative to other organizational objectives. Thus risk regulation penetrates deep inside the workings of the business organization while simultaneously embedding it in a widening web of strengthened regulation involving multiple players.

One important hybrid form of regulation that exemplifies these trends is enforced self-regulation which involves a mix of state and corporate regulatory efforts. The government lays down broad standards which companies are then expected to meet.[4] This involves companies in developing risk management systems and rules to secure and monitor compliance. Where compliance is not being achieved then companies are expected to have procedures in place to deal with non-compliance. Regulatory officials oversee this process. They undertake monitoring themselves and can impose public sanctions for non-compliance. Moreover the state co-opts other sources and methods of regulation, notably in this case the regulatory capacity of the company. Ayres and Braithwaite (1992, pp. 6 and 103) describe this as a middle path between self-regulation and command and control regulation.

Enforced self-regulation is popular for a variety of reasons, notable among which is that it is seen to maximize the advantages, and avoid the major pitfalls, of pure state regulation and of pure self-regulation. So regulation is not left entirely to the willingness of companies to regulate and neither is it so heavily dependent upon state systems of control. Instead it builds on corporate regulatory capacity and affords companies the flexibility to devise systems and rules which meet the broad standards but which are adapted to their particular circumstances and the risks associated with their particular workplace. Meanwhile, the efforts of the regulatory agency are directed to those companies which are either unable or unwilling to effectively self-regulate. Another advantage of this system is said to be that companies will be more committed to rules and systems which they have devised themselves. Indeed it is speculated by some that this could lead to innovation in techniques and systems of risk management and regulation. Finally, enforced self-regulation is seen to have major cost benefits, notably for the state. At one level this model could be seen as a form of subcontracting regulatory functions to private actors. Certainly much of the enforcement and monitoring work is devolved to the company. But there are also a number of limitations to such an approach.

Enforced self-regulation is very dependent upon the regulatory capacity of the company. Generally it is most suited to large, well-informed and well-resourced companies and crucially it is also reliant on the readiness of companies to self-regulate. It is also reliant upon a balance being established and maintained between too much and too little state oversight of corporate self-regulation. If state agencies exercise too much oversight then the ambition of companies taking full regulatory responsibility may be lost. Too little over-sight may result in poor levels of compliance and lower standards of risk management than are either required or desirable. From a business perspective another possible limitation of this approach is that it moves the costs of regu-lation more firmly onto business. But these costs may be mitigated if the companies own risk management practices are aligned with state require-ments. Where they are not aligned there may be fewer incentives for self-regu-lation. The success of the enforced self-regulation model very much pivots around the commitment and capacity of companies to self-regulate and the ability of the state agency to find and maintain an optimal monitoring and oversight role. Thus the spotlight falls onto organizational risk management systems and the capacity of businesses to take responsibility for the risks they generate.

BUSINESS ORGANIZATIONS AND THE REGULATED POPULATION

Regulatory understandings of business organizations have become more sophisticated over the past 20 years. Business organizations used to be seen as coherent, hierarchical, instrumental and above all wealth maximizing (Sigler and Murphy 1988; Stone 1975). Increasingly these assumptions have been eroded by a different perspective on organizations which regards them as less coherent and less efficient than do neo-classical models. Rather they are seen as complex, comprising different interest groups with different goals. Indeed, their goals may be multiple and conflicting and they may be unable to achieve agreed upon objectives (Fisse and Braithwaite 1983; Wilthagen 1993). An important part of the criticism focuses on the neo-classical view that without regulation the market would be unregulated. Critics argue that all markets are regulated but not necessarily by the state. The focus of regulation studies should thus embrace the state and the plurality of other regulatory influences operating in regulatory space.

An important aspect of understanding regulation and risk management is an appreciation of how differentiated a population the so-called regulated popula-tion is. It comprises different industries and individual companies and busi-nesses which range from complex, well-organized and multinational companies to simple, small-scale and local firms. Organizational responses to regulation from all sources may vary between different sectors of an industry, between different parts of one site and over time. It may also vary within an organization, for example, between different categories of people such as employers and employees; specialists and generalists; the skilled and unskilled; the experienced and inexperienced. The research literature suggests that this structural model is typically adopted by regulatory enforcement officials. So inspectors judge corporate responses according to such factors as the company's commitment to regulatory objectives; the attitude their staff have towards compliance; their record of compliance; the quality of the management; their ability to comply; and also according to more normative criteria such as their treatment of their staff or consumers (Hutter 1997).

The size of a company may also influence the way it manages risks and responds to risk regulation. Some authors have identified a considerable gap between standards of health and safety in large and small firms (Dawson et al. 1988). This is partly related to the capacity of organizations to comply (Grabosky and Braithwaite 1986; Hutter and Jones 2006; Yeager 1991) and also their greater capacity to challenge how deviance is defined (Snider 1987; Yeager 1991). There are crucial power differentials between businesses. The concept of regulatory capitalism captures this well. Braithwaite (2008) remarks on the power of large corporations to encourage regulation, such as industry-led regulation, which small businesses simply cannot meet. He further remarks on the powerful position of some large corporations in relation to the state and hence their ability to dominate some areas of state and beyond the state regulation. Such discussion underlines the need to differentiate the regulated population as there is a massive gap between small micro businesses and large multinational organizations whose turnover may be greater than those of some national economies.

It is important to appreciate that large companies do pose risk management and regulatory problems. This is well summed up by Di Mento (1986, p. 156) when he writes 'Size correlates with differentiation in a firm and the greater the differentiation the greater the possibility of non-compliance' (see also Hutter 2001; Vaughan 1982). The research literature on organizational risk management supports this view. It underlines the importance of focusing on organizations as the sites of producing, managing and exporting risks (Hutter and Power 2005; Short 1992). Thus the larger, more complicated and more transnational an organization, the greater is its potential to generate risks, perhaps on a global scale. There are of course many cross-cutting caveats to such generalizations. As we might expect from the regulation literature the evidence is that there is immense variability between and within organizations in their management of risks. This variation relates to a variety of factors such as organizational capacity to manage risks both financially and in terms of the required knowledge and expertise. Studies have also shown that there may be very different understandings of risk within one business organization, with variations occurring according to such factors as hierarchical position in the organization, specialization, professional training and departmental culture (Hutter 2005; Vaughan 1989). The routines and practices of different groups and individuals within organizations demand attention. For example, risk taking may be normalized or even unwittingly incentivized (Vaughan 1996). The Barings Bank case is illustrative: the case of remuneration incentives based on short-term trading performance led to excessive risk taking which was supported, rather than questioned, by the company. In this case the poor risk management of individual behaviour led to the demise of an entire bank. Moreover, there are important interdependencies within organizations (Kunreuther and Heal 2005). These are well illustrated by the cases of AIG and UBS in 2008, where varying risk management practices in different parts of their transnational organizations led to financial crisis. In the case of AIG, a large multinational insurance corporation, the activities of 80 of its London-based staff brought down a company which was at the time employing 125,000 people worldwide. This led to a massive rescue package for AIG from the US Federal Reserve Bank, the largest they had ever provided to a private company.

These examples highlight some of the characteristics that studies of major risk events have identified as contributing to failures of organizational risk management. Some relate to features of the organization itself, in particular difficulties in the interactions between the human and the organizational systems for managing complex risks. Other organizational features which have been found to contribute to vulnerability include organizational fragmentation, communication difficulties, a lack of commitment by senior staff, a lack of foresight, problems with the multiple organizational cultures which may be found within broader organizational boundaries, the influence of production pressures and human error. Other contributory factors may relate to the external environment within which the organization operates, for example, the financial, social, political, technical and regulatory environments. Typically there are multiple, complex explanations of failures involving a coincidence of several of these predisposing factors (Perrow 1999; Reason 1990; Turner 1978, Vaughan 1996).

Major risk events do of course lead to reorganizations and often new regulations to try to prevent a repetition of the event. There may be competing accounts of why risk management broke down (Jasanoff 2005) and undoubtedly the reorganization which ensues will generate risks of its own (Hutter and Power 2005). As Pidgeon and O'Leary (2000, p. 17) observe '... to understand how vulnerability to failures and accidents arises does not automatically confer predictive knowledge to prevent future catastrophes'. The demands on risk management are considerable as they are constant and continuously shifting. Moreover expectations are that organizations should be able to prevent the recurrence of risks that have already materialized and also to anticipate as yet unrealized or even unimagined risks (Vaughan 2005). It is partly for these reasons that we have witnessed a growth in the use of formalised risk management tools which seek to assess, measure and quantify risks.

Inside the Business Organization

Risk management tools are just part of a broader range of techniques which may be used by businesses to manage the risks generated by their organization. They may, in part depending on their size and complexity, have their own rules and disciplinary procedures, they may provide training and have various ways of communicating risk management messages to their staff. These may be voluntary systems or they may be mandated by the state as in systems of enforced self-regulation (see above). Studies have suggested that a company's internal organization and management are key in influencing their work practices. Howard-Grenville et al. (2008), for example, found that variations in managerial incentives, organizational identity and organizational self-monitoring were all strongly related to differences in what they term the 'internal licence to operate'. Other work suggests that understandings of business risk management systems vary between different parts of an organization (Hutter 2001). Moreover whilst supervisors, structures and policies might be in place the real difficulty is operationalizing and sustaining them (Dawson et al. 1988; Hutter 2001).

Business risk management is contingent on a multiplicity of factors and existing research suggests a variety of intra-organizational factors which might facilitate or hinder risk management within a business. Some studies refer to a broad concept of business safety culture to denote the overall approach to risk within an organization (Fennell 1988; Vaughan 1996). In practice this overall culture comprises subcultures which may shift between groups and over time (Howard-Grenville et al. 2008; Turner 1988). These different cultures embrace management style (Kagan 2006) and their perceived commitment to risk management (Hutter 2001). It also relates to the power and sophistication of staff, their education, professional training and also the power of employees, for example, through union representation (Gunningham et al. 2005). Colleagues are another important source of learning and control, indeed informal mechanisms of social control are significant in promoting (or detracting from) risk management (Gunningham 1991). In turn these may be shaped by economic constraints (Kagan 2006).

Risk regulation therefore involves the coincidence of different regulatory spaces inside and outside the business organization. Figure 1.1 represents just some of the internal influences in business and some of the external relationships which cross boundaries and may become incorporated into the internal world of the business. For example, some are bought in, such as consultants, trade associations, industry groups and insurance companies. Some are a matter of imposition, for example, the state and possibly the unions, or a matter of constitution, for instance, professional groups. Seldom are these unidirectional relationships, rather businesses have a reflexive relationship with these different actors.

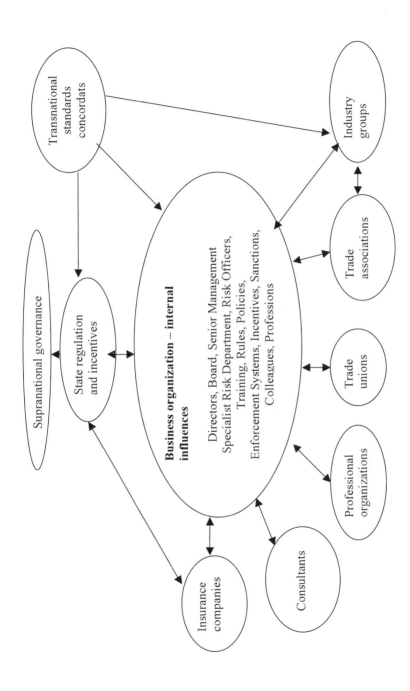

Figure 1.1   The business organization: internal influences and external interactions

The following labels appear within the figure:

Transnational standards concordats

Industry groups

Supranational governance

State regulation and incentives

Business organization – internal influences

Directors, Board, Senior Management Specialist Risk Department, Risk Officers, Training, Rules, Policies, Enforcement Systems, Incentives, Sanctions, Colleagues, Professions

Trade associations

Trade unions

Professional organizations

Insurance companies

Consultants

The remainder of this book addresses some of the gaps in the current theorizing about risk governance regimes. It also contributes to some of the gaps in empirical data surrounding risk governance issues. There are, as we have seen in this chapter, many general claims about risk regulation but there is not much empirical research into the veracity of many of these claims. For example, there are a number of assertions about the importance of some non-state influences in risk governance and a variety of assumptions underpinning policy making about regimes of enforced self-regulation and the ability of business to cope with these regimes. It is important to connect theory, policy and practice and understand better the connections between these different levels and the ways in which risk governance demands and practices are shaped by ground level understandings of risk. Theory and empirical work are inextricably related and it is important that we develop theories that can enhance our understandings through empirical research and, in turn, feed into evidence-based policy making (Cane and Kritzer 2010; Hutter and Lloyd-Bostock 1997). We also need a much deeper understanding of the roles played by forces external to a business and the internal world of the business organization. These issues generate specific themes which have been raised in this chapter and which will run through the book. These include consideration of:

- The influence on business risk management practices of risk governance regimes, specifically state regulatory regimes and broader governance regimes. We ask what sorts of non-state organization are relevant in these discussions and what is their relative importance alongside state regulatory regimes?
- The understandings of risk and risk governance held by those working in the food retail and hospitality businesses. What do they think are the main food hygiene/safety risks posed by their activities? How do these understandings interact with regulatory requirements? Do they, for example, feed into responses to state, non-state and organizational risk management and regulatory systems? And do these understandings influence compliance? We have not sought to present respondents with a formal, technical definition of risk but have focused on their understandings.
- How do different business organizations cope with the demands of enforced self-regulation and how do they manage their risks?
- And what are the implications of the research findings for theorizing and policy making? An important issue is the importance of refining theory and using this and the empirical findings as a basis for improving practice.

The book is structured around the issues introduced in this chapter. Part I focuses on the retail and hospitality food sectors in the UK. Chapter 2 outlines the key characteristics of the sector and the research approach adopted in collecting the data for this study. Chapter 3 considers the food industry and risk, paying particular attention to how those in the food retail and hospitality sectors in the UK understand food safety/hygiene risks. Part II examines risk regulation by the state, by non-state actors and by business itself. This analysis looks at these issues from the perspective of those working in the food sector and Part III draws out the implications of their views for the theoretical issues raised in this introductory chapter and also the policy implications of the research.

NOTES

1. This section is based on Hutter (2006b).
2. The term economic is being used here broadly to refer to the market economy and its constitutive institutions and actors, it is not being used in the narrow sense that the term economic regulators is often used in the UK to refer specifically to price regulation.
3. Indeed for Majone (1994, 1996) it is the rise of these agencies at both state and European Union levels which is the defining characteristic of the European regulatory state.
4. See Braithwaite (1982) and Hutter (2001). Note that others write of similar arrangements using different terminology. Coglianese and Nash (2001, 2006) use the term 'management based strategies' to refer to regimes of enforced self-regulation.

PART I

The food retail and hospitality industry and risk

2. The food retail and hospitality industry in the UK: a research approach

The empirical focus of this study is the management of food safety and food hygiene risks in the food retail and hospitality sectors in the UK. These are key parts of the UK food chain which in turn are part of a global industry which the UK is part of as an exporter and importer of food. This chapter considers the economic and employment characteristics of these sectors at the time data for this study were collected, that is, 2003–06. The latter part of the chapter outlines the research approach adopted to collect the empirical data used in this book, data which will be used to feed back into the literatures and debates raised in Chapter 1.

THE FOOD RETAIL AND HOSPITALITY SECTORS IN THE UK

A variety of businesses comprise the UK retail and hospitality sectors.[1] The food retail sector is generally taken to refer to:

- Grocers
- Butchers
- Fishmongers
- Greengrocers
- Delicatessens
- Supermarkets (including in-store bakeries).

It also applies to businesses where food is only a part of what they do such as:

- Food shops at petrol stations
- Newsagents
- Convenience stores
- Online food retail.

The food catering sector refers to:

- Banqueting
- Clubs
- Contract and in-house catering (in the workplace, institutions, schools, healthcare establishments, prisons and so on)
- Delivered catering and 'Meals on wheels'
- Fish and chip restaurants
- Food on the Move (trains, coaches, boats, aeroplanes)
- Hotels and guest houses
- Mobile snack vehicles and market stalls
- Outdoor and event catering
- Private party caterers (including catering operations conducted from domestic premises)
- Public houses
- Restaurants and cafes of all types
- Sandwich bars
- Takeaway and fast food restaurants.

Collectively their importance to the UK economy is considerable. In the third quarter of 2005 nearly 20 per cent of consumer expenditure in the UK was spent on food, drink and catering (DEFRA 2006, p. 37). In the previous year the UK agri-food sector accounted for gross value added (GVA)[2] of £78.2 billion and over half of this was contributed by the retail and catering sectors.[3] They are also of key importance to the UK economy as a major employer. In 2005 the retail sector employed 1.18 million people and the hospitality sector employed 1.39 million and the evidence from the research period was that these are growing sectors.[4] Moreover, they are labour-intensive sectors and ones characterized by a part-time workforce.[5]

The skill levels of staff in the food retail and catering sectors vary. A small proportion have degrees,[6] the large majority range from A level/NVQ level 3 to those with no qualifications, the most poorly qualified staff are kitchen and catering staff.[7] Many of these low skilled staff are very young, for example, 42 per cent of restaurant employees are 16–24 years old.[8]

Staff turnover rates in the food sector are high. This is most especially the case in the hospitality sector where the Labour Force Survey shows that in 2004–05 turnover rates in the food service were 46 per cent and the turnover of chefs and cooks stood at 32 per cent. The same survey indicates that 40 per cent of kitchen and catering assistants went into their jobs from full-time education and 54 per cent of those leaving these jobs changed occupation. Thirty-three per cent of chefs moved into their work from other occupations and 55 per cent leaving their jobs changed occupation. Labour turnover in the food retail sector is also fairly high, the food industry average is 35 per cent.[9]

Interestingly, 59 per cent of all employees in the grocery sector are employed by six grocery retailers. This reflects the concentrated structure of the retail food sector and by implication some of the risk factors inherent in the industry. VAT registrations give us some further insight into the structure of the food industry – in 2005 these numbered 172,945: 86 per cent of these were micro firms (so they employed less than ten people); 14 per cent were small and medium enterprises; and 0.4 per cent were large firms (DEFRA

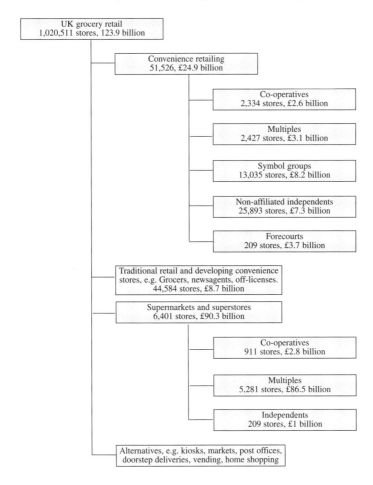

Source: IGD (2006b).

Figure 2.1   UK food retailing

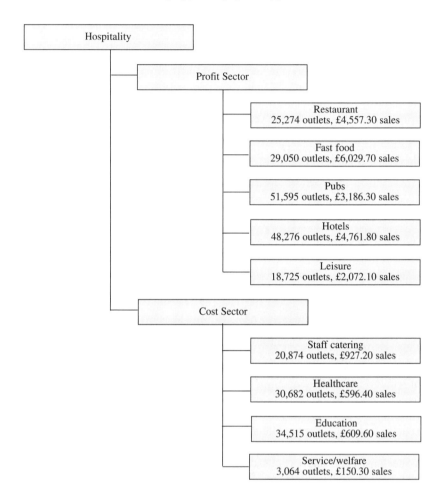

Source: IGD (2006a).

Figure 2.2   Food service sector

2006). The distribution of these businesses across sectors is outlined in more detail by the Institute of Grocery Distribution in its fact sheets: see Figures 2.1 and 2.2 which are derived from these.[10]

These diagrams highlight the diversity of food retail and hospitality premises. They also reveal the dominance of the supermarkets and superstores and their expansion to convenience store markets. This dominance has raised concerns about unfair competition and the impact on independent food retailers and suppliers (DEFRA 2006).

NON-STATE ORGANIZATIONS OF RELEVANCE TO THE FOOD SECTOR

There are a number of generic organizations of relevance to the food sector and some which focus more specifically on the food retail and hospitality sectors and also on food safety/hygiene issues. Some of these represent business, others are more consumer focused.

Business Organizations

There are a variety of membership organizations representing food business interests. At a very general level the British Chambers of Commerce represents businesses at a national, regional and local level, the latter being where they are considered to be strongest. The Federation of Small Businesses (FSB) promotes the interests of businesses. It describes itself as 'the UK's largest campaigning pressure group promoting and protecting the interests of the self-employed and owners of small firms. Formed in 1974, it now has 213,000 members across 33 regions and 194 branches.'[11] The Institute of Directors (IoD) also represents businesses from a wide range of sectors with an emphasis on the privately owned business. Retail businesses are also represented by the British Retail Consortium (BRC), a relatively strong national trade association which covers the full spectrum of retail in the UK; indeed it claims to represent 90 per cent of retailers in the UK, covering large, medium and small businesses[12] although the interests of larger retailers are not always those of the smaller retailers. The BRC provides information and advice to retailers; lobbies and campaigns on behalf of retailers at both UK and EU levels;[13] and produces technical standards which are updated to take account of changes in legislation. The BRC has a specialist Food and Drink section, for example, it has a food policy team which among other things covers food safety issues. It also has a number of food-related technical standards: The BRC Technical Standard and Protocol for Companies Supplying Retailer Branded Food Products; the BRC/IOP Technical Standard and Protocol for Companies Manufacturing and Supplying Food Packaging Materials for Retailer Branded Products; and the BRC/FDF Technical Standard for the Supply of Identity Preserved Non-Genetically Modified Food Ingredients and Products. These standards are auditable and the BRC accredits certification bodies and lays down standards for evaluators.

Food retailers are represented by the more specialist Institute of Grocery Distribution (IGD) which was formed in 1908.[14] IGD focuses on the food chain and is concerned to develop and disseminate best practice. It undertakes research and training but does not lobby. IGD has over 700 corporate members drawn from across the food chain and from across the globe.

The British Hospitality and Restaurant Association (BHA), established in 1907, is the trade association representing hotels, restaurants, motorway services, food and service management organizations and student training. This is a national trade association which also has a lobbying and promotional role for the hospitality industry at local, national and international levels. It also links to national tourism efforts. As a trade association BHA also has an informational, educational and advisory role for businesses and provides a number of business services.[15] For example, it keeps its members up to date with industry and legislative changes.[16]

All these trade associations have policy advisors who specialize in risk and regulation although the position they take on regulation varies – not surprisingly – to suit the interests of their members. Some of the above organizations often adopt an outright anti-regulation stance rarely mentioning the benefits it brings to society, whereas others are more measured in their approach, particularly where regulation builds consumer trust within their sector or favours their members over non-members in the same sector. All are potential sources of information and advice on food safety/hygiene matters.

There are also a number of producer organizations which operate certification systems of relevance to the whole food chain. These include, for instance, organic food organizations such as the Soil Association.[17] There are also regional certification schemes such as the Scottish Beef Cattle Association.

CONSUMER ORGANIZATIONS

The UK's largest consumer body is Which. This is an independent organization which provides a number of consumer services. It is perhaps best known for its product testing service which is reported in its magazine *Which*, but it also provides advisory services, such as its legal service, and has a campaigning role. Its informational role focuses on the provision of independent information and also an awards scheme which positively rewards those providing good products and services. Which has a separate focus on food and drink issues through specific reports linked to food and drink issues, for example, reports on 'Diet, nutrition and safety', 'Eating and drinking' and 'Labelling and shopping'. It also runs a number of related campaigns. For example, its campaign on 'Regulation and safety' includes campaigning for hygiene scores to be adopted by all restaurants, such as, through making public the results of environmental health officer (EHO) inspections. It also calls for greater openness and transparency in official decision making about food risks.[18]

The other main consumer body in the UK at the time of the research was the National Consumer Council (NCC) which was 60 per cent funded by government and 40 per cent funded by contracted income. Like *Which* the NCC had particular food interests, especially in diet and nutrition standards and with a particular concern for low income consumers and children. Its approach was partly educational, with a concern to raise awareness of these issues among consumers, and partly lobbying the food sector to encourage healthier choices. Its emphasis here was on promoting information disclosure, advertising and provision of nutritious school meals. In 2004 and 2005 it conducted surveys of supermarkets focused on standards of labelling and consumer information and the provision of healthier products.[19]

In addition to these general consumer organizations there are a number specifically focused on food issues but these tend to be single issue organizations such as GM Watch (http://www.gmwatch.org) or Friends of the Earth.[20]

At the European level, Foodaware has a contract from the Food Standards Agency and a Secretariat provided by European Research into Consumer Affairs to coordinate the UK consumer movement's work on food safety, nutrition and standards, to give consumers a voice on food policy by bringing together their representing organizations and to consult and support UK consumer representatives on food-related committees.[21] Its activities are centred around publications on food-related topics.

These organizations form part of the institutional landscape within which food retail and hospitality businesses operate in the UK.

THE RESEARCH APPROACH

The food retail and catering sectors were selected for this study partly because they embraced a good cross-section of businesses across the UK. My previous work on business responses to risk regulation examined a large national company, British Railways (Hutter 2001). The food retail and catering sectors represented a distinct contrast to this with the full range of large multinational outlets, small and medium-sized enterprises (SMEs) and a large number of micro businesses. Moreover these sectors and the focus on food safety and food hygiene covered a range of risks, many of which are relatively low-tech and straightforward, while others are more technical and risk based. Food safety/hygiene risks have been known and regulated for a long time. New risks have emerged as food production changes and our knowledge of risk has developed, as have regulatory approaches and the structure of the industry. Yet many of the fundamental risks and approaches have remained relatively stable, thus highlighting one of the major changes of risk management, how to maintain awareness and interest.

The issues raised in this book are not easy to research. It is very difficult to untangle the impact of law and the various non-state influences discussed.

Organizations and those working within them are variously motivated (Ayres and Braithwaite 1992; Etienne 2010) and the regulatory environment is fluid. The most appropriate methods to examine how those working in the food sector make sense of all of this are qualitative methods. This is especially the case as the basic orientation of this research is to map out the food governance terrain as it is seen from within the industry and then refine the questions asked and data collected as the research develops. The research employed a number of research methods, including the usual literature reviews and documentary searches. It also necessarily involved a good deal of primary data collection in England and Scotland during the period 2003–06. In order to develop and refine the research, data collection was divided into three phases – each building on the preceding phase.

Phase 1 we have termed the 'The Consultation Phase' because it comprised the collection of data through a literature survey and preliminary discussions with industry representatives, central and local government representatives, regulators and consumer organizations. While the researchers were familiar with the academic literature about risk and regulation they were not experts on food safety and food hygiene. The purpose of this phase was therefore to understand the main issues of relevance to this domain of risk management, for example, to gain an appreciation of the major risks involved in the domain; to identify the range of potential sources of regulation external to companies; to recognize the main risk management tools in use in the sector; and to collect information about the structure of the industry in England, Wales and Scotland, and the range of professionals likely to be involved in risk regulation.

Bridget Hutter and Clive Jones conducted these meetings during January–September 2003. Interest in the study was very high from the start and many extremely busy and senior people readily gave us their time, knowledge and above all enthusiasm for the project. In fact only one set of relevant people we approached refused to meet with us. They were from a government department but we did manage to interview a significant advisor to this department and were able to gain ready access to other relevant departments and agencies. Many of the Phase 1 respondents were in fact part of a rolling sample as each interview led to new potential participants.

The first phase involved consultations with 49 experts related to the food industry and its regulation (Table 2.1). They include managing directors, chief executives, group technical managers and risk managers in industry and trade associations, and directors, senior policy advisors, economists and enforcers from the public sector. Some individuals held multiple roles to the extent that they occupied more than one position in the food industry, some serving on government committees or acting as independent consultants on a part-time basis. Some also held positions on international food boards and committees.

Table 2.1   Participants in Phase 1 of the research

	England and Wales	Scotland	Total
Policy makers from central government	6	2	8
Regulators – central government related	9	9	18
– local government related (Greater London)	2	5	7
Trade associations	5	4	9
Food businesses	10	1	11
Consumer organizations	2	2	4
Total	34	23	57

Discussions, which lasted on average an hour, were broad-ranging and offered a variety of perspectives on the state of food safety and food hygiene in the retail and catering sectors in the UK. They covered a range of topics including the main food safety and food hygiene risks which characterize the food retailing and hospitality sectors; the main state and non-state sources of regulation; the key legislation and enforcement bodies; the main risk management principles and tools which may emerge in the Phase 2 survey; discussion of the structure of the food retailing and hospitality sectors; and discussion of the research, in particular the sampling frame and approach to be adopted in Phase 2 of the research project.

These discussions formed the basis of our sampling approach in Phase 2 and were also crucial to the development of the questionnaires we developed for Phase 2 of the research.[22] This is in a number of respects. The Phase 1 interviews ensured, for example, that we had an accurate and comprehensive understanding of the main issues and how the industry and the food governance regime are structured. It also enabled us to develop questionnaires that were comprehensible and meaningful to participants in Phase 2. Some Phase 1 participants very kindly commented on draft questionnaires, this was especially valuable as the majority of questionnaires were intended for self-completion. This process took several months and underlines the importance we attributed to developing and refining the project as it progressed.

Phase 2 comprised a questionnaire survey seeking respondents' knowledge, understandings and views on a range of key issues raised in Chapter 1 and crystallized into meaningful questions through the discussions in Phase 1. Respondents were asked about their understandings of the food safety and food hygiene risks associated with their business and also how they and their staff found out about these risks. They were asked about how their organization managed these risks in terms of communication, training and putting in place systems to ensure compliance with risk management demands. Sections of the questionnaire sought their knowledge and views of external regulation including questions about how much they knew about state regulation of food safety/hygiene and also the influence which might be exercised by non-state influences which were suggested as relevant in the academic literature and Phase 1 discussions (see Appendix 2).

The Sampling Frame

Phase 1 discussions and the literature survey suggested two main variables for the sampling frame, namely, the size of the business and the type of business, retail or catering. The business size definitions we used were those used by the European Commission (1996) and Department of Trade and Industry (DTI) (2006):

- large firm: over 250 employees
- medium firm: 50–249 employees
- small firm: 10–49 employees
- micro firm (including sole trader): 0–9 employees

These two variables are represented in the industry segment matrix (Table 2.2). The matrix was used to orient selection of the sample so that a cross-section of relevant businesses was included.

The researchers considered the inclusion of a regional variable very seriously. After lengthy discussion it was decided that the resources available would be best used to concentrate the sample in the London area where a range of different environments, enforcement practices, retailer types and size of business could be incorporated in the study. But there was one major exception to this, namely, the case of Scotland where a limited amount of data collection also took place. The researchers visited Scotland twice and spoke to representatives from central and local government, business, trade associations and a consumer group. Phase 2 of the research project included two large businesses which had both Scottish and English branches and managers from both regions in both companies took part in the survey. One was a supermarket and convenience store operator, the other a branded restaurant chain. Phase 3 also included Scottish representatives in the sample. The findings did reveal interesting variations which are reported in this book.[23]

The Sample

Securing access for Phase 2 of the research was very time consuming. While some companies were decisive and keen to participate, the majority took longer to persuade. Some companies were nervous of research and despite numerous

Table 2.2   The distribution of respondents across the sampling grid

Business size	Retail sector responses: company and number of responses	Hospitality sector responses: company and number of responses
Large: over 250 employees	Orange – 46 Green – 38 Director/senior managers – 2	Blue –19 Red – 7 Yellow – 18 Pink –38 Director/senior managers – 5
Medium: 50–249 employees		Brown – 10 Director/senior managers – 1
Small: 10–49 employees	Director/senior managers – 1	Director/senior managers – 4
Micro/sole traders 0–9 employees	Director/senior managers – 3	Director/senior managers – 12

meetings eventually failed to grant the researchers access. In some cases there was concern about commercial sensitivities, there was suspicion that we were researchers from a publically funded centre and this might mean we worked for the government. Indeed these discussions brought to our attention very early in the research the importance food businesses attach to reputation. But there were other important constraints, most notably freeing up the time for employees to complete the questionnaire. The most difficult sector to target was the medium, small and micro businesses. We eventually only increased participation in this area by face-to-face interviews with interviewers agreeing to interview during quiet periods or in between serving customers. This does of course underline the very real commitment made by those who did participate, who gave up their own time and often that of their managers to participate in the research.

A total of 204 individuals across 28 businesses responded to the survey. Table 2.2 gives a breakdown of the 28 companies and how they were allocated according to size and sectors. The six large businesses and one medium-sized business had multiple respondents.[24] For reasons of anonymity we refer to these businesses as Pink, Brown, Blue, Yellow, Orange, Green and Red Companies. They may be characterized as follows:

- Pink Company is a large contract catering business operating in a range of sectors including workplaces and catering to the public throughout the UK.
- Brown Company is a medium-sized business operating several restaurant- bars in South East England.

- Blue Company is a large restaurant business operating at sites throughout the UK. The sample includes sites located in Scotland in addition to those located in London.
- Yellow Company and Red Company are large hospitality companies whose branches are both 'take away' and eat-in businesses operating in South East England.
- Orange and Green Companies are two separate retail business units within a larger business whose operations include supermarkets and convenience stores throughout the UK. Orange represents the sites in Scotland and Green represents the sites in South East England.
- The 22 medium, small and micro businesses included several convenience stores, sandwich shops, bakers, coffee shops, cafes and restaurants identifying their styles of food variously as Italian, French, Spanish, Chinese and Thai. These were all located in London.

Two forms of questionnaire were used in Phase 2. One version was for site managers of the six large and one medium-sized companies who agreed to their staff being circulated copies of the questionnaire (manager's questionnaire).[25] A longer version was sent to directors or senior managers with head office type responsibilities of these seven companies, and also the most senior member of staff in the 22 micro and small businesses in the sample (director's and senior manager's questionnaire).[26] The director's questionnaire included almost identical questions to those in the manager's questionnaire but had additional questions which assumed a more strategic view of the market. The questionnaires used are reproduced in Appendix 2 and Table 2.2 shows how respondents were distributed across the sampling frame.

Clive Jones undertook the majority of the Phase 2 interviews with the SME and micro business managers and owners. These questionnaires and the completed managers' questionnaires were processed by an external data processing firm and then analysed using SPSS statistical analysis software. The data are presented in Chapters 3–7 of this book.

Appendix 1 gives a basic profile of respondents from the six large and one medium-sized companies whose managers responded to the Phase 2 questionnaires.

Once Phase 2 was completed each of the seven main participating companies were sent confidential reports on the findings relating to their company and how they compared with the overall findings. Great care was taken to preserve anonymity of the participants, none of whom were known to have participated by the company employing them as we sent questionnaires directly to a sample of managers we selected from a regional list and they responded directly to us.

Phase 3 developed out of Phase 2 and further refined the research questions. It comprised 25 in-depth interviews with representatives of five of the large businesses and the medium business included in Phase 2.[27] Twenty-two of these interviews were with people included in the Phase 2 survey and the other three were their replacements as the original participants had moved onto new jobs.[28]

The interview schedule was constructed after the analysis of the Phase 2 questionnaires. It broadly followed a similar format to the Phase 2 question-naire but allowed for much greater depth replies and probing of responses (see Appendix 3). It also included some new topics, such as a section on reputation and questions on consultancies. These topics emerged as relevant in Phase 2 and appeared to warrant further exploration.

Clive Jones conducted these interviews, 18 were face-to-face, in England, and seven Scottish interviews were conducted over the phone. The face-to-face interviews lasted from 34–63 minutes and the telephone interviews from 20–42 minutes. The length of interview, like the availability of people for interview, very much depended upon how busy respondents were, and some interviews had to be curtailed because premises became busy which is why the response rate to different questions varies.

Table 2.3 gives details of the positions Phase 3 respondents held in their companies. The number of employees these managers were responsible for varied from 2 to 170. This of course reflects the varying seniority of these staff, four of whom held responsibilities across several sites in different loca-tions and most of whom were responsible for one branch, although the size of each branch varied considerably: the range being from large canteens to eat-in and take away cafes and from chain grocery stores which varied in size to micro businesses which had few employees.

Respondents' responsibilities varied, most were responsible for stock control; financial control; the recruitment, training, management and welfare of staff; health and safety; food safety and hygiene; implementation of corporate policies; and store presentation. The overwhelming majority had previously

Table 2.3   Phase 3 respondents

Position in the business	Number interviewed
Director	2
Area manager	2
Branch manager	19
Assistant manager	1
Supervisor	1
Total	25

worked in the food sector. At the time of interview, they had been in their present jobs from two days in the case of one respondent through to 17 years for one Orange Company manager, indeed Orange Company managers had worked noticeably longer in their jobs than other respondents.

The data generated by these three phases of research form the basis of the following chapters.[29] In these chapters the empirical data will be interwoven with the existing academic literature. This includes the literature relating to the food sector and also to other domains. This is partly because there is a dearth of relevant empirical data relating to the food sector but also to enable comparison of our data with data from other domains. It is important to be alert to areas where effects are common to domains and those where they differ. This is especially the case as many claims made in the academic and policy literatures are couched in generic terms, for example, assumptions about enforced self-regulation and the role of non-state influences. It is important to take a broader view of the existing evidence to help us better assess the usefulness of some of these general theoretical and policy assumptions.

In the next chapter we turn to the food industry in the UK and consider the official data regarding food hygiene/safety risks it poses. We then examine our research findings about the understandings of risk held by those working in the industry.

ACKNOWLEDGEMENT

The author wishes to thank IGD for granting permission to include figures 2.1 and 2.2.

NOTES

1. These definitions are drawn from two guides by the Chartered Institute for Environmental Health (CIEH) in response to the Food Safety (General Food Hygiene) Regulations 1995 and Food Safety (Temperature Control) Regulations 1995: one guide for retail which was produced by the British Retail Consortium and the other, for caterers, was produced by the Joint Hospitality Industry Congress (JHIC). Local Authorities Coordinators of Trading Standards (LACOTS) and the Department of Health contributed to both.
2. GVA is the difference between a sector's sales and the value of its purchased inputs.
3. Food and drink retailing generated £20.16 billion (2 per cent UK GVA) and non-residential catering generated £21.8 billion (DEFRA 2006, p. 10).
4. In the period 2000–05 the catering sector in the UK grew by 11.2 per cent and the food retail sector by 8.8 per cent (DEFRA 2006).
5. Whereas 31.8 per cent of all UK jobs are part-time, 62 per cent of food retail jobs are part-time and 57.1 per cent of hospitality jobs are part-time and 60 per cent of these are women, especially in the hospitality sector (DEFRA 2006).
6. See Labour Force Survey (2004–05). Nineteen per cent of restaurant and catering managers and 13 per cent of those in the food retail sector are educated to NVQ level 4 and above.

7. Twenty-one per cent in these occupations have no qualification (Labour Force Survey 2004–05).
8. Labour Force Survey (2004–05).
9. http://www.personneltoday.com/Articles/2005/07/05/30654/supermarket-sweep-tesco.html (accessed 2 November 2007).
10. The four grocery sectors identified by the Institute of Grocery Distribution (IGD) refer in part to the physical size of the selling space and the range of products on sale. Convenience stores have sales areas of less than 3,000 square feet and sell products from at least eight different grocery categories; traditional retail and developing convenience stores have a sales area of less than 3,000 square feet; supermarkets have a sales area of 3,000–25,000 square feet; and superstores have a sales area over 25,000 square feet (IGD 2006b).
11. http://www.fsb.org.uk/about (accessed 25 October 2010).
12. http://www.brc.org.uk/defaultnew.asp (accessed 25 October 2010).
13. The BRC has a Scottish sister organization which was launched in 1999 to represent Scottish retailers and lobby the Scottish Parliament.
14. http://www.igd.com (accessed 25 October 2010).
15. Food manufacturing interests are represented by the Food and Drink Federation and the National Farmers Union (NFU) represents farmers and growers in England and Wales.
16. http://www.bha.org.uk (accessed 25 October 2010).
17. http://www.soilassociation.org (accessed 25 October 2010).
18. http://www.which.co.uk (accessed 25 October 2010).
19. In October 2008 the NCC became part of Consumer Focus, a statutory organization, created through the merger of three organizations – Energywatch, Postwatch and the National Consumer Council (including the Scottish and Welsh Consumer Councils) – by the Consumers, Estate Agents and Redress Act 2007.
20. http://www.foe.co.uk.
21. http://www.foodaware.org.uk.
22. At the end of Phase 1 in 2004, we produced a research report on Phase 1 which was circulated to all participants.
23. Sadly we were unable to raise further funds to explore this in more detail although various attempts were made to do so. Hutter and Jones published an article on their Scottish findings for the magazine of The Royal Environmental Health Institute of Scotland (REHIS). Variables such as corporate culture; position in the market and profitability are acknowledged as possible influencing factors by the researchers; but this research programme was not designed to test the significance of these variables.
24. Six large companies and 22 SMEs participated in the research. One person per SME was interviewed and on average seven per large company.
25. These questionnaires were sent out as printed booklets by the researchers and included a stamped addressed envelope for direct reply. No company manager knew which of his or her staff had been included in the sample. In all cases the senior manager responsible for food safety/hygiene in the company provided a letter to accompany the questionnaire assuring the company's support for the project.
26. Many were owner managed with several being family businesses – most operated on a single site.
27. The numbers from each company are as follows: Orange Company – 5; Green Company – 1; Blue Company – 6; Pink Company – 4; Red Company – 4; Brown Company – 5.
28. Staff turnover made it very difficult to arrange these Phase 3 interviews.
29. Where Phase 1 and 3 quotations are used in this book we note in parenthesis that these data are from these phases. Phase 2 quotations do not mention the phase but do identify the category of staff and the company for which they worked or if they are from the director/senior manager category.

3. The food industry and risk: official data and workplace understandings

The food safety and food hygiene risks associated with the food retail and catering sectors have the potential to cause considerable suffering to the public and cost to the economy. This chapter will consider the main food safety/hygiene risks that require managing in the retail and hospitality industry in the UK. It will then turn to the empirical data to examine how much is known about these risks by those working in the food industry. Their understandings of food hygiene and food safety risks affect the wellbeing of us all as their levels of comprehension may well influence their capacity to manage risk and their propensity to comply with food safety/hygiene regulations.

RISKS ASSOCIATED WITH FOOD SAFETY/HYGIENE IN THE HOSPITALITY AND RETAIL SECTORS: OFFICIAL DATA

Foodborne diseases are perhaps the best known risks associated with the food sector. Foodborne disease is defined by the World Health Organization (Food Safety Act 1990) as 'any disease of an infectious or toxic nature caused by or thought to be caused by the consumption of food or water'. It is also used, along with its more populist counterpart 'food poisoning', to refer to a group of infectious intestinal diseases (IIDs) which may be spread by a variety of pathways including microorganisms and parasites which may be found in foods of plant and animal origin: diseases which can be transmitted from animals to humans are called 'zoonoses' (see generally Federal Institute of Risk Assessment, http://www.bfr.bund.de/en/food_safety-737.html (accessed 20 April 2011)).

Data on foodborne diseases in the UK are available from a variety of sources. For example, National Statistics keep details of deaths from food poisoning in the UK,[1] more detailed information concerning outbreaks of Salmonella and so on can be found at the DEFRA website in *Zoonoses Report 2000* which includes major sources of food and waterborne zoonoses including *Salmonella* and *E. Coli* 0157.[2] The most general source of data on food poisoning deaths is the *Health and Personal Social Services Statistics for England,* an annual Department of Health publication. Other data can be found on the Food Standards Agency (FSA) website and in the reports of the Chief Medical Officer. An important source of data emerged during the research period when the FSA produced its first *Annual Report of Incidents 2006* (FSA 2007a).[3] It reports that 11 per cent (146/1342) of all incidents in 2006 were the result of microbiological contamination. Seventy-two per cent (105/146) of these were bacterial contamination with *Salmonella* accounting for 41 per cent (43/105) of these incidents and *Listeria* 65 per cent (28/105). The majority of these microbiological incidents relate to the manufacturing sector; 12 per cent (17/146) relate to the retail sector; and 3 per cent (5/146) to the catering sector.[4] Two foodborne incidents were classified as high during 2006: one of these was a national outbreak of *Salmonella montevideo* in chocolate products produced by Cadbury Schweppes; the origins of the other *Salmonella* outbreak remain unknown.

According to the various sources available the data suggest that at least 70,000 people in 2004 suffered from food poisoning in England and Wales (Health Protection Agency 2010). However, it is accepted that endemic under-reporting of food poisoning is severe for cultural, technical and bureaucratic reasons. The DEFRA *Zoonoses Report 2000* highlights the problem:

> … the reported cases represent only the 'tip of the iceberg' as many patients do not seek medical attention or their doctor does not request a laboratory investigation, or a positive result is either not notified or the occurrence of the disease is not notifiable. Reports also tend to be biased towards more clinically severe cases in high risk groups. (DEFRA 2001, p. 1)

For example, among the intestinal diseases that are not notifiable, and thus may not be reported by GPs, is *Campylobacter* which helps to reveal the scale of underreporting as *Campylobacter* is cited by one expert as the main cause of food poisoning in the UK: Professor Hugh claims it 'causes diarrhea in people far more often than all other food poisoning bacteria put together' (2003).[5]

Adak and Long (2002, p. 832) attempted to overcome some of the limitations of the official data by using multiple sources of data such as routine surveillance data, special survey data and hospital episode statistics. They estimated that one in 5.8 cases of intestinal disease is not reported so adjusted their data accordingly and also to take into account travel-associated infections. They estimate that in 2000 'over 5 million people in the UK suffered from acute gastro enteritis which they ascribed to contaminated food' (Adak and Long 2002). Of this group, over 20,000 were admitted to hospital with food-related illnesses and 480 died.[6] Their findings suggest a fall in intestinal disease in England and Wales for the period 1992–2000: overall a reduction of over 50 per cent in illness but just a 3 per cent fall in hospital admissions.[7] They relate these improvements to changes in eating habits, notably a fall in the consumption of red meat, and the introduction of a vaccination programme against *Salmonella* among chickens (2002, p. 808).

In addition to those affected by foodborne illnesses are others who may suffer from the effects of a variety of different food risks.

Natural chemical contamination. 13 per cent of incidents reported to the FSA in 2006 were caused by natural chemical contamination. By far the largest group of reported incidents in this category were caused by mycotoxins. These are toxic chemical substances produced naturally by moulds. They may affect crops, nuts, dried pulses and fruit, or enter the food chain through animal feeds or drinks via contaminated cereals and grapes. Mycotoxins tend to survive storage and high temperatures so can be found in cooked foods if contaminated ingredients are used, for example, in bread making. Prevention is seen as the best cure. The FSA (2007) attributes the high figures of mycotoxin contamination in its 2006 report partly to being the result of high levels of reporting caused by increased sampling; 113 of the 168 reported incidents of contamination were rejected imports from West Africa, the Middle East and Asia (FSA 2007, p. 44).

Physical contamination accounted for 10 per cent ($n = 140$) of incidents reported to the FSA in 2006: 33 incidents were related to pests; 26 by metal; and 17 by plastic.

Food tampering is defined as 'a malicious act of sabotage that turns food into a risk for its consumers' (FSA 2007). Tamperproof packaging is commonplace and there have been few reported cases of food tampering. Allied Bakeries suffered two incidents in 2005 and 2006: one involving incidents of foreign bodies in pre-packaged bread and one involving foreign objects found in the packaging.[8] A more dramatic case occurred in 1989 when razor blades, pins, caustic soda and glass were found in jars of baby food across the UK. The scare had its origins in late March, when a blackmailer (who later turned out to be a former Metropolitan detective sergeant) informed the British unit of H.J. Heinz that unless the company paid him $1.7 million he would contaminate Heinz products.[9]

Bioterrorism is much discussed but again there is little evidence of its occurrence in the UK. The threat is very much regarded as a global one:

> The malicious contamination of food for terrorist purposes is a real and current threat, and deliberate contamination of food at one location could have global public health implications. This document responds to increasing concern in Member States that chemical, biological or radionuclear agents might be used deliberately to harm civilian populations and that food might be a vehicle for disseminating such agents.[10]

Environmental contamination refers to chemical spills or leaks and fires. Twenty-eight per cent of the FSA's major incidents for 2006 fell into this category; of the reported incidents 317 were organic and 46 inorganic (FSA 2007, pp. 39ff.), 245 of the organic incidents involved polycyclic aromatic hydrocarbons (PAH) which are one of the most widespread organic pollutants, formed by the incomplete combustion of carbon fuels: they thus tend to be linked to fires and smoked foods. Indeed the main source of organic contamination was fires. There were multiple sources of inorganic contaminants, 67 per cent of which were caused by chemical spills or leaks (FSA 2007, p. 39).

Costs: most of us are likely to experience a foodborne disease at least once in our lifetime. WHO observes that food contamination is very common, even in the most developed countries (WHO Regional Office for Europe). The illnesses caused occur in varying degrees of severity. Symptoms typically involve vomiting, diarrhoea, fever and general incapacity from a few hours to a few days. For those in general good health the ill-effects are usually short-lived but occasionally these diseases do result in death or lifelong disability. Such severe outcomes are often restricted to vulnerable groups such as the very young, the very old, pregnant women and those with impaired immune systems.

In addition to the human costs of food safety and food hygiene risk events, there are also considerable costs to the economy. In the UK the costs to the economy have been estimated as £1.5 billion a year (CIEH 2007). The Regulatory Impact Assessment undertaken by the FSA on proposals by the EU to consolidate EU food hygiene legislation[11] estimated the overall actual cost of those suffering from Indigenous Foodborne Disease (IFD) in England and Wales in 2000 to be £164 million[12] (FSA, 2003, p. 26). They also attempted to estimate the cost of the pain, grief and suffering endured by individuals suffering from IFD and these were estimated to be £964 per IFD case in England and Wales in 2000 (FSA, 2003, p. 28).[13]

The costs of food risks can be very high for the economy and also very serious for individuals. How well understood are the risks to those working in the food retail and hospitality sectors? In particular, what do we know about workers' understandings of the role they might play in exacerbating these risks?

Workplace Understandings of Food Risk: The Literature

There is a modest literature on understandings of food risks and even less on the understandings of food handlers in the retail sector: much of this is published in specialist journals and as conference proceedings.[14] There is a broader literature on the risks associated with other industry sectors, but the focus of this work tends to be on more 'dangerous' occupational settings such as the nuclear, oil or railway industries; and typically the focus is on workers' perceptions of the risks to themselves rather than the risks they may pose to others.

Although the directly relevant literature is limited, it is clear that workplace understandings of risk can have a very real impact on the risk management practices of the food sector. The proceedings of an EU Risk Analysis Information Network conference on *Catering Food Safety* (European Union Risk Analysis Information Network 2003, p. 8) identified the important contributing factors to food poisoning: most of these related to the activities and behaviours of food handlers. The conference heard evidence that food handlers constitute 'a major but underestimated risk' (2003, p. 9).

In 2002 the FSA reported the results of a major survey of catering workers' hygiene which found a neglect of basic hygiene among a significant proportion of those interviewed. For example, survey responses suggested that 39 per cent did not wash their hands after visits to the lavatory and 53 per cent did not wash their hands before preparing food. A study of 444 food handlers in the UK similarly found that crucial aspects of food hygiene were not understood (Walker et al. 2003). In a study of small and medium-sized food businesses in Wales, 63 per cent of respondents reported that they do not always adhere to food practices (Clayton et al. 2002). Interestingly, this study found that food handlers did have a good knowledge of the actions they should be adhering to, but believed their businesses to be low risk. This is similar to the FSA (2002) research which found that just 32 per cent of managers believed that food hygiene practices were important to their businesses. These findings are in stark contrast to work from New Zealand where managers considered staff with good food safety practices as the most important aspect of ensuring safe food (Kramer and Scott 2004). It also contrasts with work from this UK research project where managers thought that the most important point affecting consumer differentiation was food safety and food hygiene practices (see Chapters 4–5; Hutter and Jones 2006).

Understandings of risk have been found to be socially situated and influenced by social location (Douglas and Wildavsky 1982; Heimer 1988). For example, they are influenced by the department or business workers are located in, the extent to which their working day is influenced by production pressures and organizational routines, and their place in the hierarchy (Fleming et al. 1998; Heimer 1988; Hutter 2001; Nelkin and Brown 1984; Vaughan 1998).

Research in the food industry suggests that understandings may vary according to the size of a business and according to the sector of the industry workers are employed in. SMEs and micro businesses are typically considered to have less understanding of the risks they are dealing with than larger businesses. This may result in their being slow to take up risk-focused systems such as Hazard Analysis Critical Control Point (HACCP)[15] and this may be an obstacle to compliance (Fairman and Yapp 2004; Taylor 2001). Other research has found that understandings of food hygiene and HACCP are markedly lower in the retail and catering sectors of the UK food industry compared to the manufacturing sector. Mortlock et al. (1999) found differences between the retail and catering sectors, with 59 per cent of retail and 48 per cent of catering staff regarding their business to pose a low risk to food safety. Public perceptions research supports this view. A 2005 study found high levels of concern in Britain about hygiene in restaurants with 78 per cent of consumers expressing concern about the risk of contracting food poisoning in restaurants (Mori 2005). The literature seems to support the finding that understandings are sectorized.[16]

Research suggests that the most successful programmes for improving risk awareness are those focusing on worker and supervisor attitudes and behaviour towards risk (Bailey and Peterson 1989). Knowledge of risk has been identified as necessary for developing a safety culture (Fleming et al. 1998) and understanding how workers perceive risk is important for developing safer policies (Kivimaki and Kalimo 1993). A number of studies focus on the possibility that food hygiene training can increase awareness of the risks held by food workers and in turn improve their handling of risks (Kirby and Gardiner 1997). The evidence is equivocal. Some argue that there is no relationship between the level of knowledge held by staff and the hygiene standards of premises (Powell et al. 1997). Others are more positive towards the value of and need for training but argue that current approaches are not most effective (Coleman and Roberts 2005). It may well be that training is regarded positively for effecting higher standards but is regarded as an expensive operating cost.[17]

The Research Findings

How do our data from the food industry compare with this literature and our general knowledge of this area?

Phase 1: the view of the experts
The full range of food safety and food hygiene risks was mentioned by respondents in the first phase of this research. The main food safety and food hygiene risks involved in food retailing and food catering were identified as:

- physical contamination by foreign bodies from either the production or preparation process;
- chemical contaminants in food such as pesticide, fertilizer and veterinary drug residues (including prophylactic use of antibiotics and growth hormones);

- industrial and environmental contaminants;
- microbiological contaminants such as *E. coli*, *Salmonella*, *Campylobacter* and *Listeria*;
- tampering – deliberate contamination, for example, bioterrorism/extortion or malicious communication of false information (hoax);
- zoonoses such as BSE and tuberculosis (TB);
- non-compliance with food safety and hygiene standards; and
- reputational risks from any of the above and also from perceived, but unproven, food safety and health risks.

Opinions varied as to which risk is the most important. Some regarded chemical contaminants as the greatest risk. A senior regulator cited the example of Chinese blended honey, which in 2002 revealed traces of an antibiotic used in veterinary medicine, chloramphenicol, a drug banned in foodstuffs. A similar example is the widespread contamination in 2005 of food by banned dyes from the Sudan family of red/brown food colourants; these were found in several manufacturers of branded and supermarket private label products. The discovery of such a contaminant prompted the FSA in the UK to issue a series of Food Alerts to EHOs, manufacturers, retailers and the public, leading to a major product recall of over 500 products from some of the UK's major food brands and food retailers.[18]

Another view was that 'people' are the greatest risk to food safety and food hygiene, whether this be through poor personal hygiene or incompetent animal husbandry. Alternatively it could be because of a high turnover of transient staff in the food industry when issues of training and management could be especially acute. Bioterrorism and tampering were the key concerns cited by a government advisor and industry representatives. These risks were very much in peoples' minds post 9/11. Industry felt quite vulnerable to incidents of intentional food tampering. Some businesses in central London were also concerned about being targeted by terrorist explosive devices.[19]

Others identified particular areas of the food industry as being especially risky. Small businesses and the catering sector were cited as most risky:

> ... the hazards are in the OMBs [owner-managed businesses]. (Senior representative of a major food company)

> Small restaurants are the dynamite area ... this is where EHOs should concentrate their efforts. (Government advisor)

The view that the catering sector is the most risky is one that is echoed in a report by the IGD (1998) which found that 'Restaurant standards were questioned most often by the consumers, and some people avoid certain meats because of this.' Not surprisingly representatives of the catering sector were quick to refute these suggestions, claiming that 'levels of food poisoning attributed to the hospitality industry are over estimated' (Trade association representative).

The term food safety is to some extent a shifting category and interviewees differed in their views as to which issues should be regarded as food safety issues. This was particularly the case with topical food concerns. Some expressed the view that some risks need to be treated seriously not because they are regarded as intrinsically risky by the industry but because the public so regards them. Businesses were therefore considered to prioritize reputation risk management in these instances, forgoing the sale of certain foodstuffs primarily because of the risks to reputation that may be associated with them. Three examples of foods falling into this category were cited: genetically modified (GM) products; irradiated foods; and foods that raised concerns about animal welfare. Large supermarkets were considered to be especially likely to react in this way with one senior representative claiming that they are 'more scare led than objective led'.

Discussions with experts during the first phase of research were broad-ranging and offered a variety of perspectives on the state of food safety and food hygiene in the retail and catering sectors in the UK. It is clear that there is no broad consensus about what the state of food safety and food hygiene is in the UK today. It was also among this group that risk was discussed as something which had an upside as well as downside. Risk taking was seen as an important and conscious part of running a food business:

> Safety doesn't exist; it is what risk you are prepared to take. (Senior representative of major food company)

> The food chain is about taking risk and managing risk. (Government advisor)

Another argued that the more risk is controlled, the more likely it is that food will be processed and this may adversely affect flavour. In essence he believed that there is a trade-off between risk and taste.

Phases 2 and 3: the view from the shop floor

In Phases 2 and 3 we sought the views of those closer to the shop floor. Respondents were asked a variety of questions about food safety and food hygiene risks. Figure 3.1 details the Phase 2 responses to a question asking what respondents regarded as the *main* food safety and food hygiene risks encountered by their business.[20] These responses were spontaneously given rather than pre-coded but we have grouped them here under eight risk headings for ease of analysis.[21]

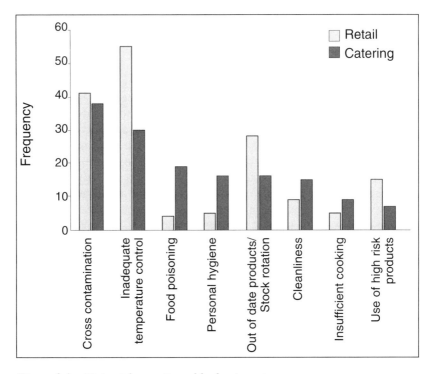

Figure 3.1   Main risks mentioned by business type

There was a high response rate to this question but concerns may be raised by the fact that 17/204 (8 per cent) of managers could not name any food safety and hygiene risk encountered by their business and an additional 10/204 stated that they 'didn't encounter any' food safety and hygiene risks in their business:

> My business has not encountered any risks. (Interviewee 787, Manager, Pink Company)

> No main risks. This place is organised properly, never had a problem. (Interviewee 712, Manager, small restaurant)

Most managers across the sample identified similar risks. The most frequently cited risks were temperature control which 85/204 (42 per cent) of the sample considered to be a major risk, followed by cross contamination (79/204 or 39 per cent) and then by out of date products (44/204 or 21.5 per cent) – 'Raw & cooked foods being allowed to contact. Incorrect temperature control. Food which is damaged or out of code'[22] (Interviewee 41, Manager, Orange Company).

Phase 3 respondents were asked 'what are the most dangerous food safety, food hygiene activities you oversee?' and their responses coincide with those of Phase 2.[23] One additional factor was mentioned by respondents in this phase, namely, 'untrained or inattentive staff':[24]

> Employees are on a very low wage, therefore it's a big challenge to motivate them: this can be a source of risk ... . Everything is a risk in this business ... there is no bible to tell you where the risk is, but you have to be able to spot them: this is good risk management. (Interviewee 867, Manager, Red Company)

There were no significant differences in responses according to the size of the business respondents came from. However, there were differences between different types of retailer. Three significant variations emerge from our Phase 2 data. The first concerns food poisoning which was mentioned as a 'main risk' by just 23/204 (11 per cent) of the sample. The majority mentioning this as a risk were from the catering sector. Second, grocers were twice as likely to mention inadequate temperature control.[25] Third, those in the retail sector tended to mention more risks than those in catering businesses.[26]

> Avoid cross contamination, stock rotation, regular cleaning of surfaces, hands and equipments, organizing courses for new recruits. (Interviewee 76, Manager, Yellow Company)

> Stock rotation, poor personal hygiene of staff. Insufficient cooking of products. Cross contamination. (Interviewee 21, Manager, Blue Company)

> Possibility of food poisoning due to poor standards of kitchen management, or contaminated food through out of date foodstuffs delivered, cross contamination, poor personnel hygiene. (Interviewee 826, Manager, Pink Company)

> Fresh meat preparation/handling. All kitchen tasks. Cross contamination. Staff awareness. (Interviewee 839, Manager, Brown Company)

> Inadequate regulation of raw materials in food preparation, temperature abuse, shelf life abuse. (Interviewee 184, Manager, Green Company)

Regional Differences

Phase 2 of the research project included two large businesses which had both Scottish and English branches. One was a large retailer, the other a branded restaurant chain. The data from these businesses are interesting.

Variations emerged in the identification of risks. More than half of both samples consider that temperature control of food was a major risk, with a slightly greater concern in the Scottish stores. One of the most striking differences centred on concerns about products perceived to be 'high risk' such as raw/uncooked meat and eggs with 13/53 of the Scottish sample referring to this as a risk compared with 9/147 of their southern counterparts. Just over half (28/53) the Scottish sample considered that cross contamination was a major risk compared to 48/147 of the South East England sample.

> Cooked meats and raw meats are the main high-risk elements. (Interviewee 141, Manager, Orange Company)

Questionnaires from the restaurant chain revealed few notable differences between Scotland and England. There were few differences in understandings of risk between the two regions. But in both the convenience store and the restaurant chain respondents, there were higher levels of knowledge of EHOs and their role in Scotland than in the English sample.[27] It is uncertain what accounts for these differences between the Scottish and South East England samples although the government and industry responses to the 1996 *E. Coli* 0157 outbreak in a Wishaw butcher's shop in Scotland may be a partial explanation (see Chapter 2).[28] This resulted in major investment in food safety and food hygiene training in Scotland. The apparent differences between the Scottish and English cases reveal some potentially interesting data about the effects of greater investment in education and training on food hygiene and food safety practices. Also, the suggestion that consumers as well as those in the food industry were so influenced by the events in 1996 is worthy of further exploration. One conclusion might be that the dreadful events of 1996 did, in concert with the subsequent inquiry and investment in food safety and food hygiene training, have a longer term impact in improving the management of these risks in the industry in Scotland.

The difference in the understanding of risk between the convenience store chain and restaurant chain also seems to be explained by their organization. Whereas the restaurant chain has a highly centralized UK wide organization, the convenience store organization is more federated and therefore potentially more sensitive to regional developments.

Comparative Risk

In order to gain some idea of how serious Phase 2 respondents find food safety/hygiene issues relative to other risks we asked if they could identify (a) risks more serious and (b) risks less serious than food safety and food hygiene risks. Forty out of 204 (20 per cent) respondents did not respond to the question about more serious offences and 82/204 (40 per cent) did not answer the question about less serious risks. Of those who did respond most were able to prioritize risks: just 12/164 (7 per cent) claimed that all risks are equally important[29] – 'It's all serious – food, employees – 'buck stops with me, I have to keep an eye open' (Interviewee 528, Owner-manager, micro-sized catering outlet).

Of those who did respond, 38/164 (23 per cent) stated that nothing is more important than food safety and food hygiene.[30] The overwhelming consensus, however, was that occupational health and safety issues are more serious. This was particularly the view of managers in medium and large-sized businesses. Few differences existed between the retail and hospitality sectors regarding occupational health and safety issues. The occupational health and safety issues mentioned were cuts, falls, slips and trips, strains, burns and scalds – 'No risk could be more serious than that of a food safety risk. However, I also consider safety risks/slips, trips etc. and accidents to be a serious issue within our business' (Interviewee 761, Manager, Pink, Company).

The second most cited risk was violence towards staff which was considered by 25/164 to be more serious than food safety/hygiene issues. Bodily assaults and fear of assault were most cited by micro and sole traders and managers of large businesses and feature most prominently in the retail sector. Regional differences were also apparent with 11/53 (21 per cent) of respondents referring to this in the Scottish sample and 14/147 (9.5 per cent) of the London/South East sample. Those in the retail sector were very concerned about violence to staff which was associated with drug use and alcohol consumption: 'physical violence from junkie shoplifters' was a phrase that stood out particularly. Phase 3 respondents explained:

> I've always worked in hospitality – the alcohol creates a high risk environment to work in – you are putting yourself in the front line 11 or 12 o'clock at night, in respect of your personal safety it is quite a high risk job. (Interviewee 843, Manager, Brown Company)

> This is more risky than a standard office job as there are more hazards, for example, violent and aggressive customers when drunk, I've been hit by a customer, handling food and handling glass. (Phase 3 Interview, Manager, Brown Company)

Evidence of confusion among managers over what precisely constitutes food safety and hygiene risks emerged in response to the question 'Give an example of risks you consider more important than food safety and food hygiene risks'. Ten out of 164 (6 per cent) respondents gave examples of risks which actually qualify as food safety and hygiene risks, specifically chemical, physical or biological contamination.

Interestingly, those who did respond to questions about risk issues of less importance than food safety and food hygiene drew on the same comparators as those citing risks which are more serious. Those risks that could be categorized were defined as either broad occupational health and safety risks such as trips, slips, falls, back strain – 'Minor cuts and scrapes from packaging'

(Interviewee 153, Manager, Orange Company) – or crime risks – 'Violence from the public tends to be directed at one individual and is easily dealt with, usually with common sense' (Interviewee 175, Manager, Green Company). In addition respondents mentioned a miscellaneous list of 'lesser risks', these included the risks related to the use of computer keyboards and screens; verbal assault; and the competence of staff.

Phase 3 allowed some more in-depth exploration of these topics. Interestingly 17/20 (85 per cent) of respondents said that they believed the food sector is a risky industry to work in. But of the nine questioned about their own company or branch and the risks it carried, only one thought that the risks were high and the risk here was from drunk customers. The remaining eight deemed the risk low, with two specifically stating that this was because they did not have raw meat on site.

The factors which rendered the sector risky varied. There was particular concern about the possibility of incidents: 4/17 (23 per cent) explicitly mentioned incidents, others referred to the risks of prosecution (3/17 or 19 per cent) or civil litigation (2/17 or 12 per cent).

> Yes, it's a risky business, the risk of prosecution is greater now than it used to be in the past. (Interviewee 262, Manager, Blue Company)

> If something goes wrong I'd be totally held responsible. People could sue us – if I/we made a silly mistake – if someone fell ill – then this could have complications for the reputation of the company … and for my job. (Interviewee 860, Manager, Red Company)

Four out of 17 (23 per cent) regarded staff issues as a major risk, especially the low pay and risks of low motivation.

Given their concerns about incidents, Phase 3 respondents were not very aware of their occurrence. Nine out of 18 (50 per cent) of those asked how many major or minor incidents there were on their site last year, replied none. Some were unaware 'hopefully none' (one), 'not many' (one) and the remaining 7/18 (39 per cent) thought between one or two a month to two or three minor incidents a year, to 3 in 5 years. The sorts of incident they could recall were primarily a 'foreign body in food' (7/12 or 58 per cent) and out of date products (2/12 or 17 per cent) – '… milk may pass its use by date as the stock is not rotated correctly, new stock put behind old stock which is moved forward' (Interviewee 860, Manager, Red Company). Such incidents were attributed to staff not following procedures or making silly mistakes – 'When people are lazy and sloppy accidents happen' (Interviewee 842, Manager, Brown Company). There was general agreement however that incidents are preventable through training and sticking to the rules – '… ask them why they have done it, get it into his head and make sure it does not happen again, if they do it again give them a warning' (Interviewee 860, Manager, Red Company) and 'Food poisoning can be prevented if you don't use out of date food' (Interviewee 29, Manager, Blue Company).

There was a general feeling that standards have improved:

> I don't think there are as many now because of recent outbreaks of the E.coli and the salmonella things have really tightened up over the last couple of years and I've seen the difference in our own company and how many more regulations have gone in and now it is an awful lot stronger. (Interviewee 155, Manager, Orange Company)

Any problems that do exist are with other parts of the sector:

> I can compare because I used to work in a privately owned restaurant and the procedures there are not followed as they are at [XXX (present employer)] – shelf of food etc. and the hygiene was not much good because they intended to save money on it. (Interviewee 29, Manager, Blue Company)

Food Safety and Food Hygiene Risks in UK Food Retail and Catering

Phase 2 respondents were asked a series of questions about their views of food safety and food hygiene at the industry level. These were relatively difficult open-ended questions and they did produce some interesting data on how our respondents regard risk. A general question 'Do you feel that more could be done to improve food safety and food hygiene in your industry?' was answered by 197/204 (97 per cent) of the sample.[31] Half of the sample believed that more could be done to improve food safety and food hygiene in the industry and 62/204 (30 per cent) thought that no more could be done to improve the industry in these respects. Just 32/204 (16 per cent) did not know what could be done.

Those in the catering sector were more inclined than those in retail to see room for improvement[32] as were those in London and the South East.[33] Size of businesses was also of relevance in this area. Fifteen out of 20 (75 per cent) of respondents from micro and small businesses believed that more could be done to improve food safety, compared with 88/184 (48 per cent) of respondents from medium and large businesses. Size of business was also related to the number of risks mentioned by businesses. A distinct and significant correlation exists between type of business and quantity of risks mentioned: grocer businesses tended to mention more risks than hospitality businesses.

When they were asked to suggest what could be done to improve food safety and food hygiene in the industry almost all the managers in the micro and small businesses made suggestions, whereas in the large business between two thirds and a half of managers did not make any suggestions. Two clear avenues for improvement were suggested. The most popular was training and this was followed by a call for more checks/audits and inspections. Thirty-five out of 76 suggested more training and this was especially the case among SMEs and the catering sector. They advocated more frequent, higher quality and compulsory training.

The influence of training on managers was examined. Training was generally considered to be a very strong influence in encouraging higher standards of risk management regarding food safety and food hygiene.[34] It was most particularly valued in the hospitality sector where 74/89 (83 per cent) regarded it as a very strong influence compared to 54/82 (66 per cent) in the grocery sector. The strength of food safety and food hygiene training appears to diminish over time as it was particularly valued by those in their present job for less than two years rather than those with longer work histories in the industry. Those who had received training were the most likely to believe that more could be done to improve standards in the industry. Training also emerged as the most valued aspect of a business's food safety and food hygiene risk management.[35] Conversely where training was absent or judged insufficient it was identified as the issue of most concern.[36]

More checks, audits and/or inspections emerged as the second largest cluster of recommendations for improvement. These suggestions tended to come from medium and large-sized businesses (15/20 or 75 per cent). In some cases they related to internal business procedures – 'More freezer & fridges. Regular internal food & hygiene inspections weekly, fortnightly not monthly, especially when I am on holidays (!)' (Interviewee 808, Manager, Pink Company). In other cases respondents advocated more frequent and tighter inspection by state regulators particularly of small and medium-sized businesses. They believed that this would assist in maintaining the reputation of, and trust in, the industry – 'Too many small business operating with no legal responsibility to hold an advanced food hygiene certificate. Not enough EHO activity or EHOs to keep a check on these small businesses' (Interviewee 813, Manager, Pink Company).

Some managers in larger businesses perceived that small businesses are subject to a light regulatory touch whereas large businesses are tightly regulated and they disagreed that this should be so. Strict state regulation was called for, especially for competitor businesses and for those who were felt to let the industry down through poor quality of risk management and failure to comply with minimum regulatory standards. Many responses exhibited a genuine concern for the good of customers in the industry.

Future Challenges

In order to encourage broader thinking about the state of food safety and food hygiene in the UK we asked a very general question 'What do you think will be the greatest food safety and food hygiene problem facing your industry in

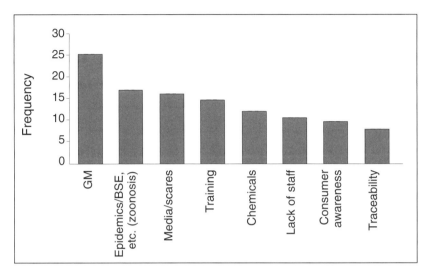

Figure 3.2   Future food safety/hygiene problems facing the food sector

the next decade?' This is a relatively difficult and open-ended question although the response rate of 139/204 (68 per cent) indicates that the sample did not experience too much difficulty answering it. Moreover, almost all the micro and small business respondents answered this question: the leading responses are detailed in Figure 3.2.[37]

These answers have a tone of genuine concern for the good of the industry. A broad range of concerns were communicated but the main ones centre on external factors which constitute the environment within which the business operates, especially more general societal concerns about health-related issues. Internal factors, management, regulation and consumers figure as less influential than one might have expected.

The main industry concerns of the future centre on contamination of the food chain, whether through GM, animal welfare/health issues (for example, BSE) or chemical contamination (for example, pesticides or additives). This also related to issues of traceability and confidence in the quality of suppliers. The GM and BSE issues had clearly concerned respondents and there was a worry that another such incident could currently be incubating – 'BSE still only [the] tip of the iceberg. Food standards reports on quality of chicken, out of date, then repacked and re-dated. Quality of sausages and what goes into them. A mystery to most of us' (Interviewee 826, Manager, Pink Company). A related concern was the consequential 'food scares' which may be generated by these events and the attendant media focus 'too much media attention confusing more *(sic)* people' (Interviewee 865, Manager, Red Company).

'Food scares' appeared to cover both inaccurate media coverage – coverage which claimed a risk existed where there was no risk – and media coverage of known risks. Food scares were seen by some as being exacerbated by poor quality risk communication campaigns which they believe leads to confusion among customers. Indeed customer expectations are seen to be partly related to media coverage with a number of respondents citing these as major challenges for the food industry in the next decade indicating that this may be the beginning of a worsening trend:

> Customer expectations (GM/pesticides/diseases etc.), media coverage (tv shows), not enough officers. (Interviewee 839, Manager, Brown Company)

> Genetic modification, media pressure/public opinion. (Interviewee 21, Manager, Blue Company)

> Consumers are becoming more aware of risks with food such as abuse of pesticides, mercury in tuna, PCBs in salmon, whether it is the media trying to scare us or the truth people will become more wary of what they eat. (Interviewee 271, Manager, Blue Company)

It is important to realize here that consumers are regarded as a major influence over risk management practices (Hutter and Jones 2006) so respondents were especially sensitive to anything which might be of concern to consumers.

Concern about staff shortages, especially the availability of trained staff, was of significant concern – 'Paperwork gets more and more. Untrained staff – staff not coming into our industry, food awareness in schools' (Interviewee 749, Manager, Pink Company). There were a few complaints about increasing bureaucracy but generally concerns about regulation focused on under- rather than overregulation, that is, a perceived laxity of external government controls (regulations). Respondents advocated more frequent and tighter inspection and regulation of all businesses in the industry. However, for several participants this did not necessarily apply to their own businesses but rather to others who were possibly competitor businesses – 'More accountability for smaller "backstreet" operations that give a well run business like ours a bad name…when bad practices are shown on TV I think people think that all catering businesses are run the same. Not right!' (Interviewee 744, Manager, Pink Company).

SUMMARY AND DISCUSSION: THE RESEARCH FINDINGS IN CONTEXT

We should keep in mind that risk means different things to different people (Slovic 1992) but patterns in understandings are discernable. We are interested in the way in which risks are understood by those working in the food industry. What do they think is a risk? How important do they consider it to be? Answers to questions such as these give us some insight into understandings which may influence their everyday work activities and in the risks they pose to us as consumers of food.

Overall it is clear that food risks are taken seriously by those we surveyed. Where they were not regarded as the most serious workplace risk they were regarded as second to health and safety or violence risks. Senior representatives interviewed in the first phase of the research differed about whether the main food safety/food hygiene risks could be seen as technical, chemical, biological or human. The second phase of research with managers highlighted some significant variations in understandings of risks.

The understandings of risk held by those in the food sector are very broadly held views which are not based on precise technical calculations. As with other work focusing on understandings of risk the distinction between risk and uncertainty is not one which resonates with how daily working life is conducted (Hutter and Lloyd-Bostock 1992). Central to these understandings are notions of control. The greatest risks are considered to be those relating to unpredictable events.

Understandings of risk differentiate factors internal to the business respondents worked in and factors external to their business. Internal risk factors connect to the immediate working environment and also to human sources of risk. External risk factors relate to other parts of the food chain and food industry and more broadly to consumer perceptions of risk and health and safety procedures.

This research strongly supports the finding that understandings of risk are socially situated, in particular that they vary according to place in organizational hierarchies and are also related to task environment, specialism and regional location. Sector differences between those from the grocery sector and those from the hospitality sector centred around particular topics which were related to tasks most associated with these environments. For example, hospitality staff were more likely to cite temperature-related risks and grocery staff were more likely to mention inadequate temperature control and stock rotation. Generally those in the hospitality sector were also most likely to see room for improvements.

The size of business respondents worked for also influenced their understandings of risk although this pattern is much weaker than that relating to sector. The variation was most pronounced with respect to general understandings of risk: those working in small businesses perceived more risks than those from larger businesses and they also considered that there is more scope for improving risk management in the food sector. Regional differences between Scotland and South East England suggest that organizational differences

between larger companies may also be important: some of which are region-
ally devolved and others which have centralized control systems, although this
is a far from conclusive finding at this stage but is rather suggestive and
worthy of further investigation. The importance of organizational factors
receives some support in the literature. For example, a study of offshore workers found that perceptions of risk were influenced by organizational factors
such as production pressures, job satisfaction and job situation (Fleming et al.
1998). Also relevant may be 'production pressures' which encourage hard
pushed, low qualified staff to cut corners (Hutter 2001; Vaughan 1998).

Of the factors perceived to be especially helpful in promoting good risk
management practices one relates to internal factors, namely, the food safety
and food hygiene training offered. This accords with respondents' broader
concerns about future risks to the industry where two internal factors were
prominent, namely, human sources of risk – a lack of staff and concerns about
training needs not being met. These findings are particularly important in a
sector which is so heavily dependent on human resources. Other studies have
identified human factors as a major source of risk (European Union Risk
Analysis Information Network 2003). Some of the reasons for these concerns
are structural features of the food industry where staff turnover is high and
where there is a high proportion of part-time and poorly educated staff
(Coleman et al. 2000). It is perhaps for this reason that training is so highly
valued by our respondents. It is seen as crucial to improving standards of food
safety and food hygiene and this view resonates with the broader literature.
Work in this area makes the point that knowledge and understanding of risk
are necessary but not sufficient in the promotion of higher risk management
standards. As Walker et al. (2003) point out, a common and striking finding is
that there is not a strong relationship in the food sector between training and
improvements. This may be related to a number of factors, for example, the
need for 'continuous' rather than 'one off' training (Coleman et al. 2000) and
also the nature of the employment market in this sector.

External factors are generally regarded as a greater source of risk than internal factors: the environment within which businesses work is seen as less
predictable and more volatile. For example, the food chain is not regarded as
entirely within their power, it may be complex and global and pose serious
difficulties to business traceability systems. Of particular concern are the
'unknown unknowns' and scares about them. These are regarded as inevitable
and potentially costly risks most especially because they are believed to influence consumers. Other research in the UK suggests those in the food industry
are concerned about public perceptions which are seen to be increasingly
sensitive to food issues, especially to 'food scares' (Shaw 1999). Some
research on public perceptions counters this view as it reports that consumers
are not especially anxious about food matters and do not differentiate between

food establishments according to food safety (Eurobarometer 2006; Green et al. 2003). However, the concern here is what those in the industry believe to be the case as it is these beliefs, rather than the accuracy of them, which mould their actions.

External factors are perceived to be especially helpful in promoting good risk management practices, most particularly regulation and perhaps perversely the impact of a major disaster. The importance of regulation in promoting good risk management is a finding supported by the literature which reveals that regulation is often valued at the micro level of the individual business. It is valued for raising standards, maintaining a level playing field and protecting industry reputation. And more often than not respondents think about regulation as something which is needed by 'others' rather than themselves (Gunningham et al. 2005). Regulation does of course very often link with major risk events as much regulation takes place in the shadow of disasters (Hutter and Power 2005). And the research does suggest that one such disaster, namely, the 1996 *E. coli* 0157 outbreak in Scotland, may have encouraged a lasting awareness of risk within the industry and also among consumers. It also led to a massive education campaign targeted at retailers and caterers: again this may help to explain the regional differences we found between respondents in Scotland and South East England.

These findings add to our knowledge of the social factors which may be relevant to shaping understandings in the workplace and are suggestive of organizational features which may be important. But there is a great deal of work to be done on the subject of the ways in which directors, managers and their workforces in different work domains understand both the risks to themselves and the risks they may pose to others during the course of their working day and lives. We know that understanding risk is important in promoting risk management but we also know that it is insufficient. In the next part of the book we consider in much more detail some of the external and internal factors shaping risk management in the food retail and hospitality sectors.

NOTES

1. http://www.statistics.gov.uk/StatBase/ssdataset.asp?vlnk=3983&Pos=1&ColRank= 2&Rank=272 (accessed 25 October 2010).
2. http://www.defra.gov.uk/animalh/diseases/zoonoses/zoonoses_reports/zoonoses_2000.pdf (accessed 25 October 2010).
3. This is the first incident report of its kind and contains data for 2006 only, no prior data is available. The report covers the UK and also covers the processing, distribution, retail and catering sectors.
4. The report unusually details the source of contamination in this case, other parts of the report give generic figures for the food chain.
5. 2003 report of the Parliamentary Office for Science and Technology (Postnote).

6. The figures for the USA are considerably higher. For example, it is estimated that some 76 million cases of food poisoning occur per year in the USA, over 300,000 of those affected are hospitalized and 5,000 die from foodborne illness and disease (Nayga 2003).

7. They report that in 1995 there were 2,365,909 cases of illness, 21,138 hospital admissions and 718 deaths. In 2000 there were 1,338,722 cases of illness, 20,759 hospital admissions and 480 deaths.

8. See http://www.food.gov.uk/news/newsarchive/2006/oct/allied and http://www.food.gov.uk/enforcement/alerts/2005/sep/alliedbakeries (accessed 25 October 2010).

9. http://query.nytimes.com/gst/fullpage.html?sec=health&res=950DE4DC113EF931A35756 C0A96F948260 (accessed 25 October 2010).

10. http://www.who.int/foodsafety/publications/fs_management/terrorism/en (accessed 25 October 2010).

11. Report on the *Sixth Summary of Progress on the Consolidation and Simplification of Food Hygiene Legislation* (11 August 2003).

12. This is considered to be an underestimate as it does not include long-term illness.

13. There are no cost analyses for physical/chemical contamination/bioterrorism/food tampering.

14. A more popular topic is public perceptions of food risks (Eurobarometer 2006; Frewer et al. 2002; Green et al. 2003; Shaw 1999).

15. The FSA explains that HACCP stands for 'Hazard Analysis Critical Control Point'. 'It is an internationally recognised and recommended system of food safety management. It focuses on identifying the "critical points" in a process where food safety problems (or "hazards") could arise and putting steps in place to prevent things going wrong. This is sometimes referred to as "controlling hazards". Keeping records is also an important part of HACCP systems.' See http://www.food.gov.uk/foodindustry/regulation/hygleg/hygleginfo/food hygknow (accessed 1 September 2010). See also Chapter 6 below.

16. Of particular interest here is work in the biotechnology industry which indicates that those working in this industry have an especially heightened awareness of risks and regulations because of their professional training. Moreover many of these firms are small start-up firms, thus providing an exception to the tendency for small firms to be less knowledgeable (Corneliussen 2004).

17. Worsfold (2005) found this to be the case with small manufacturing firms in the food sector.

18. This incident led to a major review undertaken by an independent review panel to identify lessons learnt by all sectors involved, including manufacturers, retailers, enforcement authorities and the Agency. The review highlights a number of recommendations directed towards all sectors, covering four main areas: incident prevention, incident handling, communications and relationships. See FSA (2007b). As a consequence of this report the FSA established the Food Incidents Task Force to strengthen controls in the food chain and to reduce the possibility of future contamination incidents.

19. The bulk of the research took place prior to the terrorist bombings on the London transport network on 7/7 2005. Five out of 204 of the entire sample mentioned terrorism as a greater risk than food safety and food hygiene risks and all these were in large businesses.

20. These categories are neither entirely mutually exclusive nor are they entirely independent; although some are interdependent, that is, under certain circumstances food poisoning is the outcome when cross contamination and insufficient cooking has occurred.

21. Note that 102/204 (50 per cent) of respondents gave examples of more than one different type of risk with many naming up to four separate risks. Some risks were coded into multiple categories and some responses fell within a single category.

22. A reference to an expired 'sell by' date.

23. Temperature control was mentioned by 11/23 (48 per cent); stock rotation/out of date products by 9/23 (39 per cent); and cross contamination by 6/23 (26 per cent).

24. Phase 3 respondents also gave multiple responses to this question.

25. Fifty-five out of 91 (60 per cent) grocers cited this compared to 30/113 (26.5 per cent) of caterers.

26. For example, 15/91 (16 per cent) of grocery respondents did not cite a risk compared to 36/113 (32 per cent) of hospitality respondents. More than one risk was cited by 55/91 (60 per cent) of grocery respondents and 47/113 (42 per cent) of hospitality respondents.

27. We should note that this was a relative difference, overall knowledge of EHOs was very high.
28. In addition to 0157 other outbreaks of verocytotoxin-producing *E.coli* (VTEC) have occurred in subsequent years resulting in death and illness but none on such a scale as the 1996 incident.
29. Three out of 164 (2 per cent) replied in this way for the 'More risk' question (all worked for the same large catering company) and 12/122 (10 per cent) for the 'Less risk' question.
30. There was no patterning of responses across type or size of business.
31. Seven out of 204 (3 per cent) did not respond to this question, all were from large companies, most from one large catering company. Thirty out of 32 who did not know what could be done were from large companies.
32. Sixty-seven out of 113 (59 per cent) cf. 36/91 (40 per cent) retail.
33. Eighty-three out of 147 (56 per cent) cf. 19/53 (36 per cent) Scotland.
34. One hundred and twenty-eight out of 171 (75 per cent) considered it a very strong influence.
35. It was cited by 22 per cent (45/204) of the sample as the most valued aspect.
36. It was cited by 10 per cent (21/2004) as the issue of most concern.
37. There is an 'other' category of 60 (a total of 199/204 or 98 per cent)) comments, many of which we could not easily categorize such as 'high rents' and 'animal feed'. We had smaller clusters of around four and five responses around 'too much paperwork', 'budget pressures' and 'production techniques'.

PART II

Risk regulation

There has been a broadening conceptualization of risk regulation over the past century and a shift that some term a move from government to governance. So regulation is no longer regarded as the exclusive domain of the state and governments and the role of non-state actors in regulation is now widely acknowledged.[1] Some non-state sources are new and represent a growth of regulation. But many of the sources of regulation are well established, they have existed for a very long time in one form or another. What is new is the growing recognition of these alternative sources as regulation, their formal co-option by the state and an increasing coordination of activities between various regulatory sources.

One way of making better sense of the complex of regulatory pressures upon business organizations is through the notion of risk regulation regimes. This concept is analytically helpful in teasing out some of the main risk regulation pressures on business organizations. Hood et al. (2001, p. 9) define a 'regime' as 'the complex of institutional geography, rules, practice, and animating ideas that are associated with the regulation of a particular risk or hazard'. It allows for varying scales of operation, from the local to international, varying levels of integration or fragmentation and differing levels of formality and practice. The institutional geography takes into account such characteristics as the scale, scope, integration and focus of institutions comprising the regime. Consideration of the rules embraced by the regime includes their degree of formality; their targets, whether they are inputs, processes or outputs; and any penalty or incentive structures attaching to them. And the animating ideas focus on professional and cultural biases, the rigour with which regulation is pursued and associated preferred policy instruments and approaches. A further distinction drawn by Hood et al. is between the context and content of regulation – the former refers to 'the backdrop of regulation' and the latter to 'regulatory objectives, the way regulatory responsibilities are organized, and operating styles' (2001, p. 28). With reference to the content of regulation Hood et al. (2001, p. 31) do note the importance of considering the extent to which regulation involves a mix of private and public sector actors. And it is important in the context of this book to develop these concepts beyond state risk regulation regimes. In particular it is important that the concept is extended to take into account more independent non-state regulatory actors and to identify the types of regulatory role they play in influencing business risk management.

The first section of Chapter 4 will examine the state risk regulation regime for food safety/hygiene in the UK. The second section of this chapter will present the empirical findings from this research to assess how much our sample knew about the state regime and their views of it. Chapter 5 will extend the notion of regulatory regimes to consider the influence of organizations and groups beyond the state. Much of this chapter will present the empirical findings of our research on the subject of regulation beyond the state, juxtaposed with the existing literature on various non-state influences. These discussions highlight the importance of empirical work as much of the supposition about the potential regulatory role of non-state actors is theoretical and not supported by much empirical data. Chapter 6 will focus in particular on the role of business organizations in their own self-regulation, something which is viewed from a policy perspective as the ideal form of regulation. The emphasis will again be upon considering the existing literature alongside our research data.

NOTE

1. See Baldwin et al. (1998), Black (2002) and Hutter (2001) for discussion of varying definitions of regulation.

4. State governance of food safety and food hygiene: the regulatory regime and the views of those in the food sector

The regulation of the risks associated with food safety was part of the dramatic extension of state interests and power in nineteenth-century Britain when the Adulteration of Food Act, 1860, and the Food and Drugs Act, 1860, were passed. Paulus's (1974) detailed study *The Search for Pure Food* argues that the Food and Drugs Acts are representative of nineteenth-century welfare legislation in their use of the criminal law to protect consumers from the damaging practices of business and the ways in which they accommodated the needs of different interest groups (see Hutter 1988; Paulus 1974). Draper and Green (2002) also regard this early legislation as protective of consumers with regard to fraudulent and then negligent behaviours by food manufacturers and sellers. At first this focused on fraud and food composition (including chemical adulteration), but later in the nineteenth century it also extended to bacterial contamination and the risks of food poisoning. Draper and Green explain that there then followed a long period of relative quiet from the government and public with respect to food and food safety. The exception was the debate on the pasteurization of milk. But to all intents and purposes the subject aroused little interest until the 1970s when food came onto the agenda as a result of concerns about the relationship between diet and health. And in the late 1980s a series of food scares placed food and its safety firmly on the public and political agendas. These events brought public confidence in the state, experts and the food industry to a serious low point. This partly contributed in the latter parts of the twentieth century to a change in the role of the public to that of consumers who could make informed choices. And at the end of the twentieth century there was a move to a much more active citizen who could participate in policy formation (Dryzek 1990; Rothstein 2004).

In this first section of this chapter we consider the state regulatory regime in place for food safety/hygiene at the time we collected the empirical data for this research. This includes discussion of the relevant legislation, institutional regime and series of crises which led to fundamental changes in the UK food regulation in the late 1990s. We will then consider the research data regarding how much those in the food retail and hospitality sectors knew about the state regime and how influential they felt it to be on their risk management practices.

THE UK REGULATORY REGIME FOR FOOD SAFETY/ HYGIENE

Legislation

The food retail and catering sectors in the UK are subject to an array of laws and regulations. These include the registration of food premises; licensing laws regarding the sale and supply of alcohol, providing entertainment, and selling hot food between 11pm and 5am; health and safety legislation; fire safety; VAT registration; and food labelling, description and pricing. In addition are the areas which are the focus of this study, namely, food safety and food hygiene and these are subject in their own right to a number of laws and regulations.

Food safety issues at the time of this research were covered by three main laws – the Food Safety Act 1990, and two EU laws: the General Food Law Regulation 178/2002 and the General Food Regulations 2004. These endeavour to ensure that food is fit for consumption and has no adverse health effects and also that food is 'of the nature or substance or quality demanded by the purchaser' (S7, Food Safety Act 1990). The 2002 Regulations relate to provisions about the import and export of food from and to the EU. There are also requirements relating to not misleading consumers, to traceability systems and to the withdrawal and notification of non-compliant food. The 2004 Regulations specify breaches that constitute criminal offences and the penalties for these breaches.

Food hygiene is subject to separate legislation. Until January 2006 the main legislation relating to food hygiene was the Food Safety (General Food Hygiene) Regulations 1995 and the Food Safety (Temperature Control) Regulations 1995. These regulations laid down general requirements to ensure activities were carried out hygienically with respect to such areas as food preparation, food processing, manufacturing, packaging, storage, distribution, handling and offering for sale or supplying foodstuffs. Its general application was inclusive of products not already covered by product-specific hygiene laws and regulations. Since January 2006 these laws and any subsequent amendments have been replaced by the Food Hygiene (England) Regulations 2006[1] which sought to consolidate and simplify EU food hygiene laws. It requires all business from 'farm to fork' to have in place HACCP[2] based food safety management procedures and to keep up-to-date records.

The UK's membership of the EU is crucial to these regulations which are derived from the EU. Most EU food legislation is either a regulation or a directive: regulations are 'directly applicable' so become the law of a member state from the time they are enacted by the EU; directives are binding on member states but only become law when implemented into national legislation. The Food Hygiene (England) Regulations 2006, for example, are regulations which were enacted in the UK immediately they became law in the EU.[3] Some of this legislation is vertical so it covers all aspects of particular foods. Some EU legislation is horizontal so it deals with a particular aspect such as labelling or hygiene and is applicable to all foods.

On a broader international level there are a number of transnational influences on the UK and EU food law. Perhaps the best known of these is the Codex Alimentarius Commission (Codex) which was established in 1962 and which is jointly sponsored by the WHO[4] and the Food and Agriculture Organization of the United Nations (FAO).[5] All EU member states are members of the Codex and the EU also has observer status. Its mission is to set international food standards (Demortain 2007), raise awareness of food issues and increase consumer protection. The Codex does not place any obligations on member states but the establishment of the World Trade Organization (WTO)[6] in 1995 greatly enhanced the status of the Codex. The WTO does place obligations on its members to abide by the rules and one of these rules specifies that member countries should base their food safety standards on the standards of the Codex (Article 3(1) Agreement on Sanitary and Pytosanitary Measures). The Codex has general standards for such matters as food labelling, food hygiene, food additives and pesticide residues, and specific standards for particular foods, for example, meat, fish and dairy products.

UK legislation thus partially derives from international bodies and standards. In each case of course the UK does contribute to the formation of these standards.

Food Safety Crises in the UK in the 1980s and 1990s

Historically the Ministry of Agriculture for Fisheries and Food (MAFF) took the lead in the UK government's handling of food issues related to food standards, labelling, composition and food contaminants, while the Department of Health took the lead on microbiological contamination of food. Also historically the DTI took the lead on weights and measures issues – many of which relate to food retail and hospitality outlets. These responsibilities changed with the creation of the FSA in 2000 (see below) and the Department for Environment, Food and Rural Affairs (DEFRA) in 2001. These changes were the result of a series of food incidents in the 1980s and 1990s which shook confidence in the system of food regulation in Britain, most especially confidence in MAFF and the government's handling of food safety. These crises merit brief discussion given their importance to food governance regimes in the UK.

The major food risk event of the 1980s–1990s was the BSE epidemic. BSE is a fatal, neurodegenerative disease in cattle which causes the brain and spinal cord to degenerate and become 'spongy'.[7] The first confirmed case of BSE was in cattle in Britain whose authorities (MAFF) were slow to identify this officially as a case of BSE. The cow was first examined in 1985 and was suspected to be BSE in 1986 but it was not until June 1987 that this was finally confirmed as a case of BSE.[8] In 1988 the first suspicions arose that animal foodstuffs were the cause of BSE and in June 1988 a ruminant food ban[9] was announced. In addition the compulsory slaughter of infected animals was announced as was a compensation scheme for farmers.

The mid to late 1980s witnessed growing public concern and media pressure over BSE, most especially concern that BSE posed a threat to humans. As a result of this pressure MAFF established, in May 1988, an Inquiry chaired by Sir Richard Southwood, who held the Linacre Chair in Zoology at the University of Oxford. Its remit was to establish whether or not BSE posed a threat to humans. The Southwood Committee reported in 1989 (Southwood 1989), focusing on the threat to cattle and asserting BSE to be an 'animal disease'. Nevertheless it was far from definitive in its conclusions, stating that the risk of transmission of BSE to humans 'appears remote 'but that if there were any implications, they would be extremely serious'. It recommended excluding high-risk material from baby food and recommended that there should be a new committee set up to give advice on BSE and similar diseases.[10] Despite these caveats MAFF took the Southwood conclusions as definitive rather than qualified and thus did little to promote confidence in the official responses to BSE in the UK.

Rates of BSE infected cattle rose despite the ruminant ban and suspicions grew that other species were at risk from BSE. In 1992 the first cases of human variant BSE Creutzfeldt-Jakob disease (vCJD) were recorded but it was not until March 1996 that there was official recognition that BSE was the likely cause of vCJD. In the meantime there were repeated government denials that there was a link between BSE and vCJD. This furthered a serious lack of confidence in official and governmental sources of information in the UK. There were particular concerns about the prime source of information throughout the crisis, namely, MAFF which the Phillips Inquiry (2000) was later to criticize for its interpretation of the Southwood conclusions as definitive rather than qualified. The eventual statistics of the crisis make for depressing reading. The UK was responsible for 99.5 per cent of recorded BSE cases in the EU; between 1996 and 1999 3.3 million cattle were slaughtered; and the estimated economic loss of UK GDP was £3.7 billion.

BSE was not the only food crisis the UK witnessed in the 1980s. In the late

1980s it experienced a panic involving *Salmonella enteritidis* in eggs and poultry. 1988 saw a dramatic rise in human infections of *Salmonella enteritidis* in England and Wales. There were outbreaks across the country with 11,000 cases reported by the end of October. These outbreaks were linked to eggs and poultry leading a junior government minister, Edwina Currie, to announce that most of the country's egg production was infected. This triggered a crisis of confidence in eggs with sales falling dramatically and the destruction of nearly 400 million surplus eggs. The government introduced a number of measures such as the slaughter of chickens, new laws and tighter controls on the sale of eggs. Meanwhile the egg producers were furious and supported by MAFF a compensation package was established to pay for the cull of chickens. Edwina Currie was severely criticized by a select committee of Parliament for panicking the public and eventually she was forced to resign her ministerial post. Interestingly she was never asked to withdraw or repudiate her comments (Doig 1989). It is, however, now acknowledged that her remarks did help to improve the safety of eggs in the UK but at the expense of a great deal of panic and a crisis which could have been avoided (Hickman 2006).

The third major food crisis in the UK occurred in 1996 when central Scotland experienced Britain's worst outbreak of food poisoning from *E. coli* 0157. It resulted in 20 deaths and left 272 people ill, 127 of whom were admitted to hospital (Pennington 1998b). The outbreak was traced to cold and cooked meat products sold by a butcher, John Barr and Son, in the Lanarkshire town of Wishaw, who had supplied 85 outlets throughout central Scotland. Inspection of his premises revealed a number of defects including a general lack of proper food hygiene for which the company was fined for breaching regulations. The Sheriff's report found that the shopkeeper, John Barr, had been ignorant of food hygiene procedures and had deceived food inspectors. The environmental health service was also criticized for acting too slowly in linking the outbreak to Mr Barr's shop. A subsequent inquiry led by Professor Pennington (1998a) made a number of recommendations about food safety and risk-based HACCP systems and also the management of livestock, slaughterhouse and butchers' shops practices and hygiene, and enforcement.

The cumulative effects of these crises were so undermining of the UK food governance regime and the food industry that, in anticipation of a forthcoming election victory, Tony Blair, then leader of the opposition Labour Party, commissioned Professor Philip James on 6 March 1997 to produce interim proposals for the establishment of a new structure for the control of food safety which would establish public health and consumer protection as priorities.

The James Report

The James Report was published on 30 April 1997. A key theme of the report was the loss of confidence in British food. It identified 'secrecy' in decision making, perceptions that 'inappropriate political and industrial interests' were at work and a fragmented, poorly coordinated food chain (James 1997). Public surveys discerned public concern in four main areas, namely, the microbiological safety of food, for example, prompted by the *E. coli* and *Salmonella* outbreaks; the chemical safety of food relating to particular concerns about pesticide and drug residues; apprehension about GM novel foods; and concerns about the nutritional quality of the diet and the role of food labelling in this. In order to restore public confidence James recommended a separation of institutions protecting the public and promoting business at governmental level and measures to combat uneven enforcement. The report then outlined proposals for the function and structure of the FSA. These proposals were largely incorporated into the new Labour government's White Paper *The Food Standards Agency: A Force for Change* (Cm. 3830), published in January 1998.

The White Paper attracted a great deal of interest. It proposed the new independent FSA, a non-ministerial department which would undertake responsibilities previously held by multiple government departments and would oversee local authority enforcement. A key objective was to restore consumer confidence in the safety of food. The new body would coordinate information and advice to government departments and to the public and act both at the national and international levels. It would have an integrated approach with 'from plough to plate' responsibilities. Food safety would be paramount and the agency would represent concerns and educate the public about food safety, food standards and nutrition. The independence of the agency from government was stressed as was its public role where it would 'put consumers first' and have a policy of openness and transparency. In 1999 the Food Standards Act formally established the FSA and set out its remit and powers (see below).

The creation of the FSA changed the institutional landscape at a national level. Further changes ensued in 2001 when MAFF merged with part of the Department of Environment, Transport and the Regions and with a small part of the Home Office to create DEFRA. The department was created after the perceived failure of MAFF to deal adequately with an outbreak of foot and mouth disease which seriously disrupted agriculture and tourism in the UK (Winter 2003). DEFRA is now responsible for environmental protection, food production and standards, and agriculture, fisheries and rural communities in England. It is also the lead department for the UK in the EU on agriculture, fisheries and environmental matters.

European Organizations[11]

The EU was also touched by the food crises experienced by the UK in the

1990s. BSE in beef cattle was an issue that had repercussions in Europe and, as in Britain, there were questions in the EU about the competence and the effectiveness of the existing systems to protect consumers. This led in 1997 to the creation of the EU Food and Veterinary Office to monitor compliance with food hygiene, veterinary and plant health legislation within the EU. An important aspect of this role is to maintain confidence in the safety of food consumed in Europe. As part of its remit the Food and Veterinary Office carries out audits and spot checks on food safety controls.

January 2000 witnessed another move to tighten up EU procedures and consumer protection relating to food. In January 2002 Regulation (EC) No. 1787 of the European Parliament and Council laid down general principles and requirements of EU food law and the establishment of a new EU regulatory body for food safety, namely, the European Food Safety Authority (EFSA). EFSA was a response to low consumer confidence in food safety (Chalmers 2003; Vincent 2004). Its role is to work with national food authorities, to consult and to provide 'objective scientific advice on all matters with a direct or indirect impact on food and food safety' (http://efsa.europa.eu/).[12] Risk assessment and risk communication are central to EFSA's remit and key to achieving this remit is EFSA's Scientific Committee and its Scientific Expert Panels which provide risk assessments.

UK Institutional Arrangements for Food Safety and Food Hygiene Regulation

State regulatory arrangements for food safety in the UK are organized on both a national and local basis (Figure 4.1). The 1999 Food Standards Act formally established the FSA and set out the organizational arrangements for the FSA's constitution and appointments; set out its main functions and objectives, for example, the development of food policy, provision of advice and information and monitoring of enforcement action; and contains a number of miscellaneous provisions. In April 2000 the FSA became operational as a policy-making body with responsibility for guidelines, standards and codes of practice. It has an enforcement arm, the Meat Hygiene Service, whose activities are independent of and parallel to those of local authority EHOs (see below). Each of the home nations of the UK, except England, has a devolved branch of the FSA (Figure 4.1). Upon its creation the FSA entered into a series of concordats with other parts of national and local government working in the food area. For example, it agreed a concordat with the Department of Health about working on issues of nutrition, foodborne communicable diseases and emergencies.

The FSA has an independent board including representatives from science, consumers, and food and farming. A great deal of emphasis is placed on

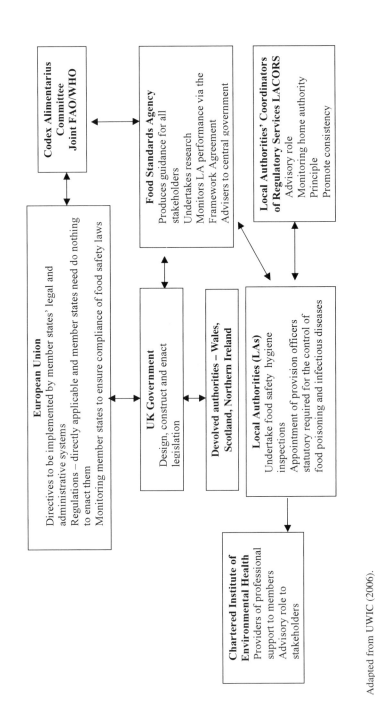

Adapted from UWIC (2006).

Figure 4.1   Organizations involved in food safety enforcement in the UK

consumers and being transparent. To this end effort is put into including consumer representative presentation on FSA committees, undertaking consumer surveys and providing accessible information to help consumers make informed dietary and food choices. Attention is also directed to promoting best practice in the food industry and ensuring enforcement of the law. The agency also provides advice to ministers and represents the UK in the EU.

While the Food Standards Act 1999 changed the national system for food governance it left enforcement of food safety and food hygiene legislation with local authorities who have long held responsibility for safeguarding public health.[13] The local system of food governance has remained broadly stable for the past century. Typically food safety remains the responsibility of local government EHOs and food standards the responsibility of local government trading standards officers (TSOs). The exception to this arrangement is in London and Scotland where both food safety and food standards are the remit of EHOs and they may have the title of food safety officer.

EHOs inspect food production, catering and retail premises on matters of food safety but they also perform additional duties such as housing standards, pollution control, health safety and welfare and noise control (Hampton 2005). In larger authorities this can be mitigated organizationally by employing specialist teams but in some areas the pressures for a more generic cross-cutting inspector remain dominant. With respect to food safety/hygiene EHOs monitor compliance with the minimum standards required by EU and UK government legislation; promote guidance and best practice on higher standards; and they may take enforcement action against businesses which are non-compliant with minimum legal requirements.

EHOs typically hold high levels of discretion about how to implement the law in individual premises and the evidence is that they deploy this discretion flexibly. Their overall approach does not take enforcement of the law to refer simply to legal action; rather it refers to a wide array of informal enforcement techniques such as education, advice, persuasion and negotiation. Securing compliance is its main objective, both through the remedy of existing problems and, above all, the prevention of others. The preferred methods to achieve these ends are cooperative and conciliatory. So where compliance is less than complete, and there is good reason for it being incomplete, persuasion, negotiation and education are the primary compliance methods. Accordingly, compliance is not necessarily regarded as being immediately achievable; rather it may be seen as a long-term aim. The use of formal legal methods, especially prosecution, is regarded as a last resort, something to be avoided unless all else fails to secure compliance. Indeed, the importance of legal methods lies in the mystique surrounding their threatened or possible use rather than their actual use (Hutter and Amodu 2008).

There are variations in the ways in which EHOs implement regulation and these differences may be accounted for by a variety of factors (Hutter 1988). Some variation, for example, is inherent in the legal framework. Differences in the size and location of the local authority may also lead to variations in enforcement approach. For example, enforcement practices are sensitive to the organizational resources available, particularly the department's budget and staff numbers, viewed in relation to the number and complexity of environmental problems encountered (see also Hampton 2005). Differences in the severity of the regulatory problems encountered are reflected in the enforcement approach as is the political salience of environmental health issues. There is, however, a potential downside for food safety in these decisions as food safety issues may be accorded less importance than more visible environmental health problems. This may be reflected in great variation in the resourcing of environmental health departments and also the financing of the different elements of their many responsibilities.

The Food Standards Act 1999 added a crucial element to the previous relationship between local and central responsibilities for food enforcement, namely, that the FSA inspects and audits the environmental health departments of local authorities. The FSA has authority to set performance standards, monitor performance, demand information from local authorities and inspect their food enforcement resources. And in the interests of transparency any reports they compile as a result of their audit can be made public. In pursuance of its duties in this respect the FSA has a Framework Agreement on Local Authority Food Law Enforcement which covers issues of agreeing standards, transparency and monitoring performance and securing improvements. The FSA website gives details of their audit scheme and also links to audit reports and follow-up audits, some of which reveal that, despite quite critical public audit reports, local authorities can be slow to respond to the reports.[14] The FSA also collects data on all food law enforcement activities and in turn reports them to the European Commission. The Commission in turn has its own team of auditors from the Food and Veterinary Office who, in effect, audit the FSA's auditing of auditors by visiting individual business premises in the presence of an FSA official and a local authority official. These data include, for example, numbers of inspections, numbers of infringements leading to formal action and details of sampling activities. This is presented in summary form and according to local authority.[15]

There are a number of bodies which could help to mitigate some of the professionalization and coordination difficulties experienced in the local authority governance system in the UK. The Chartered Institute for Environmental Health (CIEH) is the professional body which represents EHOs in the UK. It sets standards and awards qualifications as well as providing information to its members and government.[16] Another relevant body is the Local Authorities Coordinators of Trading Standards (LACOTS), which was set up in 1978 to coordinate the enforcement activities of trading standards. In 1991 it added food safety to its remit and was renamed Local Authorities Coordinators of Regulatory Services (LACORS). LACORS is located within the offices of the Local Government Association (LGA) and provides advice to local authorities on regulation and has published numerous briefing documents on food safety and hygiene.[17]

Let us now turn to consider how much those in the food retail and hospitality industry in the UK know about the regulatory apparatus in place for food safety/hygiene. Particular attention is paid to how much respondents knew about the local authority and nationally based regulators and we examine the variations in the knowledge held about these by different groups within the food retail and hospitality sectors. We also consider the views of those we interviewed about the importance and influence of state regulatory regimes.

RESEARCH FINDINGS: KNOWLEDGE AND UNDERSTANDINGS OF FOOD SAFETY/HYGIENE REGULATIONS IN THE FOOD SECTOR

Previous studies suggest that we should make no assumptions that state regulatory regimes are well understood by those subject to them. This was also the view of some of our first phase respondents who regarded the state regulatory arrangements set up in the late 1990s to be confusing. They expected that we would encounter a great deal of uncertainty in business especially among micro, small and medium-sized enterprises (SMEs) and particularly about the role of the FSA. Accordingly the research in the second and third phases did not take for granted that state regulation is familiar to everyone working in the food industry. Rather it problematized this issue aiming to discover the extent of knowledge about different regulatory systems (state and non-state).

Knowledge of the Law: Phase 1 and Phase 3 Findings

The overwhelming majority of those interviewed in the first phase of the research thought that national legislation is still the main reference point for most food businesses in the UK. They expected that most businesses would know about the 1990 Food Safety Act, the Food Safety (General Food Hygiene) Regulations 1995 and possibly more specialist regulations, with a few mentioning the 2000 European Commission White Paper on Food Safety which created the foundations for the EFSA. The third phase of the research allowed us to ask respondents direct and in-depth questions about the law and regulations governing food safety and food hygiene. Their replies indicated that they were less familiar with the law than our Phase 1 experts expected.

Rather, they were hazy when asked directly what food safety and hygiene laws they had to observe; none spontaneously cited any specific laws. Their main response was that these are encompassed by company rules, and the implication here was that they did not and did not need to know the law lying behind the corporate rules:

> ... company rules and regulation take away the necessity to look at individual laws. (Interviewee 191, Manager, Green Company)

> I've done a food safety course ... I've heard it mentioned there but I don't quote it every day to be honest. (Interviewee 86, Manager, Orange Company)

> ... they don't play a role in everyday conversations where only concrete regulations matter. (Interviewee 153, Manager, Orange Company)

Asked if they had heard of the Food Safety Act 1990 or the Food Safety Regulations 1995 11/14 (79 per cent) claimed that they had. Asked what these Acts required of them, respondents again gave vague replies about the detail or claimed that there was no need to know them because of company rules – 'don't know, fingers crossed, it's second nature, you give training to the people, the chefs and then once a week double check their records and make sure that they know what they are doing' (Interviewee 43, Manager, Orange Company).

Questions about the duties the law places on employers regarding food safety and food hygiene led to similar replies: 5/7 (71 per cent) could not give examples and four referred to company manuals which they could refer to for reference. Only two could give examples of the detail:

> Question: What do these laws and regulations require you to do?

> R: I might be able to find out as we've got manuals on this. (Interviewee 29, Manager, Blue Company)

> R: ... yes: they are explained in the health and safety folder, which is kept at the branch. (Interviewee 35, Manager, Blue Company)

> R: The training and the food alert (consultants) book has all these laws and documentation in them and it is up to the management to read them and understand them. I'm sure it is all there, it's been dumbed down when you trained so it actually goes in key bullets points. (Interviewee 843, Manager , Brown Company)

There was very much a view that the company should keep abreast of the law and through training and supervision ensure it is complied with:

Staff are aware of laws but they wouldn't be aware of the Food Safety Act 1990. People are youngsters, uneducated or different nationalities, people are not proficient in English. Senior managers know what these are. (Interviewee 860, Manager, Red Company)

Laws change all the time and it's difficult to track all changes. It's the company's duty to keep me informed so that I can in turn inform my employees. (Interviewee 867, Manager, Red Company)

Despite an apparent lack of knowledge of the law respondents did have quite strong views about food safety and hygiene laws. A range of views were expressed (Table 4.1).

Table 4.1   Phase 3 respondents' views about food safety and food hygiene rules and regulations

Views about the law	*n*	*%*
necessary/reasonable	11	69
reasonable though sometimes antiquated/unpractical	3	19
they should be stricter	1	6
they go too far	1	6
	16	100

Some felt that the laws were too restrictive but they appreciated why the laws were in place:

Some are needed, some are a little bit 'nanny state', obviously they are there for people who are not too sure about what to do and those people who don't really care or want to get away with stuff … the bad apples. (Interviewee 842, Manager, Brown Company)

They are there for a reason – to try and protect the consumer. Some are antiquated and not practical, you have to try and get on with it – you try your best. (Interviewee 780, Manager, Pink Company)

I think it's a shame that they had to be made into laws. Conscientious business people know if you want to make money you need to keep customers happy, and that involves giving them something that they gonna enjoy. (Interviewee 294, Assistant Manager, Blue Company)

Others more positively welcomed the laws as offering important protection and checks for the industry and consumers:

It does make an impact – when compared to other countries we are extra cautious, over cautious, in aspects of food management. We need to have laws, strict systems … This does have an impact on the business. (Interviewee 860, Manager, Red Company)

They need to be in place to set the standard you work to, if you don't work to it then you shouldn't be doing the job. More regular updates and training for managers so they do understand what their job entails when it comes to the legislation and legal side of things, as you are a key holder for a company and they trust you to make sure that you do everything in your power to make sure that the business runs smoothly. (Interviewee 843, Manager, Brown Company)

I think it is good, it is protection for [the] us and the staff and the customers as well. (Interviewee 113, Manager, Orange Company)

They are excellent and they have to be there because we have to make sure we are monitoring it for the customer to ensure the quality. (Interviewee 155, Manager, Orange Company)

One respondent even expressed the view that the laws should be stricter – 'I do believe that they could be a lot stricter … Temperature checks, probing of food need to be far more stringent' (Interviewee 262, Manager, Blue Company).

It is notable that it was only in the first phase of the research that any particular note was made of the influence of the EU on UK legislation. Possibly the EU did not feature in the second phase as EU legislation tends to be incorporated into national legislative regimes. No one in the third phase of the research referred to the EU in connection to any of the issues discussed, the law included.

It is of course debatable as to how much knowledge of the law food employees do need to have and how to interpret their varying levels of knowledge. Some commentators see knowledge of the law as a prerequisite to compliance (Genn 1993). Others believe that compliance is possible without a detailed knowledge of the law, moreover it may not require any knowledge of the law, most especially for employees who may have the legal requirements incorporated into company rules (Hutter 2001). Clearly there are differences between businesses according to ownership and size. Phase 3 respondents came from medium-large businesses which one might expect to have well-resourced headquarters which embody the law in their own self-regulatory systems. Such resources are typically not available to small and micro businesses and as we will discuss throughout this book, this is central to our understandings of food safety/hygiene practice in the retail and hospitality sectors in the UK.

Let us now turn to interviewees' knowledge of the law in action.

The Influence of State Regulatory Organizations

In the second phase of the research, managers of food businesses were asked a very general question about the extent to which their consideration of food safety and food hygiene risks is influenced by sources external to the business. Table 4.2 details the aggregate responses we received. Table 4.3 does the same for Phase 3. In the rest of this chapter we will consider these data alongside the other interview and survey data we collected so as to gain a better understanding of the influences of state regulation on business risk management practices. Chapter 5 will consider the influence of non-state influences on business.

Table 4.2   Phase 2: the range of influences upon managers when considering food safety and food hygiene risks

		Source of influence	Influence Index*
Most	▲	EHOs	1.35
Influence		Consumers	1.36
		FSA	1.74
		TSOs	1.90
		Media	2.46
		Insurance	2.85
Least		Lawyers	3.19
influence		Pressure group/NGO	3.23

Note: * Based on the statistical mean of all questionnaires (completed) by managers in Phase 2.

Table 4.3   Phase 3: the range of influences upon managers when considering food safety and food hygiene risks

		Source of influence	Influence Index*
Most	▲	Consumers	1.23
Influence		FSA	1.50
		EHOs	1.71
		Media	1.75
		TSOs	3.0
		Consultancy	3.0
		Pressure group/NGO	3.67
Least		Insurance company	3.8
Influence		Lawyers	4.0

Note: * Based on the statistical mean of all questionnaires (completed) by managers in Phase 3.

State Regulators: Phase 2 and Phase 3 Findings

Respondents were asked about three state regulators, the FSA and the two local authority regulators, EHOs and TSOs. In the first phase interviewees expected that the main point of contact between food businesses and state regulation is likely be EHOs and this was borne out by the second phase survey which found that state regulatory agencies were, alongside consumers, the most important external influence on food businesses and of these, EHOs were held to have the most influence (see Table 4.2). The strength of the influence is revealed in the constancy of the findings across different groups: 68 per cent of managers and 67 per cent of micro and small business managers claim EHOs are a strong influence when they are considering food safety and food hygiene risks with only 2 per cent of managers and no micro or small business managers claiming EHOs are of no influence.

Respondents were asked a series of questions about contact between EHOs and their business. These focused on their levels of awareness of organizational and personal contact with local authority EHOs. In particular they were asked if they could remember the frequency of EHO visits; when an EHO last visited their business; and how they regarded their relationship with EHOs. The majority of those interviewed (77.5 per cent or 158/204) were aware of contact between their organization and EHOs. Of those who were aware 66 per cent (135/204) could recall when EHOs last visited the company. Fewer had personal contact with EHOs (62 per cent or 127/204) and the majority of them thought that they saw EHOs annually or once every few years or after an incident.[18] The large majority of those interviewed (80 per cent or 81/102) thought that they had a very good/good relationship with EHOs, the remaining 20 per cent (21/102) were either neutral or did not know.

There were a number of variations in the responses, mainly according to the company that employed the respondents. For example, respondents from Brown and Orange Companies had higher levels of personal contact and recall than others and respondents from Yellow and Green Companies had relatively low levels.[19] There are no variations between type of retailers in evidence here but there are regional variations as Orange and Green Companies represent the Scottish and South East areas of a large retailer: the results suggest varying regional policies with respect to levels of contact with EHOs. Indeed, the point of contact in each business varies. In many businesses managers were not present during an EHO visit and in large organizations the visit was often 'handled' by a specialist from head office or a more senior manager. This was the case with Yellow Company whose managers revealed the lowest levels of personal contact with EHOs.

The case of micro and small businesses is interesting as we might expect the owner/manager to have direct and personal contact with EHOs. Yet small and micro business respondents did not have significantly higher levels of knowledge of EHOs than the rest of the sample. Indeed one of the surprising findings of the survey is that with one exception (one out of 15 respondents) none of the micro-size catering businesses proactively sought advice from EHOs. This is especially surprising as overall EHOs emerged as an important source of information for other food businesses (see Chapter 6), two thirds of managers we interviewed reported that their businesses actively sought advice from EHOs. The explanation of the small micro business responses is most probably found in EHO inspection practices whereby small and micro businesses are likely to receive infrequent visits unless there is some prior indication that a business has problems. The frequency with which EHOs are able to visit every food premise in their area varies according to local authority resources and also according to the risk a premise is thought to pose to consumers. This is judged according to the type of food and food handling involved, levels of current compliance and EHO confidence in management control systems. According to these risk ratings a premise may be visited in a range of once every six months to five years unless a complaint or food poisoning incident prompts an earlier visit. Clearly a lot may change in five years, such as a change of staff or even management. But local authorities have diminishing resources and cannot make repeated visits to low rated premises which may be in need of advice.

Inspection appears to be an important educative channel and it may be that micro businesses find these visits especially helpful when they happen yet they may simultaneously lack the confidence to actively ask EHOs for advice in the way larger businesses do.

Phase 3 data confirm that EHOs are perceived as very influential on decisions about food safety and hygiene risks management. Sixteen of the 19 respondents (84 per cent) ranked the influence of EHOs either first (six respondents) or second (ten respondents): this was relative to eight other state and non-state sources (see Table 4.3). The in-depth one-to-one interview setting in Phase 3 allowed for more detailed questions about EHOs. These started with an open-ended question which 12/25 (48 per cent) were able to answer: 'You have told me about the company's checks upon food safety/hygiene, is there anyone else responsible for checking food safety/hygiene?' This was followed by a series of detailed questions about respondents' knowledge of local EHOs and the amount they could recall of their last visit. They (13/15, 87 per cent) were able to respond to a general question about the name of their local authority but they were less certain about more detailed questions such as their ability to name or recognize their local EHO (3/5 (60 per cent) thought they could name/recognize their local EHO) despite the fact that 5/6 (83 per cent) thought that they see the same EHO for each visit. Half (8/16) could recall the EHO's last visit – how long the EHO stayed (from 30 minutes to over two hours) and the frequency of their visits (on average once every one or two years).

There was a general awareness of what EHOs did during their visits:

> [They] look at your operation, walk into the fridge, take fridge temperatures, come into the office and look at the files, look at training records, look at temperature records, look at the cleaning records, they check the cleanliness of the restaurant, they check the corners of the fridges ... they check everything. (Interviewee 860, Manager, Red Company)

> ... they don't come often for there are no problems with this site, they check problematic businesses more frequently. (Interviewee 153, Manager, Orange Company)... ask questions to check whether policies are met, quick check of paperwork. (Interviewee 35, Manager, Blue Company)

> ... inspected the kitchen, looked in the fridges, checked behind the range and checked the files, legal documentation, signed off then went. (Interviewee 843, Manager, Brown Company)

> EHOs always find something, no matter what. (Interviewee 867, Manager, Red Company)

Other visits were reactive and prompted by complaints. One reported that EHOs had investigated a complaint from a neighbour about noise from the premises, or an incident – 'He came out to condemn food after a freezer broke down due to an 18 hour loss of power. He advised on how to dispose of the food. He looks at our daily check book, checks health and safety, cleanliness, stacking safety' (Interviewee 113, Manager, Orange Company).

There was also a belief that EHOs' checks are useful for business. The majority (9/15, 60 per cent) found them comprehensive, and very helpful (11/18, 61 per cent); 3/18 (17 per cent) commented that they always find 'something minor'; and only four felt that EHO checks were less thorough than business's own checks:

> They are very helpful (for their advice). (Interviewee 858, Manager, Red Company)

> ... they are an invaluable source of information if you get to see them. Their reports are fantastic ... (Interviewee 36, Manager, Blue Company)

> ... they mention small minor issues – such as covering danish pastries – petty issues nothing serious. (Interviewee 860, Manager, Red Company)

> I've never had a problem with them, but it's good to know that they are doing checks, more from a customer point of view... It's great for consumers. (Interviewee 86, Manager, Orange Company)

It is also clear that not all of those interviewed would be comfortable approaching EHOs for advice: 10/19 (53 per cent) said that they would approach an EHO for advice while 8/19 (42 per cent) would rather approach their company resources first:

> I would always go internal first … because I'm worried that if I get into contact with the EHO I sort of make myself known to them and then I bring myself under scrutiny. It's not that I'm afraid of that but I don't want necessarily to put stress on myself. It's a paranoid subconscious thing. (Interviewee 294, Assistant Manager, Blue Company)

Going to head office is of course not an option for many SMEs working in the food retail and hospitality sectors as they have no head office to refer to.

One interviewee expressed the view that EHOs are not always so expert about food safety and hygiene issues, their expertise may lie elsewhere:

> An EHO I think is 75% health and safety focused, 25% food safety focused. This is mirrored by external consultants' work that also mainly consists of health and safety issues. (Phase 3 Interview, Director, Red Company)

This view is echoed by another:

> From my experience here not many of the EHOs which visit have as much knowledge as our quality and safety experts from head office … the people from government don't know if you are cheating or not, on shelf lives for example, but our people they do know and we get them in quite often. (Interviewee 29, Manager, Blue Company)

The examples offered of EHOs helping and giving useful advice centred on reactive situations, for example, helping with a product recall or broken equipment (a freezer).

Compliance and Knowledge of Legal Action

Compliance with EHOs' recommendations was regarded as automatic by respondents:

> … we got the EHO's notes and we dealt with them straight away. (Interviewee 867, Manager, Red Company)

> … their interpretation is always within the law and there is no reason to dispute that … Obviously if they found us, you know, in infringement breach of the law, they gonna come down on you to force up the law. You know in general we get on with these guys. We just don't irritate them so you don't cause yourself any problems. (Interviewee 153, Manager, Orange Company)

But two respondents did challenge this and in so doing raised the issue of costs and that EHOs may ask for things 'beyond the law'.

> It depends if it is a recommendation or a law. If it is going to cost a lot of money to do it and it is a recommendation not a law then the accountant will come back and say 'what is the point of doing it?' It may not be feasible where you are working. (Interviewee 780, Manager, Pink Company)

One reason for taking notice of EHOs is that they do generally work in the shadow of the law. The six interviewees asked about this in Phase 3 did know that EHOs have legal powers, four mentioned the possibility of fines and two believed that the courts could close down businesses – 'I know they can give you a letter of prohibition and they can give you a letter to make sure the changes get done they can close your store down effectively – if you don't do changes or if there is something that is a major risk to the public' (Interviewee 155, Manager, Orange Company).

The majority did not know of any legal action against their business; 13/16 (81 per cent) said that there had been no legal action against their business and two thought that other branches may have been the subject of legal action:

> I don't think so as there is never anything that serious happens, it's always picked up before that stage by us. (Interviewee 113, Manager, Orange Company)

> No, because I know we've got good procedures and I know we follow the proce-dures – I'm not saying we're 100% because there are always minor things they can pick up on … but I've never had a reason to think that we could be closed down. (Interviewee 155, Manager, Orange Company)

But not everyone is sure that they would know if their business had been involved in any legal action from EHOs – 'I'm not aware of that, I don't know, it could be that they have had an improvement notice' (Interviewee 29, Manager, Blue Company).

Legal action resulting from EHO visits did worry eight of the 13 questioned about this; 5/13 (38 per cent) were not worried but they expressed confidence that their company's own internal checks were good enough to avoid them getting in trouble with an EHO.

Those interviewed in Phase 3 were generally positive about EHOs who they believed to be important in raising standards: the majority (9/11, 82 per cent) believed that they are important in raising standards in the industry; just two believed that their value was less in raising industry standards and more related to particular businesses which would otherwise not meet the legal standards:

> Generally they do contribute to a better standard of food safety and hygiene. There should probably be more of them. (Interviewee 858, Manager, Red Company)

> It's all about how you put standards in place, the doing is the difficult bit, do the businesses want to spend the money? (Interviewee 27, Manager, Blue Company)

They don't bring higher standards, they just enforce legislation, there are not enough of them. (Interviewee 36, Manager, Blue Company)

Q: Do you think the EHO's presence makes a difference to food safety standards?

R: Yes, absolutely. Especially for smaller businesses – not specifically for us, because we already have strict policies. (Interviewee 35, Manager, Blue Company)

Interviewees did feel that EHO visits should be more frequent – 'several times a year'. These visits would not be a great burden on respondents' businesses but on 'other' less well-run establishments:

Yes, small businesses don't always spend the money they should until they are caught by the EHO. (Interviewee 27, Manager, Blue Company)

As a company their inspections don't bother us, if they come they come, they check. Privately owned restaurants should have more inspections and more thorough inspections. (Interviewee 29, Manager, Blue Company)

New businesses were identified as those needing more visits and also those with poor track records – 'it depends upon your past record, if you are known to be bad then it should be more regular' (Phase 3 Interview, Assistant Manager, Brown Company).[20]

Trading Standards Officers (TSOs)

Respondents in Phase 2 were also questioned about TSOs who are usually responsible for food standards rather than food safety or hygiene. The exceptions to this arrangement are in London and Scotland, both areas we conducted some of the research in, where both food safety and food standards are the remit of EHOs and they may have the title of food safety officer (see above). TSOs clearly influence (126/204, 62 per cent) our food businesses but not as strongly as EHOs (186/204, 91 per cent). Knowledge about TSOs was patchier than was evident in the case of EHOs. For example, when asked about TSOs 50 per cent (10/20) of micro and small businesses indicated a response of 'Not applicable' or 'Don't know' compared to 10 per cent (2/20) who did not or could not respond on the subject of EHOs. Little patterning was evident according to the size of business or whether the business was a retail or catering business. TSOs were spontaneously mentioned elsewhere in the survey by less than 2 per cent (4/204) of respondents.

This would suggest that an awareness exists of trading standards matters but managers, directors and owners have had little experience of direct contact with a TSO.[21] This is confirmed by considering the responses of the directors and senior managers where just over half of the sample (15/28, 54 per cent) said that they had no contact with TSOs; ten did have contact; and three did not know or did not answer the question. Those working in small and micro businesses had less contact than did managers of larger businesses. There was some uncertainty about how frequently TSOs were seen although eight of those who claimed to have contact with TSOs thought that they had a good relationship with them. Levels of awareness of TSOs were significantly greater in the grocer than in the hospitality sector ($\alpha < 0.05$). Contact with other government or local council officials was mentioned as influential by a minority of respondents, these included a miscellany of officials from the Heath and Safety Executive, police, fire services, planning officials, pest control and the Inland Revenue.

Food Standards Agency (FSA)

During the first phase of the research the role of the FSA was, as one might expect among this group of experts, well known. But there was a great deal of uncertainty in this group about how well known the FSA would be in the wider food industry. Yet in our second phase survey the FSA was ranked as the third most important external influence on food retail and catering businesses. This ranking did vary between businesses. Those with a detailed knowledge of the FSA tended to be at the highest levels within businesses, that is, within 'head office' specialist functions and similarly specialist functions within trade associations. It is indeed interesting that the FSA was spontaneously mentioned on just two occasions in Phase 2: once when a general manager of Brown Company thought that updates from the FSA would improve food safety and hygiene in the industry and once when a senior manager of a large retailer mentioned contact with the FSA as part of his/her interaction with state regulators. The FSA did seem to be most important in its role as a provider of information: 33.5 per cent ($n = 59$) of respondents cited the FSA as one of the manager's main sources of information about food safety/hygiene issues. And 12 per cent ($n = 22$) of respondents thought that the FSA was one of the main sources of information for staff (see Chapter 6).

The Phase 3 data tend to support the views of the experts.[22] The influence of the FSA on food management is perceived as rather low: when asked 'You have told me about the company's checks upon food safety/hygiene, is there anyone else responsible for checking food safety/hygiene?' only one of the 16 (6 per cent) asked spontaneously mentioned the FSA; when prompted four out of 16 (25 per cent) respondents had not heard of the FSA; five out of 16 (31 per cent) respondents had heard of the FSA but were not in contact with them.

Q: Do you know much about the Food Standards Agency?

R: I know from what I read about them, but I don't know more than that. So I know, to say, I think I know as much as the other person in the street that reads a good newspaper. (Interviewee 819, Manager, Pink Company)

Others claimed to have heard of the FSA but their knowledge was hazy. Five out of 16 respondents (31 per cent) have or might have received information leaflets from the FSA, but did not find that information useful: 'Yes, I think they sent me a leaflet' (Interviewee 29, Manager, Blue Company). One respondent thought the FSA had visited their premises but ranked their influence compared to other sources only third. Only one respondent seemed to have had contact with the FSA on the occasion of a food recall.

Phase 1 – the Experts' Views of State Regulation

The FSA was borne out of a crisis in food regulation in the 1980s and 1990s (see above). During the course of this research there were differences in opinion concerning the state of food safety and food hygiene in Britain today but no one indicated that they considered it in a state of crisis.

The only detailed discussions about the FSA occurred in Phase 1 where the role of the FSA was discussed mainly in relation to three areas. First, was the potential for their audits of local authority enforcement to encourage consistency. Second, was criticism of their adoption of the precautionary principle rather than principles of proportionality; this was perceived to impose major costs on business, some of which were thought to be unwarranted. The third topic relating to the FSA was the perceived differential effects of their policies, especially the effects of HACCP management systems which was a major focus of concern of the majority of those we spoke to (see below).

Views about EHOs varied widely, much as they have done over the past 20-plus years. Some were of the opinion that EHOs are an invaluable part of a national 'team' trying to improve food standards, especially in Scotland (see below). Indeed, one commentator declared EHOs to be 'much better and professional than they used to be ... now it's more an attitude of trying to help and advise people' (Phase 1 Senior Industry Representative). But the juxtaposition of different perspectives is apparent in the following criticism of EHOs and TSOs: 'The good guys [compliant businesses] don't like the fact that EHOs/TSOs don't prosecute the cowboys, those that give the sector a bad name' (Phase 1 Senior Governmental Policy Maker). As ever, regulators are criticized for either being too lax or too harsh, depending on who is spoken to.

The more difficult criticisms focus on complaints that EHOs are handicapped by their levels of training and technical knowledge and also by alleged inconsistency between different local authorities – 'Consistent enforcement across all regions is an issue ... business just wants a level playing field'

(Phase 1 Senior Industry Representative). Both areas of criticism were seen to undermine the effectiveness and credibility of EHOs. Some were sympathetic as to the causes, this was summed up by one respondent who commented that EHOs are 'overworked, underpaid and poorly co-ordinated' (Phase 1 Senior Industry Representative). The criticism is seen to be especially of concern in a new world where EHOs are required not just to inspect but to assess the quality and suitability of the businesses hazard management system in place in each food establishment.

FSA audits of local authority provision for enforcing food safety and hygiene laws were considered important but they are not without their own points of controversy. For example, there is some suspicion that while FSA activity has raised awareness of food safety and hygiene issues this has been to the detriment of other environmental health functions. Moreover, FSA audits do not necessarily result in improvements as acting on their recommendations is not mandatory (see Chapter 7).

The question of regulatory overload is a topic which one expects to emerge quite quickly in discussions about the regulation of business. It did emerge in Phase 1 but mainly in relation to SMEs. The complexity of the requirements, especially HACCP, caused concern:

> In the past few months risk as an issue for the industry has become very important … Businesses are very concerned about the wide range of subjects that now have to be included in risk assessments. (Phase 1 Senior Regulator)

But the bigger concern was the volume of overall regulatory requirements, particularly as they affected SMEs. One SME area manager from a branded chain of retail stores estimated that the manager of a single retail unit could expect between 12 and 43 compliance visits (or 'checks') per annum. The risks addressed would relate to health and safety, financial transactions and the physical security of assets and personnel, and the checks would be made by state regulators or on behalf of the company's head office. Another participant commented 'The distractions from the business are huge. The opportunity costs are enormous.' The use of the word distraction is a revealing one and apparently contrasts with the view that state regulation aligns with good business practice and can facilitate business opportunities. Interestingly some of our experts associated regulatory overload more with the regulations imposed by large supermarkets than they do with the state.

SUMMARY AND DISCUSSION: THE RESEARCH FINDINGS IN CONTEXT

Managers' knowledge of EHOs, the local authority regulators, was most widespread and most sophisticated. This is not entirely surprising as they are in most contact with the industry at shop floor level and their remit directly relates to the food safety and food hygiene risks we asked about. TSOs do not work directly to this remit but the survey responses do not seem to have such a nuanced reason for the ignorance of respondents about TSOs – the indications are that they have less knowledge of trading standards. Knowledge of the nationally based FSA is high at senior management and policy levels of large businesses but less so at junior management level. Overall, however, knowledge of the FSA among businesses was much higher than our expert group anticipated it would be.

Like other studies we found that SMEs had lower levels of knowledge of regulatory laws and state regulatory systems (BRTF 1999; Fairman and Yapp 2004; FSA 2001; Gunningham 2002; Henson and Heasman 1998; Vickers et al. 2005). They also appeared to rely on state regulatory systems for education and advice. The general levels of knowledge about the overall state regulatory system echoes the findings of other studies, although knowledge of EHOs appears to be higher than those found by studies of other regulators. Genn (1993) found great variation in levels of regulatory knowledge, with confusion about regulators highest on the smaller sites she visited. She also found little evidence of the regulated in smaller businesses being prepared to debate with inspectors, rather like the micro and small businesses in this study. In larger companies there is a greater readiness to use regulators as a resource. In Hutter's (2001) study of a national railway company the social dimensions of regulatory knowledge and understanding were striking, with senior personnel having a much greater understanding of the regulatory system than those lower down the hierarchy. This very much accords with our findings.

The literature on the impact of state regulators reveals a variable impact. The overwhelming majority of railway employees interviewed in Hutter's (2001) study thought that the state regulator was very important in bringing about higher standards of health and safety in the industry. Likewise Gunningham et al. (2003) conclude that regulation is key in shaping corporate behaviour. This contrasts with earlier studies by Gricar (1983) and Clay (1984) on Occupational Safety and Health Administration (OSHA) inspectors in the United States. Most studies argue for the necessity of maintaining some kind of outside policing of business risk management primarily to ensure that risk management objectives are established and maintained on a firm's agenda and to establish 'credible enforcement' (Gray and Scholz 1991; Gunningham and Grabosky 1998; Hutter 2001). What is less well discussed is what other influences affect business risk management practices. We turn to the subject of which pressures beyond the state are important in this respect in the next chapter.

NOTES

1. Scotland, Wales and Northern Ireland have equivalent regulations.
2. See note 15 in Chapter 3 and Chapter 6.
3. Similar regulations were simultaneously enacted in Wales, Scotland and Northern Ireland.
4. The WHO is responsible for international health, most especially a directing and coordinating role which covers such roles as developing standards and educating the public.
5. The FAO is an autonomous agency within the United Nations (UN). Its remit is to raise levels of nutrition and standards of living.
6. The WTO is the successor to General Agreement on Tariffs and Trade (GATT), its remit concerns trade negotiations regarding such issues as tariff reductions. It aims to harmonize standards based on risk assessment.
7. http://www.bsereview.org.uk (accessed 18 August 2010).
8. http://www.bseinquiry.gov.uk/report/volume3/chapterd.htm (accessed 18 August 2010).
9. This 1988 ban referred to a ban on feeding ruminant protein to ruminants. In June 1994 the EU prohibited the feeding of mammalian protein to ruminant species in all member states and in March 1996 this was extended to prohibit the feeding of mammalian meat and bone meal to all farmed livestock. DEFRA refers to this ban as 'the key BSE eradication tool' (see http://www.defra.gov.uk/foodfarm/farmanimal/diseases/atoz/bse/controls-eradication/feedban-quanda.htm, accessed 1 September 2010).
10. This led to the formation of the Spongiform Encephalopathy Advisory Committee (SEAC).
11. The Directorate General (DG) for EU food law is the DG for Health and Consumer Protection (DG SANCO). Also relevant are the DGs responsible for industry (DG Enterprise) and agriculture (DG Agriculture).
12. Its tasks are various including acting as a collator and provider of information and data, and provider of scientific advice with respect to existing and emerging risks. It also serves a coordinating role with respect to public information, scientific work, networking and research. See generally http://efsa.europa.eu (accessed 1 September 2010).
13. The first inspectors to be appointed as a permanent part of the public health administration in Britain were Inspectors of Nuisance, appointed by local Boards of Health in accordance with the 1848 Public Health Act. One of their main tasks related to food, namely, to inspect 'articles intended or exposed for the sale of food of man'. Their initial impact was limited and it was not until the twentieth century that adequate provision was made for the employment and education of these officers.
14. http://www.food.gov.uk/enforcement/auditscheme/ (accessed 2 November 2007).
15. http://www.food.gov.uk/enforcement/ocddata (accessed 2 November 2007).
16. http://www.cieh.org/about_the_cieh (accessed 1 September 2010).
17. http://www.lacors.gov.uk (accessed 1 September 2010).
18. Sixty-seven per cent (n =127) thought annually; 12 per cent (n =18) thought once every few years; 15 per cent (n =19) after an incident.
19. Significant variations among companies were found in awareness of personal contact with the organization ($\alpha < 0.01$) and recall of EHO's last visit ($\alpha < 0.01$).
20. Four out of 17 thought that everyone should have the same level of checks and 8/17 believed that some businesses should be checked more frequently than others.
21. Business managers working in Greater London would not have contact with a dedicated TSO; here the tasks of EHO and TSO are combined.
22. Sixteen out of 25 respondents were asked questions about the FSA.

5. Risk regulation beyond the state: research responses about non-state regulatory influences

In mapping out the variety of non-state actors who may play a risk regulation role it is useful to distinguish between the state, the economy and civil society (Hutter 2006a). This helps to facilitate discussion of sources of regulation which are autonomous and independent from the state[1] and consider more systematically the nature of their influence on regulatory and risk management issues.

Three main sources of regulation can be identified in the economic sector, namely, industry or trade organizations, companies themselves and those whose business is selling regulatory and risk management advice or cover to companies. The first two of these are often referred to under the heading of 'self-regulation'. This covers a wide range of arrangements (Ogus 1994) and is a prominent regulatory form (Gunningham and Rees 1997). Regulation by business itself is discussed in Chapter 6. This chapter will focus on economic sector self-regulation as mediated through trade associations[2] and the influence of those involved in selling regulatory and risk management advice, for example, insurance companies and consultancies.

The term civil society embraces a fairly broad range of actors and organizations. Accordingly the range of sources of regulation in the civil sector is diverse. Perhaps the best-known regulatory sources in this sector are NGOs, a category which itself includes a diverse range of organizations which may operate at the local, national or international levels (Hutter and O'Mahony 2004). Also important in the civil sector are standards organizations which produce standards about product quality, quality assurance and risk management (Brunsson and Jacobsson 2000) and professional organizations which have long played a very important regulatory role in regulating entry conditions to the professions and laying down standards of conduct.

There are also important hybrid forms of self-regulation, for example, enforced self-regulation which involves a mix of state and corporate regulatory efforts (see Chapter 1). There have also been attempts by the state to co-opt the influence of other actors as third parties (see below).

These organizations may influence regulation and business risk management in a variety of ways. Some will have a background and indirect influence

and others will have a much more direct influence on business risk management practices (Hood et al. 2001). NGOs, for example, may be both part of the
context and content of regulation; they may exert normative background pressure or in some cases they may be formally incorporated in business risk
management and corporate social responsibility initiatives.

The influence of non-state actors on business risk management is not well
researched and much of the work that does exist is speculative. For example,
the literature on the regulatory influence of NGOs and insurance focuses on
the theoretical possibilities of their influence rather than empirically investi-
gating its actuality. This chapter will consider the findings of our research
alongside what else is known about the influence of selected non-state organizations and pressures.

NON-STATE REGULATORS: UNDERSTANDINGS IN THE FOOD RETAIL AND HOSPITALITY SECTORS

The growth of non-state actors in regulation and risk management practices
was very well understood by our Phase 1 experts who in addition to state regulators and supranational institutions, identified a variety of non-state sources
of regulation. In the economic category they cited trade organizations,
commercial consultants, the insurance industry, lawyers, private standards and
self-regulation/best practice. In the civil category they noted professional
associations, scientists, advocacy and pressure groups, external accreditation
agencies, assurance schemes, consumer NGOs, the public and the media.
Based upon these discussions we selected the five non-state influences which
emerged as most likely to be relevant to the food retail and hospitality sectors
for inclusion in the Phase 2 questionnaires. As we can see from Table 4.3, the
most influential of these non-state groups are consumers who, along with
EHOs, exert the greatest influence over respondents' food safety and food
hygiene management.

Consumers

There is very little academic work on the role of consumers in influencing
business regulatory and risk management decisions. The most relevant
research focuses on the potential importance of consumer preferences in influencing corporate environmental policies. Grabosky (1994), for example,
argues that preferential buying or consumer boycotts may have the capacity to
influence business environmental behaviour more than state regulation. But
there is no corresponding research in the area of food safety and food hygiene.

A study in the UK found that consumers regard food safety as highly important but that they have few concerns about it as they generally agree that standards in the UK are very high (IGD 1998). Certainly our first-phase interviews did not identify consumers as having such important potential in the regulatory system and did not indicate how widespread and strong an influence they would be among the business managers interviewed in the second phase of the research.

Research findings

Most managers in the Phase 2 sample sensed a general public awareness of food safety and food hygiene risks. This is well illustrated by Table 5.1 which shows how managers responded to a question about their understandings of consumer concerns. In two companies 100 per cent of managers thought that consumers rated food safety and food hygiene issues as their most important concern. A senior risk manager from a large branded licensed catering chain commented that his business had 'over complied on GM regulations due to consumer demand'.

Table 5.1   Managers' perceptions of consumer concerns based on the statistical mean of all questionnaires (completed) by managers

	Consumer concerns	Importance Index (mean values of questionnaires)
Most Important	Food safety and hygiene	1.1
	Price (value for money)	1.65
	Labelling & product description	2.2
	BSE	2.35
	Food additives	2.4
	GM (genetic modification)	2.55
Least Important	Use of pesticides to grow food	2.55
	Organic	2.7

Two respondents cited consumers as the main food safety/hygiene risk encountered by business: one was concerned about the risk of an incident shaking consumer confidence and the second regarded consumers as a source of risk to the extent that they may not 'follow good practice after leaving the store' (Interviewee 175, Manager, Green Company). Concerns about consumer confidence were also cited by six respondents as the greatest food safety/hygiene problem facing the industry in the next decade. The issues here relate to greater consumer awareness of food risks and a belief that there are more consumer demands and expectations:

Q: What are the greatest food safety/hygiene problems facing industry in the next decade?

R: Consumers are becoming more aware of risks with food ... (Interviewee 271, Manager, Blue Company)

R: Greater awareness of consumers and changing attitudes. (Interviewee 149, Manager, Orange Company)

R: To be able to produce enough volume ... to meet growing consumer demands. (Interviewee 744, Manager, Pink Company)

The strength of consumer influence was high across the Phase 2 sample. The only variation involved a higher level of uncertainty among managers from Yellow Company where 50 per cent either did not answer or did not have an opinion. This is a high volume hospitality outlet with a high turnover of staff and this may partly explain this inability to respond.

Phase 3 data confirm the importance of consumers to the overall sample: 44 per cent (11/25) of respondents ranked consumers as the most important influence on their decisions about how to manage food safety and food hygiene risks and 52 per cent (13/25) ranked this in the top three influences (see Table 4.2). The majority (19/25 or 76 per cent) of respondents thought that customers do appreciate food safety and food hygiene issues. Indeed, customers were thought to have high expectations and to take particular notice of cleanliness and presentational issues such as the atmosphere of the outlet and the presentation and taste of food:

Q: Do customers appreciate food safety and hygiene issues?

R: Yes. They have high expectations ... You can't afford to fail on food safety, hygiene or customer safety issues. (Interviewee 867, Manager, Red Company)

R: Yes. Customers notice if food safety and hygiene is not taken seriously and they would give feedback. They would take notice if someone would be prosecuted for ignoring food safety and hygiene issues. (Interviewee 858, Manager, Red Company)

R: Yes customers come here for the cleanliness, the atmosphere and the freshness of the products. (Interviewee 27, Manager, Blue Company)

R: Yes ... And I think that's why we are doing well. Customers know that X restaurants are clean, well presented. They will probably see staff washing their hands. (Interviewee 262, Manager, Blue Company)

R: Oh yes. It's the golden rule for any business, especially restaurants and hotels: if the place [that the customer sees] if that's not clean ... You can't keep your toilet clean? You can't keep your kitchen clean? (Interviewee 294, Assistant Restaurant Manager, Blue Company)

R: Yes definitely, if the customers come in and see a bright clean deli and store overall and they are more likely to shop rather than if it is dingy and the meat doesn't look very fresh then they'll just about turn and go somewhere else. (Interviewee 155, Manager, Orange Company)

Fifty-four per cent (6/11) thought that customers do not appreciate these issues and rely on trust:

A lot of people take it for granted that a place will be safe to eat. If you see dirty tables then they have not been showing due care and attention, and if it's like that out front then what will it be like in the kitchen? That's my catering way of looking at things. (Interviewee 780, Manager, Pink Company)

Probably not as much. If they were in the industry they'd perhaps understand more. Customers trust us although they are not necessarily aware of what we are doing. (Interviewee 153, Manager, Orange Company)

I think they couldn't care less … They're into having a good time … If a fire alarm goes off, they won't go. They won't go unless somebody physically goes and says right, you have to go now. (Phase 3 Interview, Director, Brown Company)

Nine out of 11 (82 per cent)[3] believed that food safety and food hygiene standards are material to customers' decisions about where to eat or shop. Just two disagreed: one did not think that consumers took as much notice as they should and another did not think that customers are able to judge food safety and health:[4]

Q: Do standards of food safety/hygiene influence customer's decisions about where to shop/eat?

R: It depends – if they are a professional (like me) they notice. A common person would not be able to establish that [if it is safe]. (Interviewee 860, Manager, Red Company)

R: Yes, definitely. … It does definitely influence whether people want to come and eat here. (Interviewee 777, Manager, Pink Company)

R: Probably not as much as it should do. Price is the biggest influence, and obviously quality of service. (Interviewee 191, Manager, Green Company)

All agreed that an adverse food safety or food hygiene event would be damaging to their business. National chains and local businesses were both thought to be seriously affected. The majority of those asked (7/12 or 64 per cent) thought that consumers remember food recalls:

Q: How damaging would an adverse food safety or hygiene incident be to your business?

R: I'm in a Jewish area and I'm not a kosher restaurant, so my customer market is quite small anyway. If you go to a restaurant and you have a good meal you tell maybe five people. If you go to a restaurant and you have a bad meal, or you get food poisoning, you have a bad experience, you tell everybody you know … I think it's really really serious. (Interviewee 294, Assistant Manager, Blue Company)

R: I'd be pretty pissed off … They trust us, walk through the front door and we give them food poisoning … I'd be gutted and want to find out why … it could be a bogus claim. (Interviewee 842, Manager, Brown Company)

R: I think it would be very damaging, also because it is a public place not just a restaurant. It's part of the British institutions. When you've got an outbreak or food poisoning in a British institution, it's a bit different than in a single restaurant. It's like a reflection of what is happening in our institutions. (Interviewee 819, Manager, Pink Company)

R: You hear about companies being sued and the bad press in the papers which obviously no food company ever wants to see. (Interviewee 780, Manager, Pink Company)

R: Terrible as it is a local shop in the town and it wouldn't be good publicity. (Interviewee 113, Manager, Orange Company)

R: It would be pretty severe for his branch is part of the local community. Therefore, an incident would have a big impact on sales. (Interviewee 153, Manager, Orange Company)

R: Major, we'd lose a lot of customer confidence – I wouldn't go back to a store that had that previously, no way I'd shop in it … it could also have a knock-on affect on the local businesses of the shops round about that. (Interviewee 155, Manager, Orange Company)

The Media

Generally, the role of the media as a regulatory force is discussed in the existing academic literature as a theoretical possibility rather than empirical actuality. Fisse and Braithwaite (1983) considered how corporate deviance might be controlled by the use of adverse publicity since the threat of publicity targeted the desire of businesses to protect their reputations. Mason and Mason (1992) also examined the mass media as a means of enhancing taxpayer compliance, arguing that this may be a means of persuasion for moral compliance and the promotion of civic virtue. The media can play an important informational role which can influence demand for products such as food (Baron 2005; Swinnen et al. 2005). Some regard this as a positive influence. Lang and Hallman (2005), for example, refer to the media as 'a watchdog of the public interest'. Others regard the media as a source of social amplification (Kunreuther 2002; Pidgeon et al. 2003) although there is disagreement about how serious this is. Frewer et al. (2002) argue that the effects of such amplification of food incidents may be short-lived and may change according to changing levels of media reporting. Wakefield and Elliott (2003) found that although newspapers were a major source of environmental information they were also inconsistent and unreliable and thus were not trusted by the public, especially by those with access to other information networks.

Research findings

In this research the comparative strength of influence of the media was not widely recognized. The greatest recognition came from managers in the large branded retail and hospitality companies where 52 per cent (91/176) compared to 39 per cent (11/28) of directors and senior managers who ranked the media as either having a 'strong' or 'some influence'. Managers from Yellow Company were again the least likely to know or offer an opinion (33 per cent or 6/18).

In Phase 2 respondents ranked the media fifth of eight influences. Five respondents mentioned the media when responding to questions about the greatest food safety/hygiene problems facing the industry in the next decade: their concerns centred on what they believed to be media generated food scares:

> Consumers are becoming more aware of risks with food ... whether it is the media trying to scare us or the truth people will become more wary of what they eat and will expect the catering industry to. (Interviewee 271, Manager, Blue Company)

> Media issues – the 'knee-jerk' reactions to current problems. (Interviewee 48, Manager, Orange Company)

> Controlling media scares regarding food. It appears that no food is safe to consume with influences from media. (Interviewee 86, Manager, Orange Company)

In Phase 3 4/25 (16 per cent) of respondents ranked the media among the top three influences on their decisions about how to manage food safety and food hygiene risks (see Table 4.3). During the period of study it was known that some businesses in the sample had first-hand experience of direct media attention but specific details were difficult to obtain through the survey.

Respondents were more prepared to discuss the more diffuse effects of the media where either the food industry or a food product becomes the subject of media attention and all businesses are influenced. A small group of individual managers across the sampled businesses criticized the media for creating 'food scares'. Another group of managers was clearly (possibly unwittingly) 'part' of the food scare in that they would cite risk matters, of often complex and disputed risk, which were receiving extensive press coverage at the time of the study.[5] There was also concern that adverse publicity for any part of the industry had a contaminating effect on others:

> When bad practices are shown on TV I think people think that all catering businesses are run the same. Not right! (Interviewee 744, Manager, Pink Company)

Insurance Companies

Insurance companies are held to have a regulatory role in two important respects. First, according to Ericson et al. (2003), insurance is a technology of governance beyond the state. They argue that the insurance industry shares similar goals to the state, employs similar methodologies and is subject to many of the same social forces. In these respects insurance is involved in two of the three aspects of regulation identified by Hood et al. (2001). The first of these is information gathering, especially through risk surveillance based on probability statistics. Indeed, insurance companies are regarded by some as the original risk experts, producing information which is both used by the industry itself and is also a source of exploitation by governments (Freeman and Kunreuther 1997). The second aspect is behaviour modification. Insurance acts as a control and seeks to influence behaviour by calibrating premiums according to desirable/undesirable characteristics. For example, higher premiums are charged to smokers; those without home security systems such as burglar devices and window locks; and those driving high performance cars. Indeed, in a very real sense insurance companies may link standard setting with behaviour modification through pricing mechanisms.

The other important respect in which the insurance sector may be regarded as a regulator is in its role as third party enforcers. Insurance companies may be drawn into a third party role in a variety of ways, for example, through a state obligation that regulated entities hold liability insurance (Grabosky 1995). Here insurers may play a gatekeeping role by only agreeing to issue policies once certain conditions have been met or by adjusting premiums accordingly. Jweeping et al. (1998) discuss another form of third party activity, namely, a scheme adopted by the Environmental Protection Agency in the United States to use third party inspectors employed by insurance companies and to formally recognize and accredit them as inspectors, thus incorporating them into legitimate regulatory space and using them to monitor activities and check for compliance.

Insurance cover for the food industry is active in two main areas: general liability and product recall. The former is the most common and given the low level of litigation incurs relatively little cost. The latter is a relatively new form of insurance for an event which has the potential to be very costly in both monetary and reputational terms. It is for this reason that Skees et al. (2001, p. 100) believe that insurance has great potential as an alternative to regulation. But the conclusion of their article is that this has not yet been realized.[6] This is also the evidence of this research.

Research findings

We might have expected our research sample to understand insurance companies' potential to calibrate premiums according to risk-taking behaviour and their ability to impose policy conditions. Yet very few of those we interviewed and surveyed in our research regarded insurance companies as a significant influence on their management of food safety and food hygiene.

Our experts thought it unlikely that insurance companies would figure prominently as an influence on food safety and hygiene standards but there was a suspicion among these experts that their influence may be increasing. A degree of scepticism about the ability of insurance companies to play a credible role in the food sector was also expressed. Comments on this ranged from a view that insurance companies are not very good at quantifying risk to a concern about moral hazard problems – 'Insurance is the enemy of the good as it is designed to average out loss resulting in the good not being rewarded and the bad not being punished' (Industry interview respondent, Phase 1).

In Phase 2 some 65 per cent (13/20) of managers of micro/small businesses compared to 62.5 per cent (5/8) of medium and large companies[7] claimed to have insurance cover for food hygiene and food safety incidents. Conversely, micro and small business managers (30 per cent, 4/13) view insurance companies as much less influential than did managers of medium and large businesses (50 per cent (84/168)). Twenty per cent (5/28) of all managers received information on food hygiene and food safety from their insurance company but only one business (a micro/small business) reported ever having been inspected by an insurance company.

Our survey found that 15 per cent (27/174) of managers in medium and large-size businesses regarded insurance companies as having a 'strong influence' with the medium and large catering businesses being more inclined to regard them as strongly influential (20 per cent, 20/100) than the retail only businesses (8 per cent, 7/87).

Phase 3 data again confirm that insurance companies are not an important influence. Only one respondent regarded them as among the top three influences and this was countered by four who regarded insurance companies as the least influential actors of those mentioned (see Table 4.3). These findings appear to relate to two main factors. The first is that not all businesses held insurance for food safety and food hygiene. Second, there is little evidence that insurance companies do calibrate their premiums according to the behaviour of individual firms, rather they seem to calibrate them according to the behaviour of the industry as a whole which may create counterproductive moral hazard difficulties.

Lawyers

There is very little research on the role of lawyers in business risk management decisions. There appears to be no compelling evidence that liability laws do have influence on food businesses. While some authors (Holleran et al. 1999) contend that these laws are a potential incentive to food safety, others disagree. Buzby and Frenzen (1999), for example, referring to the United States where civil litigation is relatively well used, argue that product liability systems for food are weak and thus offer weak incentives with respect to promoting food safety. Henson and Caswell (1999) feel that the main influence in the UK is indirect, namely, that the 'due diligence' concept in UK product liability law is a strong incentive for the use of third party certification and the adoption of private standards. They also argue that '*ex post* liability' is of secondary importance in the UK.

Research findings
The relevance of lawyers to risk management was not well understood by our survey respondents. Lawyers were considered to have the least influence of all the external actors we asked about in Phase 3 and they were ranked 6/8 in influence in the Phase 2 survey. In Phase 2 a slight difference in influence does emerge between the catering and retail sectors with the former responding that lawyers have greater influence than was the case with the retail sector. Interestingly almost 60 per cent (12/20) of managers of micro/small businesses did not answer this question or regarded it as non-applicable.

Only two experts from Phase 1 spontaneously referred to legal influence upon food safety. This was less a comment specifically regarding lawyers as individuals and more a comment on how the legal system in its broadest sense was perceived to operate. A director of a catering company commented that their risk management approach had a bias towards viewing risk from a legal perspective in an attempt to avoid litigation possibly relating to their business operations in the United States. A senior risk manager from the headquarters of a large licensed catering chain commented on the rise in claims from customers who had 'fallen over in the car park after leaving our establishments'. He considered this an example of 'compensation culture'. Surprisingly, given the debates about the UK being riddled with a 'compensation culture' his was the only explicit mention of this phenomenon in Phase 1 and Phase 2 of the research.

One Phase 3 respondent mentioned compensation culture but interestingly thought that this was primarily a reference to health and safety issues not food safety/hygiene matters – 'An EHO I think is 75 per cent health and safety focused, 25 per cent food safety focused … customers may ask for compensation for every little irregularity that they face. Food safety … is miniscule … compared to health and safety and the claim culture' (Phase 3 Interview, Director, Red Company). He continued to explain that in his opinion this is mirrored by external consultants' work that also mainly consists of health and safety issues. We expected the compensation culture debate to be more widely discussed but it was far from the case, perhaps reflecting their daily reality. Indeed studies have found that the claims of a compensation culture existing in the UK are a myth (BRTF 2004b; Lloyd-Bostock 2010).

Pressure groups/NGOs

Pressure groups, especially NGOs, are perhaps one of the most well-known regulatory sources in the civil sector. Information gathering is an important activity for most NGOs. Braithwaite and Drahos (2000) explain that at the most basic level NGOs report 'the facts' and hope to influence, or to create opinion to accord with their own interpretation and ambitions. The conflicting interpretations NGOs offer often become a source of conflict as they challenge more established views. They provide information about 'popular' views and perceptions and advice about technical and strategic issues (Aldadeff 2003, p. 101). NGOs also offer analysis and policy alternatives to state regulators (Charnovitz 1997; Grabosky 1995) and companies (Enderle and Peters 1998, p. 5). Another form of information gathering NGOs engage in is a monitoring or auditing role, for example, monitoring governmental policies and evaluating their effectiveness (Charnovitz 1997; Grabosky 1995). NGOs are increasingly involved in the standard-setting aspects of regulation, being involved in consultation processes with governments and business and often being formally co-opted to help shape standards (Dunkerly and Fudge 2004; Hutter and O'Mahony 2004, p. 109).

Behaviour modification is perhaps the regulatory activity NGOs are best known for, most especially their use of a variety of forms of civil action such as protests, press conferences, demonstrations, organizing petitions and sometimes even arranging publicity stunts. NGOs often gain their influence through their use of the media and here they are deemed to have had some success, a prominent example being the Nestlé baby milk case when negative media campaigning led to consumer boycotts of its products (Hutter and O'Mahony 2004). The key objective here is to mobilize mass opinion, something which NGOs are particularly successful at doing in time of disaster, and in an era of mass communication (Braithwaite and Drahos 2000, p. 500). Yet NGOs did not figure prominently in our research.

Research findings

Phase 1 data revealed very different views of NGOs. A senior risk manager from a licensed catering chain commented that the Better Regulation Task Force and FSA 'even out the influence of the National Consumer Council (NCC) and other (pro-consumer) lobbyists'. A contrasting comment came from a director of a large food retailer who mentioned that as part of developing their corporate social responsibility scheme they were working with a team of academics and consumer-friendly NGOs.

One director in Phase 2 suggested that his employees would not know what a pressure group or NGO was and this is to some extent borne out by our data. Overall 42 per cent (87/204) of our sample was unable to answer questions about NGOs, with 86 per cent (6/7) of respondents in one large UK restaurant chain and 83 per cent (12/22) from a large UK takeaway chain being unable to answer at all. Generally, 31 per cent (57/184) of respondents attributed NGOs 'no influence' with just 5 per cent (7/140) indicating a strong influence (see Table 4.2). Just one respondent cited NGOs as among the greatest food safety/hygiene problems facing the industry in the next decade.

Phase 3 data confirmed the low ranking of NGOs, in this phase NGOs were ranked 7/9 in terms of their influence (see Table 4.3). This is perhaps related to the level at which these respondents were working in corporate hierarchies, we might expect that only senior managers and directors would be aware of NGO activity unless it was very widespread.

Private Consultancy Firms

Consultancies are private sector organizations which sell their declared expertise in business management. There is actually very little work on consultants despite their quite spectacular growth over the past 20 years. Saint-Martin (2000, p. 48) identifies three characteristics of management consultancy: (1) they are independent from those who employ their services; (2) their work is advisory; and (3) they are knowledge-based organizations where the production of management ideas is key, indeed they may act as the 'conduit' of business school ideas to the business world. The 1980s also saw the growing employment of management consultants by the public sector. This was part of the move to the managerialist state and the growth of non-state sources of responsibility and expertise. While management consultants still have lucrative markets in the public sector it is estimated that some 80 per cent of their revenue still comes from private sector work (Saint-Martin 2000, p. 37) and here risk management consultancy appears to be a growing sector.

Management and other more specialist consultancies focusing on selling risk management and regulatory compliance advice cover a range of risk management domains. Many such organizations exist, their trade being to sell advice which will assist businesses understand state regulations and guidance, ensure that they have compliance systems in place and even offer advice on how businesses should relate to regulators especially in registering their businesses with regulators, licensing processes, complaints procedures or legal actions.

Management consultancies' main regulatory task is advisory and centres on the behaviour modification component of regulation. This sector represents quite a growth area in market sector provision around the implementation of state regulation, self-regulation and risk management and one whose regulatory role demands to be properly researched.

Research findings

Consultancies were not included in our Phase 2 general question about the influence of state and non-state influences on risk management as Phase 1 responses did not suggest that they would be of overall importance. In Phase 2 of the research not a single manager spontaneously mentioned consultancy companies, only those at directorial level. This said, just under half of those interviewed in Phase 2 thought that consultants were employed by their business to advise on food safety/hygiene (see Chapter 6). Responses were strongly patterned. For example, two large private consultancies specializing in the food industry were well known and highly regarded for their provision of a range of technical, business, scientific, regulatory and legal services relating to risk. These were mentioned by senior policy makers and directors in Phases 1 and 2 as providing research, policy and operations support to many businesses in the sector. However, knowledge of these two consultancies was dependent upon the level of seniority in the staff hierarchy. Other consultancies mentioned by respondents were typically small consultancies run by former state regulators or former technical employees of large food companies. These were used for advice and inspection. The most direct evidence of influence came from a catering chain where the scores from consultancy audits influenced the calculation of the remuneration of the board of directors. Not a single micro or small business in either the retail or catering sectors represented in the sample used a consultancy as their main source of information about food safety and hygiene risks.

Views about consultancies were mixed. Not all consultancies were viewed positively and some received a great deal of criticism from all of the sectors represented. They were seen to be exploiting the confusion of micro firms and SMEs relating to HACCP[8] – 'consultants are making a killing out of HACCP, just pulling stuff off the net and then selling it' (Interview respondent). Others expressed concern that there is 'over-implementation of risk management practices due to the advice of commercial consultants'. This very much chimes with evidence that consultancy firms may be a source of what has come to be referred to as regulatory creep (BRTF 2004a).[9]

In Phase 3 consultancies were ranked 6/9 in terms of their influence (see Table 4.3). There were no other direct questions about consultancies in Phase 3 although they were spontaneously mentioned by eight of the 25 respondents (32 per cent). The suggestion in these comments is that consultancies provide a backup source of information and advice when food safety/hygiene related problems occur which may not happen often and also if the company cannot provide a solution internally. A minority of respondents (4/25, 16 per cent) said that they would approach consultants for advice if they had a problem and three mentioned external consultants as part of the food safety/food hygiene checks undertaken by their company:

Q: If you were worried about any aspect of food safety/hygiene in your workplace who would you talk to?

R: You'd talk to the food consultancy [XXX], they are very user friendly and they are on the end of the phone. (Interviewee 843, Manager, Brown Company)

R: The company's Quality & Safety department or [XXX], an external auditing team employed by the owners of the exhibition site. (Interviewee 36, Manager, Blue Company)

R: Someone at head office and followed by an outside consultancy. (Interviewee 842, Manager, Brown Company)

Q: Is there anyone else (except the company) responsible for checking food safety/hygiene?

R: An external company that reports back to HQ. (Interviewee 858, Manager, Red Company)

R: EHOs come in from the local council, we've had two visits in five years, didn't benchmark anything to do with food safety. We are audited once every 6 months by our consultancy (food alert) and have a mystery shopper visit every month although that is more to check on levels of customer service. (Interviewee 843, Manager, Brown Company)

Consultancies are not without influence (no respondent ranked them last) but they are not perceived to be as important as, for example, EHOs (who have legal powers) or consumers (who have economic power).

Trade Associations

Trade associations are a prominent form of economic self-regulation where businesses voluntarily join schemes involved in establishing and maintaining codes of practice (Gunningham 1995; Rees 1997). There is work on the increasing importance of trade and industry organizations and the international standards organizations (Cashore et al. 2004; Eisner 2004; Ronit and Schneider 1999). Private standards such as those promulgated by trade associations are increasingly important in the global food system and they may play an important role in making and communicating standards (see Chapter 6). Research in the environmental field suggests that they have a significant regulatory influence over environmental performance, particularly in a coordinating capacity (Bailey and Rupp 2004).

Trade associations may play an important risk management role for their members. For example, they may have an educative, training role and liaise with government over the best ways to achieve the required standards. They may issue their own codes to this end such as the British Hospitality Association Fitness for Purpose voluntary code relating to accommodation and catering standards in the hospitality sector. In this respect trade associations act as standards organizations which are discussed extensively by Brunsson and Jacobsson (2000) as a form of regulation and one which is largely located in the private sector.

Trade associations may also play a direct regulatory role where they run their own self-policing schemes, producing standards about product quality, quality assurance and risk management. For example, food assurance schemes include standard setting and inspection and in some cases may embrace food safety and food hygiene matters. But many food businesses may not belong to an association. This is particularly acute in the catering sector where one of our participants estimated that perhaps only one third of all businesses belong to an association, compared to retail businesses where over 90 per cent are thought to belong to a trade association. It is also the case that typically SMEs do not belong to trade associations so their influence is necessarily curtailed by the limits on their membership. This is reflected in our data.

Research findings
In our survey only senior staff – at director level or above – working for large organizations were aware of their firm's membership of trade associations such as the British Retail Consortium (BRC), Institute of Grocery Distribution (IGD), the Food and Drink Federation, and Association of Convenience Stores. No branch manager in any of the businesses surveyed was aware of their firm's membership of trade associations. Some directors thought they were members of trade associations but were unsure of which ones. A senior

risk manager from a large group of licensed catering chains commented that the majority of their food suppliers meet a type of 'private' standard developed by a trade association, the BRC Higher Standard.[10] This standard is thought to be widely used and valued among the larger food retailers and catering businesses. Of the micro, small or medium-sized businesses only one indicated membership of two trade associations.

A minority (25 per cent, 7/28) of managers indicated that a trade association made checks on food safety and food hygiene on their premises. Forty-three per cent (12/28) indicated that a trade association provided information on food safety and food hygiene to them and 1 per cent (4/28) indicated that this information was provided to their staff. None of these managers named or described these trade associations. It is thought that confusion exists with categories of organization – some managers may believe that a commercial consultancy is a trade organization. Similarly, some managers who mentioned using the services of a commercial consultancy may in fact be the clients of the commercial arm of a trade association. The line between the two is often unclear.

When considering food safety and food hygiene risks directors of large retail businesses were moderately more influenced by an 'industry association' than the directors of large catering businesses although in both sectors the influence is not 'strong'.

Some participants were very supportive of self-regulatory schemes such as the Red Tractor launched in the UK in June 2000 by Assured Food Standards which was created by the National Farmers Union (NFU) with government backing (Meat and Livestock Commission). Other participants preferred greater clarity about whether or not there is a regulatory requirement upon them or not, that is, a legal requirement to comply. There was a view that if schemes such as these are to have any chance of success then strong enforcement is necessary.

Several references were made by managers to what we believe are in-house schemes or proprietary standards which do not appear to have been created by trade associations or state regulators. Such schemes and standards have either been developed internally within businesses or have been introduced with the assistance of paid external technical or business consultants. These schemes and standards were referred to in passing by several of the managers, all of whom worked for the large businesses in the sample. Adherence to these schemes and standards appeared to be mandatory for those working within the business. Large supermarkets and caterers are another potential source of regulation, not just with respect to their own branches but also with respect to the supply chain. There was a very definitive view among some of our respondents that in the case of large national companies and franchises, corporate risk management systems for food safety and food hygiene take precedence over all others, the state included.[11]

SUMMARY AND DISCUSSION: THE RESEARCH FINDINGS IN CONTEXT

The influence of non-state bodies was best understood by our senior experts and policy makers who spontaneously referred to a wide range of such influences. Our survey revealed knowledge of these influences and also presented us with some surprising results. For example, the role of consumers as an important influence on business risk management practices was not flagged up by our experts yet in our survey consumers were cited as one of the strongest influences on risk management. Indeed, not only did consumers figure highly as an influence they were also deemed to rank food safety and food hygiene as the most important consumer concern.

Another surprise was that the influence of the media was deemed to be well below the influence of consumers and state officials. The other main sources of civil power, NGOs, were not well understood as an influence despite their role in opposing GM foods and promoting organic produce. Campaigns on these issues were running at the time of the research so we had expected a greater knowledge of NGOs and their regulatory role. Another unexpected finding is the fairly low influence attributed to lawyers. Given the prominent debate about the compensation culture we were surprised that respondents rarely mentioned the possibility of compensation claims or civil actions. Likewise insurance companies also appeared to have a much less influential role than attributed by some commentators.

Consultancy firms appeared to have influence and, in fact, the potential for substantial influence in some areas of the industry. The nature of this influence is controversial and an important topic in its own right. Trade associations are also potentially important especially as an area of industry self-regulation, but their influence is obviously confined to their membership and the food industry is one where there are significant numbers of businesses which do not fall within the remit of these associations.

So consumers and EHOs were deemed to exercise a direct influence over food safety and food hygiene risk management practices; private consultancy firms and trade associations sometimes had a direct influence, depending on the size of the business; the media and NGOs were more indirect background influences; and lawyers and insurance companies played a negligible role, with the latter even being described as a negative influence.

The research also identified one reason for SME reliance on state systems, namely, that many small businesses have less contact with non-state sources which provide information and advice. One feature of trade associations and regimes of enforced self-regulation is that they tend to be dominated by or favour larger businesses. Typically SMEs are not members of trade or business associations which may provide updates or even training on food safety and food hygiene matters, nor do they use consultancies (Fairman and Yapp 2004; Genn 1993). This contrasts with large businesses which have greater regulatory capacity of their own and are more likely to belong to associations, employ consultancies and take out insurance cover. Indeed, in the case of large retailers and caterers they may even become a source of regulation for other parts of the food chain as they impose standards which are sometimes in excess of state regulatory requirements.

These research data indicate that the move from government to governance is understood by those in business to the extent that they are well aware that there are multiple external influences on their internal risk management practices. These influences shape the motives and preferences of those working in business and thus affect the internal workings of the organization. Some of these influences intend directly or indirectly to exercise pressure, notably insurance companies, NGOs, the media and lawyers. The exception is one of the most potent of the influences discerned in this research, namely, consumers who are generally not coherently organized. There are exceptions to this, for example, NGOs sometimes try to organize consumers through campaigns for organic or fair trade produce, or against GM foods. Generally, however, food safety and food hygiene are not the subject of such campaigns.

Our sample believed that maintaining high food safety and food hygiene standards is crucial to sales. Whether or not this is an accurate perception is irrelevant. The important fact here is that this is what our managers believed and acted upon. Food retailing and hospitality are fiercely competitive sectors: consumers have a good choice of retail and hospitality outlets and can easily switch their preferences. Product differentiation is key to the industry and millions of pounds are spent on this each year.

Strictly speaking consumers exercising their preferences en masse and without organization would fall outside most definitions of regulation, although the finding does indicate the power that organized consumer action could have. This influence does add weight to the contention that social, economic and state influences all serve to influence the internal workings of business. It also suggests that there are domain effects to be considered. Gunningham et al. (2003, pp. 137ff.) accord environmental controls a key role in increasing performance worldwide and in the case of the paper and pulp industry argues that this has led to convergence across different jurisdictions. Our research focused on the UK only so cannot comment on the contention of international convergence. But we can say that there is no evidence of convergence within the UK. Variations did appear according to the size of the business, its type and where it was located. These differences may suggest that the domain effect is significant and worth exploring. This suggestion is strengthened by the contrasting findings for the importance of NGOs and activists, who were found to be more influential by Gunningham et al. than in this research on food.

Clearly the interaction between the state, economy and civil society is complex and may be greater than the effect of the sum of the parts. These influences seem to work differentially according to the social structure of the business. In the case of food safety/hygiene regulation in the UK we have discussed there are few formal 'joined up' connections between the state and non-state systems. There are, however, some ways in which regulatory actors do acknowledge and indirectly co-opt other regulatory players. Notable here are EHOs, some of whom 'name and shame' those with poor food safety and food hygiene practices; publicly rate or certificate premises with high standards; or certificate individuals who have been trained in food safety and food hygiene. Such information plays to other potential regulatory forces and directly to consumers. The complexities and dynamics involved are well illustrated by this case. The state, represented by EHOs, produces information which may be deployed by the media, consumers and other groups; thus they potentially influence the social reputational standing of a business and influence its commercial/economic position.

We should not automatically assume that all external forces have a positive influence on risk management practices. Certainly, consultancies have been implicated in regulatory creep. Likewise the influence of insurance companies can be problematic and deserves greater scrutiny. The background influences are variable according to topicality and size of business. The ways in which factors play out and interact are not well understood. The academic literature does suggest that each of the background influences has the potential to be a direct influence but as yet we need a great deal more evidence of this and how it might be realized and the conditions under which each influence is likely to be helpful.

We do know that businesses are subject to a complexity of pressures on their risk management practices. Some are external to their organization and others are within their organizational boundaries. Indeed different pressures may be in tension. The nature of these interactions is not well understood and the next step is to explore this further in Chapter 6.

NOTES

1. There are complicated definitional issues surrounding this topic (see Bruyn 1999 for a good discussion of these). For example, some refer to 'three sectors' but objections arise because the use of the terms first, second and third is taken by some commentators to refer to a hierarchical ordering.
2. Trade associations are classified as economic actors to the extent that they operate as meso-level business associations which are non-state and not civil sector in nature (Doner and Schneider 2000).

3. Not all respondents were asked the same questions, so the responses are difficult to compare.
4. This was a minority view as 17/22 (77 per cent) did consider consumers competent to assess a business's food safety/hygiene standards.
5. Chief among these were genetically modified organisms (GMO) in the food chain, BSE, epidemics and 'chemicals'. In the latter stages of data collection this referred to banned contamination by dyes from the Sudan family of red/brown food colourants which were found in several manufacturers of branded and supermarket private label products. See FSA, http://www.food.gov.uk/safereating/sudani/sudanitimeline (accessed 19 April 2011).
6. There is some evidence in the environmental sector that financial institutions such as insurance companies take account of environmental performance in making decisions about business (Eisner 2004; Grabosky 1994) but again opinions differ. Gunningham et al. (2003), for instance, found that financial institutions were a weak influence in the environmental area they researched, namely, pulp manufacturing.
7. Some 33 per cent of directors/senior managers responded with 'don't know'.
8. See note 15 in Chapter 3 and Chapter 6.
9. On 21 October 2004, the Better Regulation Task Force (BRTF) published a report *Avoiding Regulatory Creep*.
10. This is one of a series of standards now referred to as the 'BRC Global Standard – Food'. See http://www.brcglobalstandards.com/standards/ (accessed 19 April 2011).
11. The impact of these standards on other parts of the food supply chain was not within the remit of this study but it should be noted that the regulatory powers of supermarkets over producers is a point of some controversy in Britain.

6. Business risk regulation: inside the business organization

A central ambition of modern regulatory regimes is to emphasize risk regulation as the responsibility of business and to constitutively influence the risk management practices of business organizations. This is encapsulated by Coglianese and Nash (2001, 2006) when they use the term 'management based strategies' to refer to regimes of enforced self-regulation, thus emphasizing the fact that they are 'used by those who are *outside* an organization to change the management practices and behaviour of those on the inside' (2006, p. 15, emphasis in original). Modern regulation is a hybrid form of regulation which explicitly seeks to maximize the resources and capacity of businesses to self-regulate while simultaneously providing a degree of state oversight and control of these efforts (see Chapter 1). As Coglianese and Nash (2006) observe, the ambition is to leverage the private sector and also to give it flexibility to determine for itself how best to manage the risks it generates. This is one important reason to focus on what those inside the business know about their risk management system. Another reason to spotlight this area is because previous studies have shown that a company's internal organization and management are important influences on their work practices. Howard-Grenville et al. (2008), for example, found that variations in managerial incentives, organizational identity and organizational self-monitoring were all strongly related to differences in what they term the 'internal licence to operate'. These authors argue that this licence is shaped by internal factors such as leadership and managerial commitment to risk management, organizational cultures and structures, and managerial styles. These frame organizational risks and their solutions so shape the definition and resolution of regulatory problems and formal responses to regulators.

This chapter will focus on business risk management, paying particular attention to how much staff in the food retail and hospitality sectors we sampled knew about their business risk management systems for food safety and food hygiene. It will necessarily draw out variations in these understandings both between businesses and within them. Previous studies show that understandings of business risk management systems vary between different parts of an organization and there may be real difficulties in operationalizing the structures and policies in place (Dawson et al. 1988; Hutter 2001). In the case of the food sector it has to be remembered that we are dealing with a wide variety of businesses. Some are national organizations but others are small, micro businesses and not all of these have the capacity to manage their risks as well as the state may require. It is equally the case that some food businesses run risk management systems which exceed state requirements. Moreover, all businesses may experience difficulties at some time or another as business owners, managers juggle a wide variety of risk management demands on their time; and managing risks is a fluid, ever changing state of affairs.

BUSINESS RISK MANAGEMENT: FOOD SAFETY AND FOOD HYGIENE

Food law gives some indication of the broad areas businesses are expected to take into account when managing their food safety and hygiene risks (see Chapter 4). The UK, in line with many other global food safety regimes, has increasingly taken a holistic view of food safety/hygiene, specifying risk management requirements 'from farm to fork'. This places responsibilities on food producers, manufacturers and retailers including responsibilities for traceability schemes which have the entire food chain within their focus, the ambition being to assure product origin, quality and integrity. Food hygiene legislation also signals that everything from food preparation, processing, manufacturing, packaging, storage, distribution, handling and offering for sale or supplying foodstuff must be carried out hygienically. Since January 2006 this has explicitly included a requirement to have in place HACCP-based food safety management procedures and to keep up-to-date records; and to ensure that premises are kept clean and are properly equipped, that foods are hygienically handled, that staff are supervised, and trained in food hygiene matters, and that their managers are also adequately trained.[1]

Overall, therefore, business risk management with respect to food safety/hygiene involves risk-based systems to be in place; the use of traceability tools and the establishment of HACCP systems; knowledge of the broader food chain and processing; staff supervision; training and policies to ensure that food is handled safely and hygienically. Let us now turn to the experiences of our sample in operationalizing these requirements and their knowledge and understanding of the systems their business has in place for managing food safety/hygiene risks.

THE RESEARCH FINDINGS: AWARENESS OF BUSINESS RISK MANAGEMENT SYSTEMS

The first phase discussions revealed confidence in the systems businesses have in place for food safety and food hygiene. They were described as 'robust' by one respondent and overall references were made to a complex system of external and internal audits; the use of national league tables; sanctions; incentives; complaint investigations; sampling programmes; and 'due diligence teams'. This was not to underestimate the difficulties in operationalizing these systems. A senior business representative interviewed in Phase 1 explained how difficult the logistics of managing a retail outlet could be: ranging from transporting supplies long distance, checking suppliers and implementing traceability schemes, quality assurance and consumer care schemes, and coping with what can be a fairly high turnover of staff. The overall impression given was of a demanding regime requiring vigilance but one which was relatively well understood.

In Phase 2 respondents were asked a series of questions to discern how much those working in the food retail and hospitality sectors knew about their company's systems for food safety and food hygiene. This started with a general question about whether their business has rules regarding food safety and food hygiene and moving onto more targeted questions about their knowledge of any specialist tools employed to help manage risks.

Organizational Rules and Policies

Questions about the existence of food safety rules were readily answered by all respondents and the overwhelming majority replied that their business did have rules.[2] The majority were able to give examples, for instance, 177/199 (88.9 per cent) in Phase 2 of the research named two rules in response to a request for examples of the sorts of rules their business had in place. Table 6.1 details the most cited rules with those relating to temperature controls and checks by far the most frequently mentioned.

There were some significant variations in responses. For example, respondents from Yellow Company were most likely to refer to personal hygiene rules and those from Pink Company least likely ($\alpha < 0.01$). Both of these companies were hospitality firms where one would expect personal hygiene to be emphasized. Respondents from Orange Company were most likely to mention temperature controls and those from the group of owners, directors and senior managers least likely to do so ($\alpha < 0,01$): this difference most likely reflects daily preoccupations with managers in retail stores paying a great deal of attention to temperature controls and those in senior positions typically

Managing food safety and hygiene

Table 6.1 Top ten rules cited in Phase 2

Rule	n	% of sample mentioning rule
Temperature control	86	46
Staff training	40	21.5
Personal hygiene	36	19
Food safety/food hygiene manual/poster, COPS.*	32	17
Date control	30	16
Segregation of raw/cooked food	26	14
Cleaning	20	11
HACCP or Food Safety Management System (FSMS)	11	6
Colour coded equipment	10	5
Correct storage	9	5

Note: COPSs refer to Correct Operating Procedures Book. As with Food safety/food hygiene manual/poster, these responses do not refer to specific rules but to written documentation where these rules can be looked-up. Responses are usually limited to mentioning food safety/food hygiene manual/poster or COPS, without further specifying the rules set out in them.

paying less hands-on attention to such matters. Pink Company respondents were most likely to refer to HACCP rules ($\alpha < 0.01$); and those from Red Company least likely to refer to rules about date controls ($\alpha < 0.01$).

Phase 3 responses followed a very similar pattern, with staff training, temperature controls and date coding/stock rotation rules being the most frequently cited rules. The main difference between Phase 2 and Phase 3 data is that nearly half (47 per cent, $n = 9$) Phase 3 interviewees referred to the location of rules rather than their content. For example, they referred to manuals, posters, files and checklists:

> Managers constantly check staff. Yes, several people check the policy and also checking checkers. Managers and assistant managers check each other. (Interviewee 860, Manager, Red Company)

> Managers check constantly – it's part of the company culture that they don't sit in the office but participate in the employees' workspace. (Interviewee 858, Manager, Red Company)

> ... yes: very stringent health and safety rules, food handling rules, staff have to pass a course that says it's OK to work in the kitchen, to work with food ... health and safety file on site as reference manual, also legal notice folder, very good, very stringent, easy to monitor (i.e. easy to operate and manage). (Interviewee 35, Manager, Blue Company)

> We have a separate storage area, separate handling procedures, dedicated staff have to have a very, very big training programme and to make sure that they know how to do each of the separate areas and it is monitored on an ongoing basis and every single day there is book work to be completed to ensure that everything is as it should be. (Interviewee 155, Manager, Orange Company)

> The company has a policy for nearly everything. (Interviewee 27, Manager, Blue Company)

There was a firm belief that staff did know the rules relating to their area of work and responsibilities.[3] Part of the reason for this seems to be connected to the high levels of awareness of business checks that the rules and business policies are being followed: 95.6 per cent (195/204) of respondents in Phase 2 and 100 per cent (19) in Phase 3 were aware of such checks (these factors are significant $\alpha < 0.01$).

Managers mentioned checks they made as a manager to ensure that staff followed the rules (Table 6.2). For example, almost 40 per cent of respondents from Yellow Company referred to visual checks they made such as temperature or cleanliness checks or jewellery wearing. Managers in Pink Company referred to a range of checks, from annual checks on knowledge of food safety and hygiene matters through refresher tests to daily temperature tests. A manager from Brown Company similarly referred to the range of checks he experiences – 'Cleaning rotas that must be filled in daily. Temperature checks which are carried out twice daily on all food fridges and also hot food' (Interviewee 841, Manager, Brown Company).

Phase 3 respondents were also asked for their views of the checks in place. All of the ten that were asked this question thought that checks on the rules and policies are a good thing and necessary:

> It's a necessity to make sure people follow the law. (Phase 3 Interview, Manager, Pink Company)

> Checklists are a good reminder to check that things are getting done. (Interviewee 113, Manager, Orange Company)

> Yes, we have our [company] procedures and manual in the store. Staff meetings when we discuss temperature control and cleanliness. We have checklist book – daily things wc do and weekly things we do – chillers – temperature – cleanliness – inductions – we have our own checklists too to check the checker to make sure they have done their job correctly. (Interviewee 113, Manager, Orange Company)

> … the last thing we want is a customer falling ill because you have not carried out procedures, when it gives you a bad name it is hard to lose that you know, I've seen it with the butchers and things before … they have not followed procedures and someone gets ill and that's it you are out of business. (Interviewee 86, Manager, Orange Company)

Table 6.2   Phase 2 responses on business checks to ensure staff follow rules and policies

Type of check	*n*	% of sample mentioning check
Documentation	66	34
Managerial checks	59	30
Physical/visual checks	51	27
Training	42	21.5
Audits or supervision	18	9
Questions	9	5
Regular staff meeting	5	3
Other*	15	7.5
Not answered	12	6
Total	277	

Note: * All examples mentioned by less than 2 per cent within the sample.

Three Phase 3 respondents were critical of their company: one of his company's specific checks which he did not regard as good as those in place by a previous company he had worked for, and another because they were not fully effective – 'things don't work 100 per cent, say 80 per cent' (Interviewee 843, Manager, Brown Company). Another criticism focused on perceived over-prescription:

> the food alert manual is … overly complicated, repetitious and it asks for too much. For it to ask our managers to have a risk assessment for pretty much everything, like putting a champagne bottle on the rack, do you understand? And then updating that risk assessment. They won't do it. So it's unrealistic in its scope and because it asks for too much detail in terms of actions, it gets less detail than a much more concentrated, more … Bones, the bones of health and safety rather than the, you know, every little detail … it's all about user-friendliness really and rather than trying to do everything to the nth degree and do nothing brilliantly, I think if we did the important things, then we'd have better health and safety. (Phase 3, Manager, Brown Company)

Others took a very different view of their employer's checks:

> …very good, very stringent, easy to operate and manage. (Interviewee 35, Manager, Blue Company)

> We've got our own in-house, I guess it's like an EHO officer … Quality and safety inspector. They inspect every unit twice a year … They are very thorough and go further than what the local EHOs are looking for. (Interviewee 262, Manager, Blue Company)

Phase 2 respondents were asked a much broader question, if they were 'aware of *any* checks regarding food safety/hygiene made by your company?'. There were significant variations, as one might expect, according to the company respondents worked for ($\alpha < 0.01$). For example, respondents from Red Company were most inclined to consider they were subject to weekly checks ($\alpha < 0.05$) and Blue Company respondents either didn't know if there were any checks or thought that such checks took place after an incident, suggesting that their checks were not routine.

There were also differences according to the size of the business a respondent worked for and his/her position in a business. For example, SME respondents were least aware of checks (28.6 per cent (6/21) were aware of checks). Directors and senior managers were less likely than middle and junior managers to be aware of the checks.[4] Directors and senior managers gave much more reactive replies than the rest of our sample. They believed that company checks took place following a food safety/hygiene incident[5] ($\alpha < 0.01$) or after a failed inspection ($\alpha < 0.05$).

The main categories of people thought to be involved in checking also varied according to company. Some undertook checks as managers (see above), while others were aware of checks by line managers and specialist organizational food safety officers. Checks by others were less well understood. Respondents from Blue, Green and Orange Companies, all nationwide chains, were most inclined to believe that these checks were undertaken by a specialist manager sent by their headquarters organization ($\alpha < 0.01$). Those from Red Company, a London-based hospitality chain, were most likely to regard line managers as undertaking these checks ($\alpha < 0.05$), whereas respondents from Brown Company, another London-based hospitality company, were most likely to believe the checks to be undertaken by an external advisor, consultant or auditor ($\alpha < 0.01$). Red and Green Company respondents believed that their companies used 'mystery shoppers'. But those from Yellow, Blue and Pink Companies did not think that their companies used external staff for checking at all. Very few (4.7 per cent, $n = 8$) believed that inspectors from a trade association were used by their company.

Specialist Personnel

Interviewees were asked directly about three categories of specialist staff who may be employed by their business to advise on food safety/hygiene issues. Two of these would normally be employed directly by the company, namely, a food safety or food hygiene officer and a risk officer or risk manager. The third category of specialist help might be external to the business, such as a consultancy firm of some kind.

Overall 67.6 per cent (138/204) of managers in Phase 2[6] and 100 per cent (*n* = 18) of those asked in Phase 3 indicated that their business employed a food safety or food hygiene officer. Fewer were sure about whether a risk officer/manager was employed.[7] The second phase questionnaires asked two sets of questions about consultants – once in relation to the employment of specialist staff and once in a section on external influences on the management of food safety/hygiene risks. In both cases high levels of ignorance were revealed in the 'Don't know' and 'Not answered' categories, with 39 per cent (80/204) not being able to answer the first question asked on this topic and 37 per cent (75/204) not responding to the second. Of those who did feel able to reply the majority thought that consultants were employed by their company.[8] A high proportion believed that these consultants undertook food safety/hygiene checks of the business.[9] There was a sharp division between the owners and managers of small and micro businesses where 52 per cent (11/21) replied that consultants were not employed and 24 per cent (5/21) did not answer the question, and managers from larger companies where 47 per cent (82/176) thought that their company did employ consultants.

There were some significant variations between companies ($\alpha < 0.01$). The majority of SME owners reported that they did not employ specialist staff. This is in contrast to the responses of managers from the larger companies, where Blue Company staff tended to think that their company did employ food safety and risk officers; Orange and Green Company staff also thought that their business employed food safety officers; and Pink Company staff thought that their company employed risk officers. Some confusion clearly existed around the use of specialist personnel and this was further confirmed in the Phase 3 interviews where a number of company specialists in food safety/hygiene were mentioned. These included a wide variety of business staff. For example, company fresh food specialists, company quality and safety staff and area managers were all referred to by three respondents in Phase 3. Others mentioned a miscellany of staff, some of whom are not related to food safety/hygiene issues, for example, company health and safety officers, the marketing team and supply chain team.

Specialist Equipment

Phase 3 interviewees were also asked if they were provided with any special food safety/hygiene equipment. They all replied yes and came up with a variety of different examples: temperature probes, protective clothing, colour coded equipment, cleaning products, laser probes and checklists. One respondent was critical of what was provided, claiming it to be in poor condition, something he attributed to issues of cost.

Tools

Phase 1 participants referred to a broad range of risk management tools. Some originate from the state, others from trade associations and others from private consultancies. The main tools mentioned were HACCP, traceability, 'due diligence', accreditation, education and training, inspection, sampling, technical standards, and management and assessment systems.

Building on the information received in the first phase of the research the Phase 2 questionnaires asked specific questions about certification schemes, audit, HACCP, inspection, sampling and traceability. The results are shown in Table 6.3 and reveal that respondents were most knowledgeable about inspection, audit and certification schemes and less certain of HACCP, traceability and sampling being used as a tool for managing food safety/hygiene in their businesses.

Inspection was most frequently cited across the sample and sampling was mentioned the least. Audit was also popular, although this is particularly so among our sample companies ($\alpha < 0.01$) with the exception of Yellow Company where half of the sample either didn't know or did not answer. Senior managers and directors of the sample companies were less certain of whether audit is used by their company. This is interesting as one might have expected that they would have received the results of audit. These findings suggest that if audit is used by their organization the audit results are not widely disseminated within the company. There was a very low level of use of audit among SMEs: 38 per cent ($n = 8$) said they did not use audit; 43 per cent (9) did not answer; and just 9.5 per cent (2) said they did use audit.

Table 6.3   Phase 2: knowledge of tools used to manage food safety/hygiene standards

	Tool is used to manage food safety/hygiene standards		Don't know	
	%	n	%	N
Inspection	82	167	5	11
Audit	75	152	8	17
Certification	65	132	13	27
Traceability	53	107	17	35
HACCP	48	98	26	53
Sampling	37	75	20	41

HACCP

HACCP is a form of quality management system devised and used by the food industry.[10] It is 'a system which identifies, evaluates, and controls hazards which are significant for food safety'. By following the seven principles of HACCP a plan can be drawn up by a food business and then used by staff in their daily duties to control (or reduce) hazards and prevent harming the consumers of their products. 'New EU Food Hygiene Regulations, applicable from January 2006, require food businesses (except those in primary production) to put into place food safety management procedures based upon HACCP principles.'[11] At the time of this research, therefore, HACCP was not yet mandatory but was soon to become so (see Chapter 4).

In this research HACCP was regarded as the most controversial tool by first phase interviewees who expressed either great hope that this would promote higher standards of food safety and hygiene throughout the industry or enormous concern that it will prove unenforceable. Most agreed that it would require 'a behaviour change ... by those in business' (FSA representative). The hope was that HACCP would 'give people in business a level of understanding of hazards and of controls' (FSA representative). Our experts assumed that large companies would most probably cope with HACCP, largely by filtering to staff information on a 'need to know' basis. The expectation was that a full understanding of HACCP would reside at headquarters level only; no one thought that operatives would know much about HACCP. The major concern was how SMEs can cope with HACCP, a concern shared by nearly everyone we spoke to. A deal of scepticism was expressed about the various attempts to render HACCP comprehensible to SMEs. Others felt that HACCP is less suited to the retail and especially catering sectors than the manufacturing sector it was developed for.

A key issue seemed to pivot on trading comprehensibility against the legal requirements, the implication being that any attempt to simplify the requirements would weaken them. The role of EHOs in this process was also a point of comment, one view being that they have a crucial role to play in helping SMEs to understand what is required. The more critical view was that many EHOs do not adequately understand the requirements themselves, especially if they are not specialist food officers. A senior EHO we spoke to believed that a simplified version of HACCP was essential for SMEs and that this needed to be supported with financing for training provision for SMEs and EHO support of them. Another EHO believed that the benefits of HACCP for business needed emphasizing and promoting, for example, the possibilities of it being cost-effective and a due diligence defence.

In Phase 2 just under half of our sample said that HACCP was used by their business but there were distinct variations in the responses ($\alpha < 0.01$). As our Phase 1 respondents expected HACCP did not figure very much in SME responses: 43 per cent (*n* = 9) did not use HACCP; 29 per cent (6) did not answer; and 24 per cent (5) did use HACCP. This very much accords with concerns from, for example, the FSA that SMEs have difficulties in under-standing and implementing HACCP principles. Managers from Yellow, Pink and Red Companies believed their companies to use HACCP and those from Blue, Green and Brown Companies tended to respond that their business did not use HACCP. These variations are not related to differences in the type of business but are company-based variations.

Traceability

Traceability is a legislative demand to the extent that the Food Safety Act, 1990, required retailers to ensure the food they receive is safe. Traceability is seen as especially important in a global food market (Vernede et al. 2003). As with many other tools traceability requirements are seen to be experienced as particularly demanding on small businesses. But they are also thought to provide efficiency, marketing and legal gains (Hornibrook and Fearne 2003). A non-state industry response to traceability requirements are assurance schemes (Fearne and Hughes 1999).

Traceability was seen as very important by some Phase 1 respondents. One industry association representative regarded traceability systems as key and he explained how introducing a traceability system facilitates several outcomes. These included making complying with accreditation easier, for example, British Pork labelling which restricts veterinary drug use and animal welfare; enabling the control of potential allergens such as peanuts which present a safety risk to some people; enabling the control of ingredients and identity of preserved food, for example, GM tomato; and making it possible to act more quickly and efficiently with respect to product recall/withdrawal following possible product failure. The organic food sector was regarded as especially good in its handling of traceability tools. But there was not universal praise for traceability. One business representative thought that 'Traceability is not much use as it may give false confidence.' Certainly the Sudan 1 dye incident in the UK in 2005 does suggest that traceability systems can be vulnerable to major failures.[12]

Just over half of the second phase sample thought that traceability tools were used by their business and again there were company-related variations ($\alpha < 0.01$). Yellow and Red Company respondents were relatively ignorant of this tool with very few respondents from these companies able to answer the question; managers from Blue, Green and Orange Companies were relatively aware of their company using traceability systems. So it appears that the vari-ation is related to the size of the business and different company practices rather than the distinction between grocery and hospitality.

Trade Association Standards

The importance of trade associations was discussed in Chapter 5. Here we focus particularly upon one of their most important roles, namely, standard setting. The BRC, for example, has been involved in the development and implementation of technical standards since 1996 and there are some 30 accreditation bodies for BRC standards (see Chapter 2). Fulponi (2006) argues that trade association standards have become an important governance tool for major retailers and also that they are increasingly more stringent than those of government. Their importance in the food chain is regarded as especially important (Henson and Hooker 2001). Likewise Holleran et al. (1999) see the potential incentives for food businesses to adopt these standards. These include satisfying customer requirements and helping to meet legislative demands.

First phase respondents' views of trade association standards varied according to their source, some were regarded very highly whereas others were seen as marking a low standard. The Soil Association was regarded as having very high standards, 'copper plate standards' (FSA representative). The organics sector reported very strong systems of checks: audits, inspections and mystery shopping at all stages of the food chain.

Certification schemes, which are often run by trade associations, were apparently used by a number of businesses. Overall 65 per cent ($n = 132$) of those interviewed in Phase 2 thought that their company did use these schemes. The variations are significant ($\alpha < 0.01$) with SMEs being less likely to use these schemes than the larger companies. Yellow Company employees were the least certain about whether these schemes were used and Blue and Brown Company employees the most certain that they are employed by their companies.

SOURCES OF INFORMATION AND MEANS OF COMMUNICATION ABOUT RISK: MANAGERS

The questionnaire included two sets of questions regarding the ways in which employees learn about food safety and food hygiene risks – specifically questioning as to the main sources of information for managers themselves and their staff. In addition managers were questioned about the means of communicating this information to managers and their staff. From this it is possible to construct an impression of how risk information moves within an organization and through whom: these sources of information may not always coincide with those which the business regards as primary. If so this is in itself interesting as it is likely that the responses we received reveal the most memorable sources and means of communication.

Managers cited a range of sources of information about food safety/hygiene risks as being important. In particular there was a heavy reliance on company generated information, especially from corporate headquarters (cited by 88.6 per cent or 156/176). This was less so for managers from Yellow Company where line managers were regarded as key. Indeed line managers did figure as significant across the sample (52.8 per cent, $n = 93$) and other staff (20.5 per cent $n = 36$) also played an important role. Trainers or lecturers were specifically cited by just over half of the sample (51.7 per cent, $n = 91$). State sources of information do also emerge as important, most especially EHOs (60.2 per cent, $n = 106$) and the FSA (33.5 per cent, $n = 59$).[13]

External sources, employed or paid for by the company in some way, were not especially mentioned as sources of information about food safety/hygiene: 11.4 per cent ($n = 20$) received information from consultancies, this being mentioned by managers from Brown and Red Companies. Just 4 per cent ($n = 7$) mentioned trade associations and they were mainly from the senior manager/director category.[14] SMEs and senior managers/directors relied on fewer sources and were especially reliant on written materials from the local council and FSA. They were less likely than managers from the sample companies to receive information from training courses.[15]

How information is communicated to managers generally reflects the sources they use (Table 6.4). Overall training and operating manuals/handbooks were the most likely means of communication but as we might expect this was patterned ($\alpha < 0.01$). These sources are especially important for our sample company managers. For SMEs verbal instructions are most important and looking at the sources of their information it is likely that the source of these instructions is EHOs.

Phase 3 data reiterated, as we might expect, the sources of data mentioned in Phase 2. Particularly prominent was the information emanating from the business hierarchy (mentioned by 12/16), a variety of sources were mentioned in this respect including operations directors and generic references to 'head office'. When asked if they managed to read all of the information they received, the usefulness of documentation as a resource to be consulted became clear:

> I have read all the manuals thoroughly once in five years – I know which sections are in there, how to record a food poisoning, health and safety … it's everything you need to know. (Interviewee 843, Manager, Brown Company)

> There is a lot of information there but we have a directory which tells us which page to go to, so if we need information quickly we can get it quickly. (Interviewee 155, Manager, Orange Company)

Table 6.4 Phase 2 means of communication to managers

	Managers		SME owners		Senior manager/ director		All	
	n	%	n	%	n	%	n	%
Training course	154	87.5	8	38.1	14	50.0	168	82.4
An operating manual or handbook	150	85.2	7	33.3	16	57.1	166	81.4
Written instruction	116	65.9	1	4.8	4	14.3	120	58.8
Verbal instructions	96	54.5	11	52.4	11	39.3	107	52.5
Training video, tape or CD ROM	84	47.7	2	9.5	12	42.9	96	47.1
Training leaflet/newsletter	65	36.9	7	33.3	13	46.4	78	38.2
Magazine	35	19.9	8	38.1	5	17.9	40	19.6
Web/Internet	14	8	2	9.5	5	17.9	19	9.3
A workmate	17	9.7	1	4.8	2	7.1	19	9.3
Other	1	0.6	1	4.8	2	7.1	3	1.5
	176	100	21	100	28	100	204	100

Note: Multiple responses: percentages add up to more than 100.

External sources of information were less prominent in this phase although in this phase the media appeared as a source of information (mentioned by two respondents and trade fairs and magazines were mentioned by two also). Managers also learn of changes in the law or new regulations through a mix of written and verbal means:

> If it were a new regulation nine times out of 10 we would get a new training course for it and we would get information sent down either from attending a course, a video, brief or book work which everyone would have to fill in, or memos sent down for immediate changes we have to make and we have competency trainers who would come out to the store and do training very quickly in the store. (Interviewee 155, Manager, Orange Company)

SOURCES OF INFORMATION AND MEANS OF COMMUNICATION ABOUT RISK: STAFF

A separate question asked managers the sources of information and food safety/hygiene risks used by their staff. The replies here are very heavily focused on in-house sources in information. Managers responding to the red questionnaire, that is site managers, mentioned:

Themselves or another manager	86.4 per cent (152/176)
Trainer or lecturer	75.0 per cent ($n = 132$)
Company head office	60.8 per cent ($n = 107$)
Line managers	28.4 per cent ($n = 50$)

State sources did also appear here, although they were generally considered to be less important for staff than they were for managers themselves: 34 per cent ($n = 33$) mentioned local council officials or EHOs and 12 per cent ($n = 22$) mentioned the FSA or 'the government'. These sources are much more significant ($\alpha < 0.01$) for SME respondents.

There are some broadly similar patterns in the way risks are communicated to staff and managers, for example, the reliance on training and to a lesser extent written communication (Table 6.5). Also important here is a greater use of verbal instructions. There were also corporate differences. For example, training was mentioned by 100 per cent of Yellow and Blue Company respondents compared to a general average among managers of 78 per cent. For Yellow Company this was the main means of communication. Training video, tape or CD ROMs were mentioned by less than half of the sample, their use most prominent in Orange, Red and Green Companies. Orange and Green Companies are the Scottish and South East areas of a major grocery chain so these means are being used to try to communicate to a geographically disparate workforce.

Table 6.5 *Means of communicating to staff about risk*

	Sample co. managers		SME owners		Senior manager/directors		All	
	n	%	n	%	n	%	n	%
Company manual or handbook	149	84.7	3	14.3	10	35.7	159	77.9
Training course	138	78.4	10	47.6	17	60.7	155	76.0
Verbal instruction	100	56.8	16	76.2	22	78.6	122	59.8
Training video, tape or CD ROM	84	47.7	1	4.8	7	25	91	44.6
Written instruction	83	47.2	1	4.8	5	17.9	88	43.1
Poster	76	43.2	3	14.3	8	28.6	84	41.2
Training leaflet/newsletter	66	37.5	3	14.3	7	25	73	35.8
A workmate	37	21	3	14.3	7	25	44	21.6
Magazine	36	20.5	1	4.8	2	7.1	38	18.6
Web/Internet	14	8	0	0	1	3.6	15	7.4
Other	3	1.7	2	9.5	3	10.7	6	2.9
Not answered	5	2.8	1	4.8	1	3.6	6	2.9
	176	100	21	100	28	100	204	100

Note: Multiple responses: percentages add up to more than 100.

Training

As we can see, training is attributed a position of particular importance by Phase 2 respondents (see also Chapter 3). Training courses emerge as a major source of information regarding food safety/hygiene risks for managers, and staff and training leaflets and videos are also cited as significant means of communication (see Tables 6.4 and 6.5). Given the importance attributed to training in Phase 2, the Phase 3 interviews included a number of in-depth questions on the subject. All but one of those interviewed in Phase 3 had received training. In the majority of cases this had been a food safety/hygiene training course, in some cases leading to a certificate.[16] Nine out of 19 had been on refresher courses and interestingly five mentioned health and safety training, once again highlighting the importance of health and safety issues and their occasional confusion with food safety/hygiene issues. Most of this training had been provided by the company (10/14), the rest being provided by bona fide outside agencies:

> every single member of staff who works with food has to meet a range of training requirements/positive about extensive training of staff: multi-skilling helps manage other than food related risks as well. (Interviewee 191, Manager, Green Company)

> If we are moved into a store with a butcher then we'd have to go on this course (for dealing with raw food) to ensure that the manager is up to speed for all the regulation of the butchery. If you wanted extra training, then it's not a problem for us to get it. (Interviewee 155, Manager, Orange Company)

There was general satisfaction with the training received[17] although a number of criticisms did emerge in the interviews, for instance, the need for refresher courses and the need for there to be training at the start of the job rather than part way through. This resonates with the findings of Phase 2 where there is a correlation, albeit a rather weak one,[18] which shows that the influence of training decreases according to the number of years staff have been in their present job. This contrasts with views that experience is as important as training.

> We do risk assessments on the Health and Safety course and we also do a food safety course – I got a food safety certificate for that. It's really good but a lot comes down to experience, lots of things you can't see happening. (Interviewee 113, Manager, Orange Company)

> it takes time until 'virgin' staff is trained on food safety and hygiene and develops a basic awareness of risks … it always comes down to common sense. If new employees do have that, added training will make good staff. (Interviewee 867, Manager, Red Company)

Analysis of the Phase 2 data also reveals that the influence of training is higher in the catering than the retail sector[19] and according to company.[20] Some interviewees did note that training can be difficult to organize where staff are distributed across large geographical areas – 'Training we're not so hot on as an area … Cleanliness we're fantastic on. Reasons for the training issue are partly geographics, partly restructuring of the training department.' (Interviewee 262, Manager, Blue Company).

The Best and Worst of Management Practice

Another set of questions focused on the food safety management regime of the businesses for which the respondents worked. They were asked 'What single aspect of your company's food safety and food hygiene management are you most *pleased* with?' and 'What single aspect of your company's food safety and food hygiene management causes you most *concern*?' Respondents more readily replied to the first of these questions.[21] Also a minority of respondents (7 per cent), from all sectors, mentioned the same risk twice across the two questions.

Figure 6.1 details the Phase 2 responses to these questions. Overall the single issue most valued, across all businesses, is training. This was especially the case in Red ($\alpha < 0.01$) and Brown ($\alpha < 0.05$) Companies. Micro businesses and the directors and senior managers of our sample companies were least likely to cite training ($\alpha < 0.05$). The second most valued aspect was the quality of the documentation and manuals which constitute management systems, especially valued in one large catering company (Pink Company $\alpha < 0.01$) where the documentation/handling manual was clearly valued more highly than training which was ranked second. As one respondent from Pink Company commented – 'I have no concerns, I have been trained well and if I have any concern I know I can talk to my operations manager' (Interviewee 783, Manager, Pink Company).

Twenty-two per cent could not cite anything they were not pleased with and this varied little between size of business and type of business. Of those who could identify issues of concern the single most cited factor, mentioned by just 10 per cent, was a lack of training. Taken together with the citing of training as the aspect they were most pleased with, this indicates that training is very highly valued as a risk management tool.

The other most pressing issues referred to tended to be internal to the business. They related to staffing levels, training, maintenance, equipment and budgets (especially what was perceived as cost-cutting) which clearly can be of relevance to broader risk management issues that is, a need for higher staffing levels, new equipment and larger budgets. One manager commented that one of his greatest concerns was '… working through the

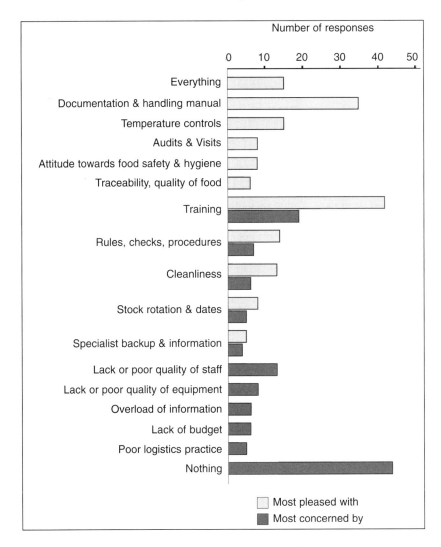

Figure 6.1 Best and worst aspects of company food safety management

food alert file and having the money and time in our budgets to complete the necessary requirements' (Interviewee 841, Manager, Brown Company). Other managers cited, once again, the importance of checks and inspections.

THE INFLUENCE OF FACTORS INTERNAL TO THE BUSINESS ON FOOD SAFETY/HYGIENE RISKS

Phase 2 respondents were asked about the influence of a variety of factors internal to their company on their food safety/hygiene practices. As we can see from Figure 6.2, three aspects of internal organization emerge as especially significant influences on staff with respect to food safety and food hygiene risk management, namely, company policy, training and senior management. Company disciplinary procedures and penalties, colleagues and company reward schemes were generally of less importance, although each of these factors were thought to be of some influence by over 50 per cent of respondents so none of them should be underestimated.

There were a few significant company variations: senior management was significantly less influential in Green Company ($\alpha < 0.01$) possibly because managers here work in small retail branches throughout Scotland and may be isolated from senior management. Perhaps for similar reasons rewards, recognition and incentives were weakest in Orange ($\alpha < 0.01$) and Green ($\alpha < 0.05$) Companies which are the Scottish and London areas of this retail business. Rewards, recognition and incentives were strongest in Yellow Company ($\alpha < 0.01$) and Blue Company ($\alpha < 0.05$) both hospitality chains.

If we add these results to those for the influence of external factors (Figure 6.2), then we can see that a combination of external and internal influences are important. Inside the business organizations the most important influences are senior management, company policies and training and externally state regulators (EHOs and the FSA) and consumers are the most important. Undoubtedly it is the cumulative and interactional effects of all of these that combine as positive pressures for risk management around food safety and food hygiene.

SUMMARY AND DISCUSSION: THE RESEARCH FINDINGS IN CONTEXT

Looking inside the business organization is crucial to understanding its risk management practices and responses to regulation. The data collected in this study re-emphasise the complexity of managing the relatively straightforward risks involved with food safety and food hygiene. The data also point to the variability in internal business practices and capacity to manage risks.

The demands of risk management range from relatively low-tech, routine hand washing by those handling food through to the more complicated risk-based HACCP and traceability systems now required by law. Each presents its

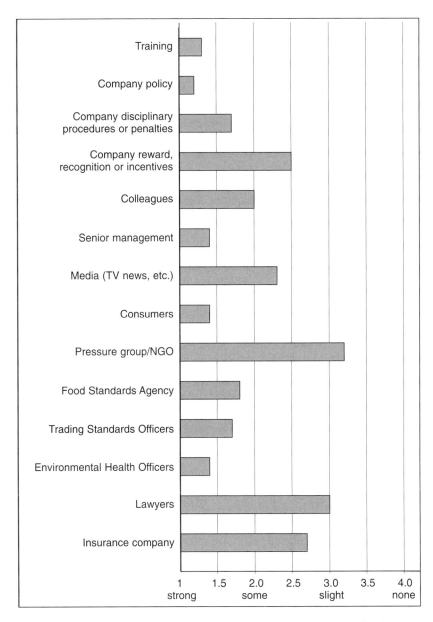

Figure 6.2 Influence of factors on the management of food safety/hygiene risks, based on the statistical mean

own risk management problems. Relatively low-tech, routine procedures are vulnerable to being overlooked, especially at times of pressure, and the catering and hospitality sector was identified as being particularly susceptible to such everyday pressures (see also Chapter 7). At the other end of the scale the more technical and risk-based systems may not be well understood. According to respondents in this study this difficulty in understanding may extend beyond business and include some EHOs especially those who are generalist and not specialist food inspectors. This latter point is to some extent reinforced by the 2005 Pennington report into the South Wales *E. coli* outbreak which identified fundamental failures in food hygiene by the butcher responsible for the outbreak, for example, failures to clean and failures to keep raw and cooked meats separate. These were not high-tech, complicated failures but simple routine failures involving well-known risks. The butcher's HACCP plan was also invalid and this was missed by repeated EHO inspections which also failed to pick up faulty working practices and procedures.[22]

More generally the literature on HACCP reveals a number of concerns with respect to its introduction, for example, difficulties in understanding the approach and questions about its general applicability and resource demands (Ehiri et al. 1995). There seems to be broad agreement that HACCP may pose particular concerns for small businesses where there is some evidence that small, and most especially micro, businesses may lack the expertise and resources to implement HACCP (Fielding et al. 2005; Panisello et al. 1999; Taylor 2001). The catering sector is also identified in the literature as encountering particular difficulties in tailoring HACCP to different menus which may not be easily standardized (Panisello et al. 1999; Worsfold and Griffith 2003). Yet most commentators have sought solutions to these difficulties. For instance, at the time of the research the FSA was working upon implementing a simplified HACCP. This is because there are thought to be very real benefits with the approach, including commercial ones such as the retention of customers and gaining competitive advantage, good practice and compliance with regulations across other parts of the food chain.

Another major challenge of managing food safety/hygiene risks is the volume of work and attention it demands. This includes understanding the risks and regulations, supplying and attending training, checking that rules, policies and procedures are being adhered to, implementing systems for tracing the origins of products, and drawing up and implementing HACCP plans. The implication of these may be costly, for example, supplying good quality training and documentation may be costly in terms of its supply but it also involves the cost of releasing staff for training. This may be especially costly where there is a high turnover of staff, as there generally is in the food hospitality and retail sectors (see Chapter 2), and also where staff are dispersed across a geographical region or nationally. This chimes with the few other studies that have examined this. For example, Worsfold (2005) found that 'resource poverty' in terms of time and money was a major obstacle to continuing training in the small food manufacturing firms. Mortlock et al. (2000) found positive attitudes towards food training and qualifications among food businesses but concerns about the cost, time and relevancy of the training. The system of checks on risk management processes may also be complicated and involve layers of daily through to annual checks involving multiple staff from the organization, if it is large and sophisticated enough, and possibly also external auditors and consultants.

What is clear from the data is that when training is well done it is highly valued by staff. Moreover, organizational rules and policies are generally known about, not always in detail but there is some basic awareness across the sample of what is needed and where to check. The managers in our sample recognized the importance of enforcement through checks and audits although there was some uncertainty and confusion about the full range of checks and who undertook them. These systems were seen to signal commitment from the top of the organization and this is reflected in the importance of senior management as an influence on risk management.

There was a general sense that food safety/hygiene is treated as important and taken seriously but the data reveal some patterns in the ability of parts of the sector to manage their risks. One clear pattern emerges over the size of a business (see also Gunningham 1991). Consistent with the wider literature SME owners and managers found it more difficult to answer questions about the sources of information on risks, training and HACCP than their counterparts in larger organizations. They were less likely to employ specialist personnel, belong to a trade association or employ consultants. And consistent with Chapters 4 and 5, the data in this chapter also identified a greater reliance on state-based regulators to provide the information necessary to organize internal risk management systems and procedures.

Variations were also found according to business. This is partly related to the size of a business, to whether they are retail or catering and how geographically dispersed their sites are. Catering establishments generally encounter greater risk management pressures because of the greater likelihood that they will handle raw and cooked foods and also because of key pressure points surrounding this handling such as around meal times. Businesses with multiple outlets in close proximity to each other find it easier to organize training and refresher courses than those where staff are dispersed across a broader area, for example, in isolated retail sites. Staff perceptions of senior management's commitment to food safety/hygiene risk management are also important and these vary between businesses. For example, senior management exercise a very strong influence over risk management in Red Company and are less strong in Green Company. These data reflect other organizational differences, for example, whereas company reward schemes figure high as an influence for managers from Yellow and Blue Companies they are less important for managers in Orange, Green and Pink Companies. Such indicators contribute to organizational culture and identity which in turn shapes how managers regard their jobs and workplace (Howard-Grenville et al. 2008).

The final pattern of note is that knowledge and understandings of organizational systems and routines are situated and informed by a respondent's position in the organizational hierarchy (see also Hutter 2001). Knowledge of routine checks was lowest at senior levels compared to middle management who routinely undertook and witnessed these checks. By comparison HACCP systems were best understood by senior management and owners, reflecting perhaps the views of respondents in Phase 1 that HACCP would be understood by those who 'need to know' and otherwise there would be ignorance of this approach to managing food safety/hygiene risks..

The flexibility offered to companies by management-based regulation or enforcement self-regulation assumes that businesses are capable of taking advantage of this flexibility (Coglianese and Nash 2006; Eisner 2004). The evidence in this research is that this is patterned and variable. While this approach is laudable in its ambitions it is important to recognize that this is not an approach where 'one size fits all', it is much more suited to larger and better resourced businesses. Although previous research suggests that they too may struggle with enforced self-regulation (Hutter 2001). The policy message deriving from this supports calls for a mix of self-regulation, third party oversights and government underpinning (Gunningham and Rees 1997). But even this is contingent on the businesses involved. For example, SMEs and micro businesses are to some extent reliant on state regulators and unable to buy in third party assistance. It is also contingent on organizational motivations to comply with regulation and risk management demands and it to this subject that we turn in the next chapter.

NOTES

1. Until January 2006 the main legislation relating to food hygiene was the Food Safety (General Food Hygiene) Regulations 1995 and the Food Safety (Temperature Control) Regulations 1995. At the time this research was undertaken the 2006 requirements, including those for HACCP, would not have been a formal requirement but its imminent introduction was clear and it was regarded as best practice. See Chapter 4.
2. One hundred and ninety-nine out of 204 (97.6 per cent) of respondents in Phase 2 and 19/20 (95 per cent) in Phase 3 thought that their business had rules.
3. In Phase 2 177/204 (86.8 per cent) thought that this was the case.
4. Twelve out of 28 (42.9 per cent) of directors and senior managers and 156/176 (88.6 per cent) of managers were aware of such checks.
5. Twenty-one per cent of this group, compared to an average of 7 per cent, said that checks followed incidents.

6. Thirty out of 204 (14.7 per cent) said their business did not employ these staff; 15/204 (7.4 per cent) were not sure; and 21 (10.3 per cent) did not reply.
7. In Phase 2 47.1 per cent (96/204) thought that these staff were employed; 18.1 per cent (n = 37) said that they were not; 17.2 per cent (n = 35) did not know; and 17.2 per cent did not reply.
8. Ninety-three out of 204 responding to the first question on this topic thought that consultants were employed by their business and 92/204 thought that they were in response to the second question.
9. Seventy-one out of 92 believed that consultants undertook checks; 16 believed that they did not; and five either did nor know or did not reply. Only those who considered that consultants were employed by the business were asked this question.
10. See Demortain (2007) for a discussion of the international development of HACCP.
11. See http://www.food.gov.uk/multimedia/pdfs/fsaguidefoodhygleg.pdf (accessed 19 April 2011).
12. http://www.food.gov.uk/multimedia/pdfs/sudanreview.pdf#page=83 (accessed 15 February 2008).
13. Significant differences were found between businesses in the use of company head office, line managers and local councils (α < 0.01) and trainers/lecturers (α < 0.05).
14. Eighteen per cent (5) of senior managers cited trade associations which were mentioned by 9.5 per cent (2) SME owners and just 4 per cent (7) sample managers.
15. SMEs – 66.7 per cent (n = 14) mentioned council sources; senior managers/directors –61 per cent (17) mentioned these sources.
16. Thirteen out of 19 had been on such a course.
17. Seven out of 11 were happy with the training.
18. Phi = 0.170, α = 0.1.
19. Phi = 0.236, α < 0.05.
20. Phi = 0.355, α < 0.01.
21. Fifteen per cent did not respond to 'most pleased' compared to 29 per cent not responding to 'most concerned'. Also almost all the micro and small businesses responded to these questions. The non-responses were from the medium and large companies with a higher rate for the retailers.
22. The report also criticized the Meat Hygiene Service, then an executive arm of the FSA, for failing to enforce existing regulations.

PART III

Conclusions and policy implications

7. Conclusions: why manage risk? What can we learn and improve?

This research has focused on how business risk management practices may be influenced by various sources of regulation and how these sway an organization's propensity to take risks. We have identified a number of important pressures for managing risks, some of which are external to the business and some internal to it. We have also examined understandings of risk and risk regulation held by those in the food sector. In Chapter 3 we found broad agreement about the risks the industry faces, with some variations relating to the social location of respondents. It was also clear that knowing what the risks are is important but that understanding them is not always sufficient to ensure compliance with risk regulation. Subsequent chapters indicated some of the factors that might be helpful in setting and maintaining high standards. In Chapters 4 and 5, for example, we found that state regulation, especially at the local level of EHOs, is an important influence on business risk management practices. But equally important are consumers, especially managerial perceptions that consumers differentiate between food businesses according to their perceptions of food safety and food hygiene standards. Chapter 6 identified factors within business organizations which are significant to their risk management, for example, training, company policies and the commitment of senior management to risk management.

What does this tell us about why businesses manage risks? Much neo-classical theory is premised on the belief that it was not in the self-interest of business to manage risk, that regulation is an external imposition which countered business's primary objective of profit maximization.[1] There are numerous studies which challenge these assumptions, demonstrating that businesses are motivated by multiple objectives, some of them financial but some moral (see below). Moreover, businesses may not be unitary in their objectives with different parts of a business organization holding different interpretations of what their objectives are and having different capacities to achieve their objectives and also to manage risk. Likewise, as we have found in this research, there are many differences among businesses.

The research data suggest two clear reasons to manage risk and comply with good food safety and hygiene practice: first, regulatory drivers, most particularly state-backed legislation and enforcement mechanisms and second, reputational issues which were generally identified as the most pressing driver. These issues relate to two risk regulation literatures, one on compliance and the other on the importance of reputation, the two issues to which we will now turn.

COMPLIANCE

Issues of compliance are an important aspect of the regulation literature. Academic research sccks to identify patterns of compliance and non-compliance, explaining them and considering how to use this information for policy making (Amodu 2008; Etienne 2010; Nielson and Parker forthcoming). A complex mix of explanations of compliance has emerged from the academic literature, relating compliance to regulatory capacity, to organizational and individual motivations and to attitudes to compliance. These in turn have been linked to notions of moral responsibility, citizenship, regulation and commercial objectives.[2] Compliance is negotiated, not just between regulators and those subject to regulation but within business organizations and also in interaction with external social and political environments (Coglianese and Nash 2006; Gunningham et al. 2003; Hutter 1997).

Research Evidence

The characteristics that emerged as important for explaining compliance in this research are state regulatory regime especially at local level, consumers and features of the business for which managers and staff worked. Phase 2 data on the issue of compliance are discussed in Chapters 4 and 5. They show that the majority of the sample was generally supportive of the law and saw compliance as important. Some of these respondents were motivated to comply because they were concerned about legal action, so there was a belief among some in the deterrence effect of sanctions. This also emerged in response to questions about compliance with company rules where some expressed a fear that they might lose their job if they did not comply – 'I don't break the rules as I may lose my job' (Interviewee 27, Manager, Blue Company) (see Chapter 6).

Ignorance of the risks involved is a common explanation of non-compliance. In this research there was broad agreement among managers in Phase 2 about the basic risks which needed managing and there was a belief among the managers we interviewed that their staff understood the importance of compliance and the consequences of non-compliance. In the case of large and medium-sized businesses this knowledge was attributed to the importance of training and internal organizational systems. In small and micro businesses local authority enforcement, officials were seen as the main source of this information and understanding (see Chapters 3, 4 and 6). In Phase 3 respondents were pushed further on understandings of the implications of non-compliance with food safety/hygiene regulations when they were asked 'Do people in the industry appreciate the consequences of non-compliance with food safety/hygiene rules and regulations?' Twenty-one out of 22 thought that their staff did understand these risks, although one felt that kitchen staff would be more likely to be aware than serving and other staff. Seven volunteered that this was because of corporate training, reminders, checks and equipment. They were less certain that staff would understand the possible consequences of non-compliance for the business: 5/12 thought that they would not understand, one thought that this would vary and six thought that they would understand. Overall there was a belief that staff were concerned about food safety/hygiene risks although it was recognized that there can be lapses – 'I like to think that all supervisors do the same job when I'm not here' (Interviewee 294, Assistant Manager, Blue Company) or '... it is ranked quite highly as it is an important part of the store. I mean if you don't get it right it could be quite bad for us' (Interviewee 113, Manager, Orange Company). Only one respondent indicated that staff could be lazy – '... they want to do the jobs the best they can, what training they should have they have. They still do things wrong everyday, they are just lazy' (Interviewee 843, Manager, Brown Company).

The impracticality of complying all of the time was generally recognized. Interestingly the main exceptions came from Phase 1 of the research when some senior officials advised that there would be little point in including large companies in our study as they are 'gold standard' and 'always compliant'. A number of high profile incidents involving large companies would suggest this to be a misapprehension. The managers in our sample (Phases 2 and 3) observed that there is not 100 per cent compliance and some argued that it is not always practical to comply (see Chapter 3). For example, in response to the question 'Have you ever ignored a food safety/hygiene regulation or company rule?' two Phase 3 managers responded thus – 'Sometimes it isn't practical to interfere with the delivery, for example when a refrigerated truck is making a delivery we don't check on the temperatures of everything being delivered – it would take all day' (Interviewee 842, Manager, Brown Company). Tensions between risk management and other factors is a recurring theme in the compliance literature, most especially production pressures. Our research suggests that the sector seen as most risk prone by our sample, namely, the hospitality sector, was viewed in this way because it was seen as most susceptible to production pressures (see Chapter 3).

One of the most fundamental tensions discussed in the literature is the relationship between compliance and costs. This is often cited in the general literature as an explanation of non-compliance. This is not straightforwardly the case in this research, in fact only one respondent cited cost as a reason for not complying with EHO demands. Nevertheless cost is undoubtedly indirectly important in a number of respects. For example, it is a reason among some medium, small and micro businesses for not providing training. It also emerged as a reason why these businesses could not afford outside consultancy and trade association advice. Few challenged food safety/hygiene regulation on the grounds of cost. Indeed, regulation was regarded as important across our sample (see Chapter 4), which generally expressed a wish to comply (see also Fairman and Yapp 2005). This wish to comply is for various reasons and among these is a belief that managing food safety/hygiene risks is regarded as cost-effective. So costs were not challenged because regulatory objectives are perceived as being aligned with good business practice. Phase 3 manager responses, for example, clearly relate food safety/hygiene risks to cost but positively so:

> It comes high, very high. I mean it's the product. It's like Ford selling a faulty car. It's going to kill the business. (Interviewee 294, Assistant Manager, Blue Company)

> ... at the end of the day if something crops up on the food side, then your revenue is going to go down anyway if you get a bad reputation after a food poisoning case or anything like that ... so you have to make sure that everything is done so you work within a clean and safe environment. (Interviewee 780, Manager, Pink Company)

This theme also emerged in responses to the direct question 'Is complying with food safety/hygiene demands costly?' Four out of 16 respondents said that it is not costly, one of these qualifying it to say '... not if procedures are followed' and two qualifying their response to say not if stock is managed skilfully. Of the 12/16 who did believe compliance to be costly all but one qualified their response. Four indicated the benefits outweigh the costs – 'It will cost you if you don't manage the problem ... but if you manage it, it won't cost you much really' (Interviewee 29, Manager, Blue Company). Two respondents replied with reference to the costs of non-compliance – 'It could ruin you' (Interviewee 753, Manager, Pink Company) or 'It may cost you your job' (Interviewee 780, Manager, Pink Company). This reinforces the findings of other studies, that where there is a strong coincidence between risk regulation and business objectives compliance is much more likely (Genn 1993; Gunningham and Rees 1997).

As the discussion above reveals, the importance of compliance directly links to our second issue reputation, most particularly through concerns about consumers' views and practices. Two respondents explicitly accounted for their compliance with company rules in terms of the adverse reputational damage which might be caused if they did not comply, one referred to business reputation because of media interest and one to his own personal reputation within the company. More generally, reputational issues emerge as the most pressing motivator to compliance through the concern respondents expressed about consumer perspectives on their business (see Chapter 4). Indeed, this is one of the major findings of the study, the acute sensitivity to what consumers might think (see Chapter 5). There was a belief that consumers differentiate where they buy their food and eat according to their views of how well food safety/hygiene issues are managed. Indeed, the directors, senior managers and owners who responded to the directors and senior managers' questionnaires believed that managing food safety/hygiene risks gave them a strategic competitive advantage.

REPUTATIONAL RISK

Reputations are especially difficult to manage given that their ownership does not reside with the organization but is attributed by others (Booth 2000; Fombrun 1996). Corporate reputations are social constructions based on a range of criteria such as legitimacy, credibility, trust, reliability and confidence (Booth 2000). They are representations of the general esteem in which a firm is held by its stakeholders (Schultz et al. 2000). Generally reputations relate to a whole organization, not part of it, so organizations are vulnerable to the actions of one part of the organization or even one rogue employee the organizational systems fail to spot or control (as happened in Barings Bank in 1995 and Société Générale in 2008). They are of course especially vulnerable at times of crisis which may occur because of external factors beyond their control (Booth 2000). For example, a crisis in one part of the sector may affect all others by association (Brammer and Pavelin 2006). Alternatively there may be significant changes in knowledge or technology which affect them, such as the 'discovery' that asbestos or cigarettes are so harmful. Such crises can have serious adverse effects on organizational reputations and market value (Fombrun and Rindova 2000). Key stakeholder groups such as customers, investors, the media, partners and regulators may react by withdrawing their support (Fombrun et al. 2000).

It is perhaps not surprising that organizations try to protect their reputations. A 'good' reputation can secure recurring sales and be transferred between products (Booth 2000). It can also 'buffer' firms when controversial events occur (Schultz et al. 2000). As Fombrun et al. (2000) explains, it takes time to build a stock of reputational capital but the literature suggests that this may well be a worthwhile investment not just to enhance reputation but also to mitigate financial losses (Altman and Vidaver-Cohen 2000; Fombrun et al. 2000). The literature devotes some space to discussing such strategies, for example, through signing up to voluntary codes of practice (Wright and Rwabizambuga 2006), corporate philanthropy (Williams and Barrett 2000) and corporate citizenship (Fombrun et al. 2000).

Reputation risk management is interesting because it requires sustained long-term activity in anticipation of reputational risks which are contingent on a variety of unspecified internal or external risk factors. These are especially difficult to manage as reputation is bestowed from the outside and involves so many stakeholders who may be local, national or even international.[3] This has led to the growth of reputation risk management as a consultancy area (Power 2007). A variety of factors are identified in the literature as affecting corporate reputation. One of these is size, the key finding being that larger firms enjoy greater name recognition, in addition to a range of other factors such as prior performance, media publicity and advertising, support of charitable causes and compliance with laws and regulations (Williams and Barret 2000).

There have been a number of high profile incidents which indicate the importance of food safety/hygiene reputation to the food industry. In the manufacturing sector there are several prominent examples, notably the case of Perrier water. In 1990 Perrier water in North America was found to be contaminated with unacceptable levels of benzene. This resulted in the recall of 70 million bottles in North America. It is estimated that Perrier lost some $40 billion sales and its stock value fell, moreover the company did not recover its previous levels of sales (Barton 1993). Another prominent case is that of Cadburys, which in 2006 had to recall over a million chocolate bars following an incident of *Salmonella* contamination. Interesting they did manage to recover their market share although their reputation remains tarnished (Carroll 2009). In the hospitality and retail sectors there have also been incidents damaging to reputations such as a BBC *Whistleblower* documentary in 2007 which alleged that Tescos and Sainsburys were selling out of date food and endangering health.[4] Indeed, every breach of food safety/hygiene regulations by leading supermarkets such as these is likely to receive considerable media attention. Likewise the local press will regularly report any local prosecutions. This was well understood by our sample although they did not rank the media as an important influence on their risk management practices (see Chapter 5 and below).

Research Findings

In our research the Phase 1 view was that reputation mattered most to large companies – 'Reputation matters most to the big boys' (Phase 1, Industry association representative). Indeed some suspected that the risk management practices of some food businesses may be primarily geared to the avoidance of scares. As one commentator observed '… the cost of scandal is enormous'

(Phase 1, Senior governmental policy maker). The view that reputation is something that affects big companies is implicit in much of the academic debate about reputation but the results of this study suggest that it is by no means confined to them. For instance, another group the respondents in all phases of this research considered to be especially mindful of reputational issues were specialist, high quality outlets, some of which were considered to be particularly vulnerable to the scrutiny of the media. Some of these are small companies that rely on their elite reputations. The evidence of Chapter 5 is that small independent retailers and hospitality outlets were also very mindful of their local reputations, the loss of which would be an adverse event which they worried could close them down.

Phase 2 respondents' identification of consumers as all but equal to state regulators in their influence on risk management practices reveals the very real value attaching to what consumers think about business and the view that this influences where they shop and eat. This was a strong influence across all categories of Phase 2 respondents. The FSA publishes quarterly tracker surveys which include monitoring of public concern about food issues. The July 2010 survey reported a significant decrease in concern since the 2009 survey (from 70 per cent to 59 per cent) with 43 per cent concerned about food poisoning. Questions about awareness of hygiene standards in hospitality outlets revealed that awareness was raised by the general appearance of the premises (73 per cent), the appearance of staff (59 per cent) and the reputation of the business (50 per cent).[5]

Phase 3 respondents were asked directly about the importance of reputation, in particular if they 'are ever concerned about food safety related risks to the reputation of your business/branch/self?'. Their responses were mixed with some (4/12) considering the sector's reputation to be 'good' or 'average' and the rest being rather more equivocal, commenting in particular on the variability of the sector – 'Hmm, it's so varied. You have your Michelin starred restaurants down to your dodgy kebab at 2 o'clock in the morning … 60% of the industry has a good reputation' (Interviewee 843, Manager, Brown Company). The hospitality sector and small businesses were specifically singled out for criticism – 'the hospitality industry hasn't got the best reputation, really. I think it's because you do have a lot of very, very small businesses that don't have a lot of advice and just wing it' (Phase 3, Director, Brown Company). Some thought the sector's reputation was improving and one attributed this to the activities of large multinationals:

[The sector's reputation is improving because] ….the suppliers also come in and audit us, [XX] are so worried about their name that they come in and audit us once a month … The [YY] rep also comes in and he makes sure that you're promoting his brand perfectly … You're governed by so many people in retail nowadays, you just take it as second nature … A [ZZ] rep was in today to make sure that her product was where it should have been, because if it is not they'll go into our head office … complain to my boss. (Interviewee 86, Manager, Orange Company)

The importance of this type of third party inspection is important and not just in the UK (Havinga 2006). In some cases the standards demanded and the enforcement may go beyond state requirements and practices.

With reference to their organization's reputation replies were again equivocal, with a minority (6/18) regarding their business as having a 'good reputation' – 'We have a very good reputation for food which was earned through incredible hard work and [through] being proactive with our customers and not lying to them' (Interviewee 843, Manager, Brown Company). The rest had concerns: some thought that there were problems with their company's reputation and others had a generic anxiety about maintaining a good reputation:

> When you have a good name your name goes very far. When you have a bad name your name goes nowhere. You have to keep a reputation … There's so much competition on the market, you can't afford to neglect customers. (Interviewee 867, Manager, Red Company)

> A reputation is very important, in this business you live and die by your reputation. (Interviewee 842, Manager, Brown Company)

> That's what we all fear … The concern is simply a general one that if a problem develops in a [XXX] store no matter how accidental the whole company will be tarred with it … immediately. (Interviewee 153, Manager, Orange Company)

The majority (11/17) were similarly concerned about their own reputation partly because they believed it to be dependent on others:

> I understand that if something happens that I'm the one that is responsible … but I know that I can't do everything on my own. I know that for a fact. And if I don't get the team working with me then it's impossible for me to do everything I need to do, and everything we as a team need to do in terms of food safety and serving the customer. So I think that if something happened somewhere else [in another branch] I'd think, you know, well, it's unfortunate, he's [the manager of the other branch] not got the people working with him that he should have. (Interviewee 294, Assistant Manager, Blue Company)

> I have a good reputation, I would not like to put myself down actually… If something were to happen of a bad sort the message would spread throughout the whole company and it would affect my reputation, and I would not like that to happen. (Interviewee 860, Manager, Red Company)

A minority (6/17) did not believe that individual reputations were at stake because others would understand how mistakes occur. The interrelationships between individual reputations and branch reputations were generally appreciated – 'People come back because of who is running it, because I've been here constantly for five years which is quite unusual in this day and age' (Interviewee 843, Manager, Brown Company). Staff and managerial behaviour are seen as crucial to branch reputation, which in the interviews is seen as essential for business survival in a competitive market.

Recognition that there is reputational leverage to manage risks is exploited by state regulators. For example, many local authorities have food hygiene awards. The best known of these is the FSA sponsored 'scores on the door' scheme which is a food hygiene rating scheme which is available to the public through websites and also displayed in catering establishments.[6] Those scoring low points on this scheme are not surprisingly rather antagonistic towards it but their reactions are testament to the power of the scheme.[7] Overall our Phase 3 research managers were positive about the scheme. Forty-two per cent (18/43) of their remarks on scores on the doors were positive, the belief being that the scheme supported customer choice and helped bring about higher standards – 'It's an excellent idea … because it would help and enhance customer confidence in the store if you get a good result. If you don't then it will be a severe incentive to get that good result the next time' (Interviewee 153, Manager, Orange Company). Forty-six per cent (20/43) of comments gave qualified support to the scheme, arguing, for example, that the scheme should be transparent and regularly updated. Some were clearly concerned by the approach, worrying it could be damaging – 'It's a very good idea as long as people know what it [a specific score] stands for' (Interviewee 819, Manager, Pink Company) and 'I think that is great for customers … [but] it would have to be done for everyone and be fair. If you are doing well you shouldn't be scared of it' (Interviewee 842, Manager, Brown Company). These sorts of concerns led to some (12 per cent or 5/43) negative comments, concerns that the scheme is based on one inspection and worries about the negative consequences of a poor rating – 'This could make or break the business, it's not a very good idea actually' (Interviewee 860, Manager, Red Company).

The use of reputation as a mechanism for regulatory control is discussed by Van Erp with reference to private sector markets, food regulation and financial regulation. She argues (2008b) that reputation is a powerful mechanism for social control which may be as effective as legal sanctions in securing compliance. She relates the use of reputation as a regulatory tool to disclosure, noting that in financial markets in the Netherlands and food regulation in Denmark and the Netherlands the disclosure of non-compliance or inspection scores was primarily established as a means of consumer information. But, she argues, it soon became apparent that this had an impact on regulatory compliance and hence was also part of a regulatory mix of enforcement tools (Van Erp 2007, 2010; see also May 2004). It is important of course to establish when and how reputation can best be targeted. Van Erp (2008a) argues exploiting reputation is most effective in private markets but this research suggests that it can also potentially be very powerful with respect to public regulation. Van Erp focuses on disclosure but it may be that other methods also need exploring. For example, other naming and shaming techniques (Braithwaite 1989) warrant greater investigation into how these can be best communicated so as to be comprehensible and available to consumers.

Understanding Anomalies and Variations

The discussion of compliance and reputation shows that those in the food retail and hospitality sectors are encouraged to manage risks through a complex of motivations and influences. Similarly business risk management is the result of a combination of influences that are external and internal to the business. The interaction of these and their cumulative effects are not well understood, partly because they are sensitive to change (Gunningham et al. 2003). One route to a greater appreciation of risk management stimuli and obstacles is consideration of the anomalies in the data and the variations which emerged in responses.

There were some apparent anomalies in the data regarding the importance of some non-state influences on reputation. Notable among these was the low importance given to the influence of the media who were appreciated to be one of the means by which reputations may be made or destroyed. One possible explanation of these results is the distinction made by Hood et al. (2001) between the context and content of regulation. The context of regulation refers to 'the backdrop of regulation' and the content to 'regulatory objectives, the way regulatory responsibilities are organized, and operating styles' (2001, p. 28). The media appear to be part of the context of regulation which is only important in the indirect impact it might have on the direct content of consumer decisions. Likewise, NGOs appear to be part of the backdrop of regulation rather than regarded as part of the content of regulation. Another possible inconsistency in the data are attitudes towards civil litigation, which was identified by one Phase 1 respondent as the third driver to risk management yet received little additional support among our sample. Interestingly, although regulatory legal action was influential (see Chapter 4) the research did not find many concerns about civil litigation (see Chapter 5). Again lawyers appear to be in a similar category to the media and NGOs, part of the context of regulation and according to our sample not a very important part of that context. It may also be that our sample had rarely come across cases of civil litigation, something academic studies and a government committee would support in their findings that the so-called 'compensation culture' is presently a myth in the UK (BRTF 1999; Lloyd-Bostock 2010).

Another explanation of the apparent discrepancies in the data may be that the extent of some of these influences is overestimated in the academic literature, where their significance is based more on theoretical possibilities than empirical observation (see Chapter 5). Our data may also be biased as most of the sample are middle managers from large and a medium-sized business and senior staff from small and micro businesses, who may be less aware of some of these influences than more senior staff in large companies would be. Nevertheless, given that the aim of the study was to find out what motivates those within the business it is a significant finding that these are the views of store and branch managers who are very much in the front line of risk management on the shop floor.

An important possibility in explaining these differences and some of the variations we will continue to discuss is that there are domain effects which hold explanatory value. For example, the relatively unimportant role attributed to the media may in part relate to the very direct experience between consumers and their purchase of food. Relational distance may be especially important in this context, much more so than in the case of large corporate cases such as those discussed by Fisse and Braithwaite (1993) where corporations were fearful of media attention.

Variations

An important objective of the research was to map out variability across businesses. Different patterns of understanding were discerned in relation to risk regulation and also with respect to knowledge of internal corporate efforts to manage risk. Our findings broadly reflect the literature. For example, the size of a business is a major criterion explaining variability; this is identified, as a key indicator of regulatory capacity. Our discussions with experts in the food sector revealed that many of them believed risk to be strongly related to size, with effort proportionate to the size of the business. But there was also a vocal minority who argued that such statements should not be too sweeping and who cited examples of large companies suffering serious and high profile risk management problems. While it is important not to generalize too much about the importance of the size of a business, it nevertheless remains the case that those from the small and micro businesses in the sample struggled the most with respect to managing risk. This is partially explained by regulatory capacity in terms both of knowledge and finance. For example, small and micro businesses typically had fewer sources of advice available to them, partly because they could not afford to employ some of the non-state sources such as consultants or trade associations. This, in turn increased their reliance on state regulators. Another important dimension of size is the power of large businesses to define regulatory agendas. This did not necessarily mean arguing for less regulation, quite the reverse, as an important observation was that some of the supermarkets had food safety hygiene standards which were deemed to be much stricter than those imposed by the state.

A second relevant factor of variability across businesses is business type. Many of those we spoke to in the research drew a clear distinction between the retailing and hospitality sectors. The hospitality sector was identified as 'the biggest challenge', partly because of the high turnover of staff and the task of handling and preparing food which also makes it more vulnerable to production pressures. Another view is expressed by one participant thus – 'the hospitality sector is a very fragmented sector, they don't tend to gel as a sector'. Moreover, the large majority are small businesses (Fairman and Yapp 2004). Hence there is a distinct overlap with the first line of variation. This accords with an IGD (1998) finding that food consumers are most likely to question restaurant rather than retail hygiene standards and with Mori (2005) data that the British are especially anxious about the risk of contracting food poisoning in restaurants. The extent to which retailers were regarded as risky partly depended upon the type of food they sold, for example, whether it is fresh or pre-packaged. Also deemed relevant was whether or not they were small independent retailers or part of a broader company or franchise. So the task environment is important, as is the organization of a business.

There are two aspects of organization that appear to be especially important in understanding variations. Most important is the commitment of senior staff (see Chapter 6) and to some extent this is taken to be revealed through organizational policies, protocols and training. Again these are areas where small and micro businesses may struggle more than larger well-resourced companies, although in these smaller businesses staff and owners will have more direct opportunities to impress their commitment through day to day interaction. There is also a suggestion in this research that how centralized or federated an organization is may explain some variations, with federated organizations being regarded as more responsive to local developments (see Chapter 3). On the downside, these organizations also seemed to encounter more difficulties in providing training for staff.

The research findings resonate with other studies regarding the socially situated nature of risk regulation knowledge and understandings. This relates to the task environment, sector and organization within which respondents work and also their place in the organizational hierarchy. Knowledge of national regulatory organizations such as the FSA, and also of consultants and trade associations is greatest among those at the most senior levels of an organization and understandings of risk varied according to place in the hierarchy (see Chapter 4). What is clear is that the lines of variation to some extent overlap. There is, as we have seen, some convergence around size of business and type of business and these in turn influence regulatory capacity.

The social situation of a business is also important. This was most exemplified in this study by the Scottish case where the FSA was better known and more appreciated than their counterpart in England (Chapter 4). This is partly because the FSA was seen as more accessible in Scotland, which to some extent relates to the size of the food community in Scotland where people tended to know each other: one respondent explained that in Scotland all EHOs could fit into one room, something which could not happen in England. There is also another facet to this regional variation, namely, that Scotland was in a post disaster environment having been shaken by the Wishaw *E. coli* disaster in 1996. This reverberated through the Scottish food community in particular and was also the catalyst for the so-called Pennington money, which was an annual payment by the Scottish Executive of some £2.6 million per year for five years to enable environmental health departments to focus on improving food hygiene in Scotland. The evidence of this study is limited but suggests that this investment had produced improved understandings of food safety/hygiene. The disaster was also perceived to have sensitized Scottish consumers to these issues.

The role of broader social concerns in influencing business has been discussed in the wider literature. The notion of the 'social licence to operate' (Gunningham et al. 2003) is possibly most forceful here. An important component in 'the social licence to operate' is the role of civil society and NGOs (Gunningham et al. 2003). These groups undertake an important monitoring role and their views, alongside those of the local community, are an important influence on business practices. Gunningham et al. (2003, pp. 153–4) also found less evidence than anticipated regarding the influence of NGO activity over pulp manufacturers, although they did accord local community activists an important role in influencing corporate behaviour. In this research, of course, NGOs did not emerge as significant but it does appear that in the Scottish case the *E. coli* disaster did, or at least is perceived, to have influenced the social licence to operate of food retail and hospitality businesses.

POLICY IMPLICATIONS – WHAT WE CAN LEARN

There are a number of policy implications flowing from the research data presented in this study. Some relate to the institutional arrangements for state governance, others to the value of non-state players in the governance system and several to principles of food governance in the UK. There are also some micro business-level lessons which can usefully be developed.

Food Governance and the State

This study underlines the persisting importance of state regulation, most especially at local authority level. Generally the FSA emerged as a useful source of information and did not attract much criticism among our Phase 2 and Phase 3 respondents. This partly reflects the fact that the FSA has gained broad public trust and overall the FSA appears to be regarded positively.[8] It is also likely to be related to the fact that many of our sample were middle managers who valued the FSA as a source of information and whose knowledge of the politics surrounding the FSA was limited. Typically the FSA was better known by those in senior positions and it was they who were more critical of the organization (see Chapter 4).

Since 2000 the FSA has come to command a budget of £152 million (2009/10) and employ some 2,000 staff. It has also experienced a series of conflicts and criticisms. These include complaints about participative regulation regarding difficulties of informational and power balances among stakeholders (Rothstein 2004). There are a number of criticisms of the FSA's handling of particular issues. For example, in 2003 and again in 2009 the FSA published research which stated that organic food is no healthier and provides no significant nutritional benefit compared with conventionally produced food. This brought the FSA into contention with organic food producers such as the Soil Association. Another issue which has attracted criticism is the FSA's handling of GM food issues where the perception was that the Agency supported GM products.[9] These issues relate to criticism about the independence of the FSA. In the organic food and GM debates FSA critics allege bias and more recently the FSA has become embroiled in more controversy over the topic of nutritional food labelling.[10] The issue of food labelling has become a highly politicized one across the globe with debates polarizing around food producers, public health campaigners and NGOs on a host of different issues. In the UK the food labelling debates were used to challenge the FSA's remit and to construct a broader argument about the Agency overextending its remit, particularly into areas of nutritional advice, although this was one of the four areas highlighted in the James Report as being an area that most concerned the public (see Chapter 4).

Regulation is a balancing act between different interests and these examples highlight the difficulties of this decision making, especially in the face of a powerful business lobby (see also Rothstein 2005). Another element of this balancing act is the government (Flynn et al. 2003; Millstone and Zwanenberg 2002) and in the case of the FSA this was exemplified in July 2010 when reports emerged that the new coalition government in the UK was considering abolishing the FSA and moving its responsibilities to the Department of Health and DEFRA.[11] This led to an outcry from the opposition, from health groups and from some food organizations. Critics of the suggested abolition were quick to remind us of why the FSA was formed, especially the concern to separate consumer interests for food safety from DEFRA's (formerly

MAFF's) remit to develop the agri-food sector. To a limited extent the back-lash was successful. The Department of Health announced that the FSA would continue to exist but with reduced responsibilities. First, their remit for the nutritional content of food was moved to the Department of Health and then responsibility for food labelling moved to DEFRA. Slowly but surely the FSA's remit is being eroded. It is alarming that just a decade after the estab-lishment of the FSA it is under threat from the government and is having its remit eroded. This suggests very little institutional learning.

The other main area of concern which has attracted criticism of the FSA is its relationship with local enforcement bodies and this was an area highlighted by the respondents in this research. The arm's length arrangement with the local authorities undertaking enforcement presents the FSA with many chal-lenges when attempting to direct the activities of individuals they neither employ nor fund. The creation of the FSA is credited with placing food safety and hygiene issues at the centre of environmental health agendas, but with the criticism that this has effected a shift in resourcing within environmental health departments which favours this aspect rather than others, not that it has drawn more resources to environmental health overall. The relationship between local authorities and the FSA is not thought to be an easy one, with many local authority officers viewing it as overly bureaucratic, impractical and difficult (Better Regulation Executive and National Audit Office 2008). While the FSA has the authority to access local government information and publish reports these are the limits of its powers over local authorities.[12]

The FSA's lack of impact at a local level did indirectly emerge in the research. The research also reflected a number of difficulties associated with the local food governance system in the UK. These centre on the profession-alism and expertise of enforcement officials; the breadth of their remit, espe-cially their non-food remit; the variations in their enforcement practices; and difficulties in coordinating food enforcement practice across the country. But some of these difficulties also reflect the merits of the system, for example, the adaptation to local circumstances, and being accountable to the local popula-tion through democratically elected councillors.

In this research there was some questioning of EHOs' expertise with some respondents concerned that not all EHOs are able to grasp the more technical aspects of food safety/hygiene control, most especially concerning the intro-duction of HACCP requirements in 2006. These difficulties in local authority food governance are highlighted in a recent inquiry report into an outbreak of *E. coli* O157 in South Wales in September 2005.[13] The inquiry was undertaken by Professor Hugh Pennington who undertook the inquiry into the 1995 Scottish *E. coli* deaths (see Chapter 4). In both inquiries Professor Pennington was critical of the local authority regulatory and inspection regimes. In the Welsh inquiry he analysed EHO inspections over eight years and found that they had repeatedly failed to identify seriously inadequate HACCP plans and breaches of the law. The inquiry raised questions about the competency and training of EHOs and criticized the local authority which permitted them to work without the necessary skills. The inquiry also criticized the Meat Hygiene Service (MHS) for its inspection of the abattoir supplying the butchers at the centre of the *E. coli* crisis. It also found some problems in the FSA's relationship with local authorities.

The case of the MHS is a revealing one. It was created in 1995 as an Executive Agency of MAFF to take over meat inspection duties from local authorities across Great Britain. In 2000 it was transferred to the newly created FSA but maintained its status as an Executive Agency. Despite these organizational changes the MHS has been subject to a variety of criticisms, many of which are similar to those levelled at EHOs. These centre on the suitability and training of veterinary staff, who proved hard to recruit to the Service, and also of their inspections. MHS inspectors were accused of inconsistency and, similarly to EHOs, they faced enforcement difficulties in an area where the financial pressures to which meat operators are subject called for a greater dependence upon external regulation and enforcement to secure compliance (Scholfield and Shaoul 2000).[14] These persistent criticisms suggest that caution should be exercised before considering organizational change to remedy the difficulties with EHO enforcement. Some of the difficulties with local authority enforcement do however point to difficulties with some higher level governance principles in the UK. Indeed, some of the merits associated with local authority EHOs also pose questions for these principles. Central here is an important message of this research, namely, that EHOs were valued by respondents and found to be particularly influential on risk management practices. They were especially important for small and micro businesses so their local base was seen to be advantageous. Yet the expertise of regulators remains problematic. There are a number of bodies which could help to mitigate some of the professionalization and coordination difficulties experienced in the local authority governance system in the UK, including CIEH and LACOTS. But these bodies are viewed by some as trade associations in that they protect the interests of their members and therefore the status quo. However, they do have the potential to initiate change.

Governance Principles

UK food safety legislation reflects a number of broad trends in UK regulation, notably the move to emphasize the responsibilities held by businesses and also the rise of risk-based approaches to regulation, particularly as embraced by the Hampton Report[15] (2005). In recent years the emphasis has been on giving businesses more leeway to determine how to manage risks themselves, which has involved them in also taking more responsibility for managing the risks they create. State regulators oversee this process of self-management and act when businesses fail to manage their own risks or fall short of the required standards (Hutter and Amodu 2008).

This research points to difficulties with both of these principles. Like other studies it raises profound questions about the ability of all businesses to manage the risks they generate. In this case this is less because of a resistance to regulation but more because of a deficit of regulatory capacity among small and micro businesses which make up a relatively high proportion of the food retail and particularly hospitality sectors. The whole self-enforcement approach assumes that businesses have the capacity to understand and manage attendant risks, which can be lacking in the case of smaller businesses. The research evidence suggests that such assumptions are ill-founded. For example, academic studies show smaller businesses can experience particular difficulties complying with their legal obligations. They may not have sufficient resources (financial or technical) to understand what the law requires of them (Grabosky and Braithwaite 1986; Hutter and Jones 2006). The food hygiene domain is no different (Fairman and Yapp 2005; see also Fielding et al. 2005). This point has wider implications for a governance system that places greater responsibility on businesses to regulate their own risks.

More space has been created for non-state actors to play a regulatory role. For example, businesses may turn to industry or trade organizations for advice on risk management and compliance issues. Alternatively, they may turn to those whose business is selling regulatory and risk management advice or cover to companies, for instance, insurance companies and consultancies. But the evidence is that it is precisely those in most need of advice who cannot afford it, namely, smaller businesses, and this leaves them reliant on the state system of regulation to learn how to manage their risks (see Chapter 5).

The research also adds to the evidence concerning the difficulties of the risk-based approached to regulation. The introduction of risk-based HACCP systems are an example. HACCP systems are only protective to the extent that the workforce and management are fully committed to their implementation (Elson et al. 2004; Fielding et al. 2005; Jones et al. 2008). Adequate training is of fundamental importance for effective HACCP programmes (Clayton et al. 2002; Little et al. 2003). The evidence is that the rigours of the regime can present particular difficulties for small businesses (Fielding et al. 2005; Worsfold 2001).

Further difficulties arise when doubts are raised about the abilities of some EHOs to understand HACCP themselves (see above). Indeed the employment of generalist EHOs, especially in a climate of fewer local authority resources, has profound implications for the collection and assessment of data required for risk-based regulation which demands expert, well-qualified staff to collect and assess data and to know how to use it to prioritize work (Lloyd-Bostock and Hutter 2008). There is evidence that EHOs are not the only food inspectors finding risk-based regulation difficult, with the 2005 Pennington Inquiry in Wales recommending consistent and rigorous enforcement by the MHS and the use of risk-based approaches. The latter was something the MHS found difficult to adopt and a joint Better Regulation Executive and National Audit Office review of the FSA's adoption of the Hampton Principles, conducted in 2008, found that the MHS was not adopting risk-based approaches. More generally, resourcing environmental health departments is a serious issue for local authorities and there may be a temptation for local authorities to use risk-based regulation and better regulation initiatives to cut resources.

Beyond the State Regulation

The potential of non-state organizations to become involved in constructive ways also demands greater attention. The literature does discuss how this might be done by a variety of organizations, but empirical examples of these translating into action are not much in evidence (see Chapter 5). One of the key findings of this research is the empowerment of consumers, with managers' risk management practices being heightened by concerns about consumer decision making being influenced by food safety/hygiene matters. Indeed a few other examples suggest that consumers do have very real influence – for example, the travel website Trip Advisor, where consumers record their experiences of hotels, and the broader notion of green markets where consumers are encouraged to buy environmentally friendly products (Grabosky 1994). Consumers' direct experiences are seen as most challenging, while the channelling or management of their views by NGOs and the media appeared to represent less of a threat in the view of our sample. This suggests possibilities in promoting regulation through increasing consumer awareness or sensitizing business to the potential of improving consumer differentiation according to risk issues. This would enable some opportunity to maximize the crucial potential of aligning risk regulation with good business practice. This is important in promoting risk management and it has been found to be crucial to compliance (Genn 1993; Rees 1994).

Appreciation of the risks that may be associated with a given activity is not sufficient on its own to promote compliance but it is an important factor in helping to manage risk. This is reinforced in the research in its identification of training as highly valued by respondents in promoting good risk management practice (Chapter 3). This refers to training as a major source of information about risk and risk management. Moreover it also emerged as the second most important influence on business risk regulation (Chapter 6). As the research underscored training can be difficult to establish. This is for a number of reasons, for example, staff may be spread across a region making it difficult to bring them together for training, staff turnover may be high, refresher courses may prove costly with respect to time and finance. Small and micro-size enterprises are especially vulnerable to these pressures and often the least able to provide adequate training. Their reliance on EHOs assumes regular contact with them but this varies considerably, because as local authorities have reduced their spending the ability of environmental health departments to maintain high levels of inspection is under pressure. Indeed cutting inspections is one objective of the UK government in reducing the so-called 'regulatory burden' (Hampton 2005).

At the micro level greater attention needs to be given to the forms and content of such training and to innovative and appealing ways of conveying risk information. This needs to take into account the high turnover of staff in the food sector, and the difficulties of communicating where staff are either spatially or financially isolated. Where staff do remain in post, consideration needs to be given to continuing education and refresher courses. Another important concern is who provides and facilitates the provision of such training. The FSA could play an enhanced role here: they are already an important player in communicating about food issues to consumers and their role with respect to supporting business education could be developed. EHOs clearly play a crucial role, indeed some environmental health departments have offered training courses for local food businesses but this varies widely according to local authority commitment to food safety/hygiene matters. But both of these options require state or local authority resources and these are far from forthcoming in an era of reduction in public expenditure.

Beyond the state, trade associations and some consultancies provide training and information for the food retail and hospitality sectors but both of these sources are often beyond the means of small and micro businesses. Again some innovative thinking is required to overcome this, perhaps involving some greater cross-subsidization by the larger and more affluent businesses to help train their poorer counterparts. There is evidence this could be a wise investment as it would improve the reputation of the sector (Rees 1994), although a counter argument of course is that people have to buy food so there would be an anti-competitive disincentive to such ideas. The risk-based regulation approach implies a system where state regulatory resources are primarily directed to businesses which are failing to manage their own risks and comply with regulation. Typically this means that regulatory resources are focused on the less able and least motivated businesses. But there are problems with EHOs having the capacity to operate such a risk-based system. This is for reasons of resource constraint and limited expertise. The latter may in part be met by improved training and specialization, with maybe the Chartered Institute for Environmental Health Officers (CIEHO) and LACORS taking a lead role. But it also demands adequate resourcing to assess risks and it might well be that some of the deregulatory policies in place are counterproductive as they diminish the ability of regulators to make these decisions. For example, the reduction in inspections decreases the ability of regulatory officials to make assessments of the current state of risk management in a business, something which is particularly important in an industry with a high turnover of staff. Limited resources have implications for regulators' ability to assemble the quality and quantity of data they need to make risk-based judgements and also for them to employ staff with the skills to assess the information they have. Restricted resources also diminish the ability of state regulators to educate and offer advice, something which has emerged as especially important for small and micro businesses.

This research reinforced the message that business risk management is the outcome of interacting influences. The size of a business emerged as material to its regulatory capacity which in turn is often associated with resources. So typically those businesses with the most knowledge and resources have the greater capacity to comply and manage risks (May 2004). In the food domain this to some extent overlaps with differentiation according to type of food sector – with the hospitality sector being much more likely to have difficulty with risk regulation than the retail sector. It is also most vulnerable to production pressures which increase the possibility of risk management rules and protocols being overlooked, even in the face of a compelling imperative to comply in the interest of strategic business objectives.

In a number of respects this research also pointed to the importance of relational distance in risk regulation. Black (1976) explained that relational distance could be 'measured by the scope, frequency and duration of interactions between people, and by the nature and number of links between them in a social network'. It has been found to be important in other regulatory settings. For example, Grabosky and Braithwaite (1986) found it important across a broad range of regulators in Australia and in the UK relational distance has been found to be significant in explaining the regulatory activities in the areas of health and safety, the environment and environmental health (Hutter 1988, 1997). In these studies the concept of relational distance is used to explain interactions between regulators and the populations they regulate and in particular the propensity of regulators to resort to law. In this study the focus has been on the regulated population and it found relational distance to be important with respect to the relationship between the businesses and regulators and also between businesses and consumers. In the case of the relationship between businesses and regulators the importance of relational distance manifested itself most particularly at the local level where relations with local authority EHOs were highly valued. It also emerged as relevant in Scotland with respect to the local offices of the FSA which were again in close spatial and social proximity to business. The indication in this research was that the close relational distance between the Scottish FSA and local businesses, EHOs and consumers led to perceptions of a closer and more positive relationship than in London and the South East where the London-based FSA was regarded as more remote.

Relational distance also appeared as important in the relationship between businesses and consumers, especially with respect to businesses maintaining the trust and custom of consumers on a daily basis. The distance between business and consumers may also be why reputation in this sector appears to be important across business size, type and to some extent region (Van Erp 2010; cf. Gunningham et al. 2005). These findings are suggestive of routes for further research such as the importance of the domain under scrutiny, that is, the task environment and industry sector. For example, in a market with multiple sellers and high dependency on a regular flow of consumers risk management can be an important marker of differentiation especially where there are risks to consumers. In such markets reputational issues may be especially important and be available as important levers for compliance with business and organizational risk management requirements.

The influence of reputational issues also warrants greater research attention. The leverage offered by the possibility of reputational damage is contingent on a variety of factors. The relationship between size and reputational damage is not simply linear. This research suggests that small local businesses are highly vulnerable to reputational damage. Large supermarkets and chains are more vulnerable to media attention but the extent of reputational damage to single risk events is unclear. It does however seem that some large companies are able to withstand such events without a significant loss of consumers.

Risk regulation in the food sector exemplifies one of the major challenges of risk management, namely, keeping risk management messages prominent and ensuring that they are adhered to at an everyday level. Devising better means of training and communication are clearly important here. Governance systems need to better exploit research findings and in particular to develop the positives rather than negatives in risk regulation. As this research has shown there are sectors and occasions when the advantages of risk regulation can clearly be linked to business advantage. This is true not just at the level of the firm but also with respect to the economy: it makes good economic sense to regulate food safety/hygiene as the health and employment costs of not doing so are very high. It is also vital to ensure confidence in state governance systems and embrace the non-state sector in smarter ways.

NOTES

1. Interestingly many of these assumptions are part of the modern 'better regulation' initiative which uses slogans such as 'lifting the burden' and 'cutting red tape'.
2. Among notable contributions to this literature are Bardach and Kagan (1982), Braithwaite and Makkai (1994), Haines (1997), Hutter (2001), Kagan and Scholz (1984), May (2005) and Parker (2002).
3. Several authors observe the global/transnational nature of reputations (Altman and Vidaver-Cohen 2000), exemplified in the very existence of international reputation ratings (Fombrun 2007).
4. http://news.bbc.co.uk/1/hi/business/6676345.stm (accessed 19 April 2011).
5. http://www.food.gov.uk/news/newsarchive/2010/jul/trackermarch10 (accessed 24 November 2010).
6. Similar schemes operate in Denmark and the Netherlands. See Van Erp (2010).
7. An example is the criticism of a celebrity chef whose pub scored 1 out of 5 in hygiene inspection, Janet Harmer, 'Worrall Thompson slams scores on the doors for being bureaucratic', Wednesday 21 July 2010 10:55, Caterer Search.Com, http://www.caterersearch.com/Articles/2010/07/21/334340/worrall-thompson-slams-scores-on-the-doors-for-being-bureaucratic.htm (accessed 19 April 2011).
8. The FSA tracking survey also monitors public views of the FSA and in July 2010 these were reported to be 63 per cent. See http://www.food.gov.uk/news/newsarchive/2010/jul/trackermarch10 (accessed 24 November 2010).
9. Dean's (2005) independent review of the FSA in 2005 criticized the Agency for appearing not to be open to debate on the issues of GM and organic foods. The issue of GM reappeared in 2006 when Friends of the Earth took the FSA to court over its failure to act in the case of imported rice, and in 2010 when two members of the FSA Public Dialogue Steering Committee resigned because they believed that the Agency was favouring the industry in a proposed public consultation on GM.
10. The FSA promoted the 'traffic light' labelling scheme on the grounds that this was best understood by consumers. This was challenged by a number of food businesses. The controversy persisted for many years, in the UK and in Europe where a proposal that the traffic light system be adopted throughout Europe was rejected in June 2009 by the European Parliament despite strong support from public health campaigners.
11. This was linked to a general, across the board cost cutting in the public sector, an exercise which particularly targeted regulation. But it also followed from criticism by the Health Secretary of the FSA's promotion of the traffic light food labelling system. A Conservative Green Paper in 2009 on health stated that the role and the remit of the FSA would be scaled back and the Agency would be put under ministerial control.
12. The limitations of these powers are illustrated by the content of some of its local authority audit reports. For example, the audit reports for the Orkney Islands reveal that repeated audit follow-ups 2005–07 were required before the local authority reached FSA standards. See http://www.food.gov.uk/enforcement/auditscheme/auditreports/auditsscotland/auditscot/coreaudits/orkneyislandscoreaudit (accessed 15 November 2007). Such occurrences do not suggest that the public reporting of audit reports is of major concern to these local authorities and no other powers of compulsion are available to the FSA.
13. This was the second largest outbreak in the UK and resulted in 157 identified cases, 31 hospital admissions and the death of a five-year old boy (Pennington 2009).
14. In April 2010 the MHS lost its separate identity and became part of the FSA, a move officially explained by attempts to become more efficient and reduce administrative duplication within the FSA.
15. Hampton's 2005 review considered how to reduce the administrative burdens on businesses, without compromising the UK's regulatory regime.

Appendix 1: Profile of Phase 2 respondents

Pink Company: all staff sent the questionnaire were site managers. They had been in the job an average of three years. Prior to working in Pink Company 75 per cent had worked in the food industry, the rest came from a range of different backgrounds including management in other sectors. They were responsible for an average of seven staff and of those responding 50 per cent used contract/casual labour. They ranked their main responsibilities as: 1. overall management; 2. financial management; and 3. staff management and training.

Brown Company: all staff sent the questionnaire were site managers. They had been in the job an average of one or two years. Prior to working for Brown Company, 50 per cent had worked in the food industry, the rest came from a miscellany of different backgrounds. Managers were responsible for an average of 11 staff and of those responding 70 per cent used contract/casual labour. They saw their main responsibilities as: 1. financial management; 2. overall management; and 3. stock management and health and safety.

Blue Company: all staff sent the questionnaire were branch managers. They had been in the job an average of between three and four years. Prior to working in Blue Company almost 60 per cent had worked in the food industry, the rest came from a range of different backgrounds including management jobs in other sectors. Managers were responsible for an average of 30 staff and of those responding over 50 per cent used contract/casual labour. They saw their main responsibilities as: 1. financial management and staff management and training; and 2. customer service.

Yellow Company: all staff sent the questionnaire were branch managers. They had been in the job an average of between one and two years. Prior to working in Yellow Company almost 40 per cent had worked in the food industry and almost 30 per cent had been in education. They were responsible for an average of five staff and of those responding over 70 per cent used contract/casual labour. They were asked to outline their main responsibilities: customer service was ranked first and food safety tied in second place with staff management and training.

Red Company: all staff sent the questionnaire were branch managers. They had been in the job an average of five years. Prior to working in Red Company almost 60 per cent had worked in the food industry, the rest came from education and other management jobs. They were responsible for an average of 30 staff and of those responding almost 60 per cent used contract/casual labour. They gave detailed and comprehensive written answers when asked to outline their main responsibilities. They ranked their main responsibilities as: 1. overall management; 2. financial management; and 3. health and safety.

Orange and Green Companies: the Scottish and South East areas of a large national retailer. With the exception of three senior officers, all of the staff sent the questionnaire were branch managers. The Scottish respondents had been in the job an average of between four and five years. And those from the South East had been in the job an average of between five and six years. Before working for their business the respondents had worked in a range of other types of employment: staff in the Scottish stores were much more likely to have previously worked elsewhere in the food industry.

Managers were responsible for a mean number of 24 staff (in Scotland a mean of 26, with 22 as the mean for the South East region). Scotland had a greater range of store sizes (as defined by number of staff employed in each). Two thirds of those responding in the South East used contract/casual labour whereas in Scotland only one third of stores used contract/casual labour. Managers were asked to outline their main responsibilities. There is broad consistency in the ranking of the main responsibilities; the order is very similar in each case with agreement that the most important responsibilities are financial management, and staff management and training. When defining their own key responsibilities, the Scots were more likely (a quarter to a third more) to volunteer information than managers from the South East and seemed clearer on their roles particularly with regard to managing the following; financial matters, staff, customer service, general management and risk (in that order).

Appendix 2:   Phase 2 questionnaires

RED Questionnaire for Managers

Introductory cover page

Who are we?
We are academic researchers which means that we have to be unbiased, independent and not represent any commercial interests. We work for CARR (Centre for Analysis of Risk and Regulation) **www.lse.ac.uk/collections/carr/** an academic research centre based at LSE, or to give it its full name, London School of Economics and Political Science which is part of the University of London. **www.lse.ac.uk**

Your senior management have very generously agreed to support this academic research project by allowing us to contact you and your colleagues. **We must emphasise that all individual responses will be treated as confidential.** You do not have to write your name or contact details on this questionnaire.

What is the questionnaire for?
The questionnaire is for an academic research project. The aim is to further our understanding of food safety and food hygiene practices and to help to promote better and more user-friendly ways of managing food safety and food hygiene risks. The results from this research will also allow CARR academics to gain insights into how your business really works. These results will be written up in a series of academic and practitioner publications by Professor Hutter. Copies of these publications will be publicly available and organisations that have taken part in the research will receive a summary of these results.

What do you have to do?
Answer the questions in this questionnaire. To do this you either have to put a tick in the box provided or write a few words on a dotted line. Remember this is not a test and there are no right or wrong answers! We are interested in what you as an individual think. We encourage you to be as honest as you can. On

completing the questionnaire put it straight into the pre-paid addressed enve-lope we've provided and put in the post.

What happens after you return the questionnaire?
We will compare your response to the other responses we get; some responses will be from people very similar to you, some very different. **Confidentiality is assured.** This is the most important thing about the way we work. Without the trust of those who help us, we would not be able to do our job. We assure you that we will not disclose any of your contact details or identifiable responses to anyone.

If you have any questions at all you may contact Clive Jones in confidence. He is a Researcher within CARR at the London School of Economics and Political Science. Tel: XXXX or email: XXXX

Please use the freepost envelope provided – no stamp needed – to return completed copies of this questionnaire to CARR by Introduction to Questionnaire
© Bridget Hutter
For CARR use only
Self Completion Research Questionnaire ref: BMH04EMPLOYEES(B)V3.0
URN

Questionnaire starts here:

Section 1 – Your Role

1 Job title:
2 How long have you been in your present job (approximately)?
Days Months Years
3 (If applicable) What did you do before your present job?
4 What are your key responsibilities in your present job?
5 How many staff are you responsible for managing?
people *(approximately)*
6 Approximately what proportion of these staff are casual or contract employ-ees?
Tick one box only
76 – 100% ❑ *01*
51 – 75% ❑ *02*
26 – 50% ❑ *03*
1 – 25% ❑ *04*
None ❑ *05*
Don't know ❑ *06*

Section 2 – Safety and Hygiene

7 What are the main **food safety and food hygiene risks** encountered by your business?

8 Please give an example of a risk you consider to be **more** serious than food safety and food hygiene risks.

9 Please give an example of a risk which you consider to be **less** serious than food safety and food hygiene risks.

Section 3 – Information and Policy

10 What are **your** main sources of information about food safety and food hygiene risks?
Please tick any boxes that apply
Your company head office ❑ *01*
Your line manager ❑ *02*
Your staff ❑ *03*
A trainer or lecturer ❑ *04*
A consultancy ❑ *05*
Advice from an Environmental Health Officer ❑ *06*
The local council ❑ *07*
The Food Standards Agency ❑ *08*
The government ❑ *09*
Trade association ❑ *10*
Other *(please specify)* ❑ *11*

11 How is this information communicated?
Please tick any boxes that apply
An operating manual or handbook ❑ *01*
Magazine ❑ *02*
Training video, tape or CD ROM ❑ *03*
Training leaflet/Newsletter ❑ *04*
The Web/Internet ❑ *05*
Training course ❑ *06*
Verbal instructions ❑ *07*
A workmate ❑ *08*
Written instruction eg, letter or internal memo ❑ *09*
Other *(please specify)* ❑ *10*

12 Does your business have rules regarding food safety and food hygiene?

Tick one box only
Yes ❑ *01*
No ❑ *02*
Don't know ❑ *03*

13 If **'yes'** please can you give two examples below:
1
2

14 Do you think that all staff know the rules that relate to their area or respon-sibilities?
Tick one box only
Yes ❑ *01*
No ❑ *02*
Don't know ❑ *03*

15 Are there checks to ensure that staff follow these rules?
Tick one box only
Yes ❑ *01*
No ❑ *02*

16 If **'yes'** what sort of checks do you have?

17 How do **your staff** learn about food safety and food hygiene?
Please tick any boxes that apply
You or another manager ❑ *01*
Your company head office ❑ *02*
Their line manager ❑ *03*
A trainer or lecturer ❑ *04*
An external advisor, consultant or auditor ❑ *05*
Advice from an Environmental Health Officer ❑ *06*
The local council ❑ *07*
The Food Standards Agency ❑ *08*
The government ❑ *09*
Trade association ❑ *10*
Other *(please specify)* ❑ *11*

18 How is this information communicated?
Please tick any boxes that apply
Company manual or handbook ❑ *01*
Magazine ❑ *02*
Training video, tape or CD ROM ❑ *03*

Training leaflet/Newsletter ❏ *04*
The Web/Internet ❏ *05*
Training course ❏ *06*
A verbal instruction ❏ *07*
A workmate ❏ *08*
Poster ❏ *09*
Written instruction eg, letter or internal memo ❏ *10*
Other *(please specify)* ❏ *11*

Section 4 – Management

19 What single aspect of your company's food safety and food hygiene management are you most **pleased** with?

20 What single aspect of your company's food safety and food hygiene management causes you most **concern**?

21 Does your business employ any of the following specialist staff?
Tick one box only on each line
Yes No Don't know
a Food Safety and Food Hygiene Officer ❏ *01* ❏ *02* ❏ *03*
b Risk Officer or Risk Manager ❏ *01* ❏ *02* ❏ *03*
c External Food Safety and Food Hygiene ❏ *01* ❏ *02* ❏ *03*
Consultants or Advisors
d Other (please specify) ❏ *01*

22 Does your business use any of the following methods to manage food safety and food hygiene standards?
Tick one box only on each line
Yes No Don't know
a Certification Scheme ❏ *01* ❏ *02* ❏ *03*
b Audit ❏ *01* ❏ *02* ❏ *03*
c HACCP/ HACCP-style food safety ❏ *01* ❏ *02* ❏ *03*
management systems
d Inspection ❏ *01* ❏ *02* ❏ *03*
e Sampling ❏ *01* ❏ *02* ❏ *03*
f Traceability ❏ *01* ❏ *02* ❏ *03*
g Other *(please specify)* ❏ *01*

Section 5 – Environmental Health Officers

23 Do you know of any contact between your company and any Council **Environmental Health** Officers?

Tick one box only
Yes ❏ *01*
No ❏ *02*
(If **'no'** go to question **29**.)

24 Do you personally have any contact with your local Council **Environmental Health** Officers?
Tick one box only
Yes ❏ *01*
No ❏ *02*
Don't know ❏ *03*

25 If yes, roughly how frequently are **you** in contact with them?
Please tick any boxes that apply
Daily ❏ *01*
Weekly ❏ *02*
Monthly ❏ *03*
Yearly ❏ *04*
Every few years ❏ *05*
After a food safety and food hygiene incident on the premises ❏ *06*
After a previous failed inspection ❏ *07*
Don't know ❏ *08*

26 Do you remember the last visit or inspection by a local Council **Environmental Health** Officer that you or your site experienced?
Tick one box only
Yes ❏ *01*
No ❏ *02*
Don't know ❏ *03*

27 If yes, roughly how long ago was this visit?
Weeks Months Years

28 If you are in contact with the **Environmental Health** Officer how would you describe
this relationship?
Tick one box only
Very Good ❏ *01*
Good ❏ *02*
Neutral ❏ *03*
Bad ❏ *04*

Very Bad ❑ *05*
Don't know ❑ *06*

Section 6 – Other Checks

29 Are you aware of any checks regarding food safety and food hygiene made by your company?
Tick one box only
Yes ❑ *01*
No ❑ *02*
(If **'no'** go to question **32**.)

30 Who undertakes these checks?
Please tick any boxes that apply
A specialist manager sent by head office ❑ *01*
Your line manager ❑ *02*
An external advisor, consultant or auditor ❑ *03*
A 'mystery shopper' ❑ *04*
An inspector from a Trade Association ❑ *05*
Don't know ❑ *06*
Other *(please specify)* ❑ *07*

31 How frequently are these checks made?
Please tick any boxes that apply
Daily ❑ *01*
Weekly ❑ *02*
Monthly ❑ *03*
Every few years ❑ *04*
After a food safety and food hygiene incident on the premises ❑ *05*
After a previous failed inspection ❑ *06*
Don't know ❑ *07*
Other *(please specify)* ❑ *08*

Section 7 – Consultancy Firms

32 Does your company engage any **consultancy firms** to help with your management of food safety and food hygiene?
Tick one box only
Yes ❑ *01*
No ❑ *02*
(If **'no'** or **'don't know'** go to question **35**.)
Don't know ❑ *03*

33 Do they undertake food safety and food hygiene checks on your business?
Tick one box only
Yes ❑ *01*
No ❑ *02*
Don't know ❑ *03*

34 How much contact do you have with them over food safety and food hygiene issues?
Please tick any boxes that apply
Daily ❑ *01*
Weekly ❑ *02*
Monthly ❑ *03*
Yearly ❑ *04*
Every few years ❑ *05*
After a food safety and food hygiene incident on the premises ❑ *06*
After a previous failed inspection ❑ *07*
Don't know ❑ *08*

Section 8 – Consumers

35 How important do you think food safety and food hygiene issues are to your consumers?
Tick one box only
Very important ❑ *01*
Important ❑ *02*
Of little importance ❑ *03*
Of no importance ❑ *04*
Don't know/No opinion one way or the other ❑ *05*

36 How concerned do you think your consumers are about the following?
Tick one box only on each line
Very important / Of little importance / Of no importance Don't know / No opinion one way or the other
Issue
a Price (value for money) ❑ *01* ❑ *02* ❑ *03* ❑ *04* ❑ *05*
b GM (Genetic ❑ *01* ❑ *02* ❑ *03* ❑ *04* ❑ *05*
Modification)
c Food additives ❑ *01* ❑ *02* ❑ *03* ❑ *04* ❑ *05*
d Organic ❑ *01* ❑ *02* ❑ *03* ❑ *04* ❑ *05*
e Labelling and ❑ *01* ❑ *02* ❑ *03* ❑ *04* ❑ *05*
product description
f BSE ❑ *01* ❑ *02* ❑ *03* ❑ *04* ❑ *05*

g The use of pesticides ❑ *01* ❑ *02* ❑ *03* ❑ *04* ❑ *05*
to grow food
h Other *(please specify)*
I ❑ *01* ❑ *02* ❑ *03* ❑ *04* ❑ *05*
II ❑ *01* ❑ *02* ❑ *03* ❑ *04* ❑ *05*

Section 9 – The Food Industry

37 When you are considering food safety and food hygiene risks what is the influence of the following on you?
Tick one box only on each line
Strong influence / Some influence / Slight influence / No influence / Don't know / Not applicable
a Senior management ❑ *01* ❑ *02* ❑ *03* ❑ *04* ❑ *05* ❑ *06*
b Colleagues ❑ *01* ❑ *02* ❑ *03* ❑ *04* ❑ *05* ❑ *06*
c Company reward, ❑ *01* ❑ *02* ❑ *03* ❑ *04* ❑ *05* ❑ *06*
recognition or incentive schemes
d Company disciplinary ❑ *01* ❑ *02* ❑ *03* ❑ *04* ❑ *05* ❑ *06*
procedures or penalties
e Company policy ❑ *01* ❑ *02* ❑ *03* ❑ *04* ❑ *05* ❑ *06*
f Training ❑ *01* ❑ *02* ❑ *03* ❑ *04* ❑ *05* ❑ *06*
g Insurance company ❑ *01* ❑ *02* ❑ *03* ❑ *04* ❑ *05* ❑ *06*
h Lawyers ❑ *01* ❑ *02* ❑ *03* ❑ *04* ❑ *05* ❑ *06*
i Environmental ❑ *01* ❑ *02* ❑ *03* ❑ *04* ❑ *05* ❑ *06*
Health Officers
j Trading Standards Officers ❑ *01* ❑ *02* ❑ *03* ❑ *04* ❑ *05* ❑ *06*
k Food Standards Agency ❑ *01* ❑ *02* ❑ *03* ❑ *04* ❑ *05* ❑ *06*
l Pressure Group/NGO* ❑ *01* ❑ *02* ❑ *03* ❑ *04* ❑ *05* ❑ *06*
m Consumers ❑ *01* ❑ *02* ❑ *03* ❑ *04* ❑ *05* ❑ *06*
n Media (TV news etc) ❑ *01* ❑ *02* ❑ *03* ❑ *04* ❑ *05* ❑ *06*
o Other *(please specify)*
I ❑ *01* ❑ *02* ❑ *03* ❑ *04* ❑ *05* ❑ *06*
II ❑ *01* ❑ *02* ❑ *03* ❑ *04* ❑ *05* ❑ *06*
* NGO is a Non-Governmental Organisation

38 Do you feel that more could be done to improve food safety and food hygiene in your industry?
Tick one box only
Yes ❑ *01*
No ❑ *02*
Don't know ❑ *03*
39 If **'yes'** what would you suggest?

40 What do you think will be the greatest food safety and food hygiene problems facing your industry in the next decade?

END OF QUESTIONNAIRE

Thank you for taking the time to complete this questionnaire.

We may wish to follow up a cross-section of replies. If you are willing to be contacted again then please let us know your personal details below.

Please note that providing this information and agreeing to contact is entirely **voluntary** and any information will be treated as **confidential**.

Title: Ms ❑ Mrs ❑ Mr ❑ Other ❑

Your full name:

Position:

Name of Business:

Business Address:

Contact telephone number or email address:

Date:

Signature:

If you have any questions regarding this questionnaire please contact either:

Bridget M Hutter

Clive Jones

Centre for Analysis of Risk and Regulation (CARR)

The London School of Economics and Political Science

Tel: xxxxxx

email: **xxxxxxxx**

www.lse.ac.uk/collections/carr/

WHITE Questionnaire for Research into Risk Management Practices of UK Business in 2004 for Directors, Owners, Senior Managers

Who are we?

We are academic researchers which means that we have to be unbiased, independent and not represent any commercial interests. We work for CARR (Centre for Analysis of Risk and Regulation) **www.lse.ac.uk/collections/carr/** an academic research centre based at LSE, or to give it its full name, London School of Economics and Political Science which is part of the University of London. **www.lse.ac.uk**

What is the questionnaire for?

The questionnaire is for an academic research project. The aim is to further our understanding of food safety and food hygiene practices and to help to promote better and more user-friendly ways of managing food safety and food hygiene risks. The results from this research will also allow CARR academics to gain insights into how your business really works. These results will be written up in a series of academic and practitioner publications by Professor Hutter. Copies of these publications will be publicly available and organisations that have taken part in the research will receive a summary of these results.

What do you have to do?

Answer the questions in this questionnaire. To do this you either have to put a tick in the box provided or write a few words on a dotted line. Remember this is not a test and there are no right or wrong answers! We are interested in what you as an individual think. We encourage you to be as honest as you can. On completing the questionnaire put it straight into the pre-paid addressed envelope we've provided and put in the post.

What happens after you return the questionnaire?

We will compare your response to the other responses we get; some responses will be from people very similar to you, some very different. **Confidentiality is assured**. This is the most important thing about the way we work. Without the trust of those who help us, we would not be able to do our job. We assure you that we will not disclose any of your contact details or identifiable responses to anyone.

If you have any questions at all you may contact Clive Jones in confidence. He is a Researcher within CARR at the London School of Economics and Political Science. Tel: xxxxx or email: xxxxxxxxxxx

Please use the freepost envelope provided – no stamp needed – to return completed copies of this questionnaire to CARR by

Introduction to Questionnaire

© Bridget Hutter

Section 1 – Your Business

1 What is your business?
Tick one box only
You own and manage the business yourself ❏ *01*
A family owned business ❏ *02*
A franchise ❏ *03*
Part of a national chain ❏ *04*
Part of an international chain ❏ *05*
Other *(please specify)* ❏ *06*

2 Which sector is your business in?
Tick one box only
Vending kiosk ❏ *01*
Market stall ❏ *02*
Convenience grocery retail ❏ *03*
Specialist grocery retail ❏ *04*
A department store ❏ *05*
Supermarket ❏ *06*
Take away food market stall/kiosk ❏ *07*
Take away food shop ❏ *08*
Contract/In-house caterer ❏ *09*
Conference/Event caterer ❏ *10*
Hotel ❏ *11*
Pub/Bar ❏ *12*
Café/Restaurant ❏ *13*
Both food retail and hospitality ❏ *14*
Other *(please specify)* ❏ *15*

3 How many sites does your business have in the UK?
Tick one box only
100 plus sites ❏ *01*
50 – 99 sites ❏ *02*
10 – 49 sites ❏ *03*
2 – 9 sites ❏ *04*
Just 1 site ❏ *05*

Section 2 – Your role

4 What is your relationship to this business?
Tick one box only
Owner ❏ *01*

Owner and Manager ❏ *02*
Manager ❏ *03*
Franchisee ❏ *04*
Other *(please specify)* ❏ *05*

5 What is your official job title?
Job title:

6 How long have you been in your present job (approximately)?
Days Months Years

7 (If applicable) What did you do before your present job?

8 What are your main responsibilities in your present job?

9 How many staff are you responsible for managing?
people *(approximately)*

10 Approximately what proportion of these staff are casual or contract employees?
Tick one box only
76 – 100% ❏ *01*
51 – 75% ❏ *02*
26 – 50% ❏ *03*
1 – 25% ❏ *04*
None ❏ *05*
Don't know ❏ *06*

Section 3 – Safety and Hygiene

11 What are the main **food safety and food hygiene risks** encountered by your business?

12 Please give an example of a risk you consider to be more serious than **food safety and food hygiene risks**.

13 Please give an example of a risk which you consider to be **less** serious than food safety and food hygiene risks.

Section 4 – Information and Policy

14 What are **your** main sources of information about food safety and food hygiene risks?

Please tick any boxes that apply
Your business head office ❑ *01*
A consultancy ❑ *02*
Trade association ❑ *03*
Your employees ❑ *04*
The Food Standards Agency ❑ *05*
The local council ❑ *06*
Advice from an environmental health officer ❑ *07*
The government ❑ *08*
A trainer or lecturer ❑ *09*
Other *(please specify)* ❑ *10*

15 How is this information communicated?
Please tick any boxes that apply
Verbal instructions ❑ *01*
The Web/Internet ❑ *02*
Magazine ❑ *03*
An operating manual or handbook ❑ *04*
Training video, tape or CD ROM ❑ *05*
Training course ❑ *06*
Training leaflet/Newsletter ❑ *07*
A workmate ❑ *08*
Written instruction eg, letter or internal memo ❑ *09*
Other *(please specify)* ❑ *10*

16 Does your business have rules regarding food safety and food hygiene?
Tick one box only
Yes ❑ *01*
No ❑ *02*
Don't know ❑ *03*

17 If **'yes'** please can you give two examples below:
1
2

18 Do you think that all employees know the food safety and food hygiene rules that relate to their area or responsibilities?
Tick one box only
Yes ❑ *01*
No ❑ *02*
Don't know ❑ *03*

19 Are there checks to ensure that staff follow these rules?
Tick one box only
Yes ❏ *01*
No ❏ *02*

20 If **'yes'** what sort of checks do you have?

21 How do **your employees** learn about food safety and food hygiene?
Please tick any boxes that apply
You or another manager ❏ *01*
Your business head office ❏ *02*
Their line manager ❏ *03*
A trainer or lecturer ❏ *04*
An external advisor, consultant or auditor ❏ *05*
Advice from an environmental health officer ❏ *06*
The local council ❏ *07*
The Food Standards Agency ❏ *08*
The government ❏ *09*
Trade association ❏ *10*
Other *(please specify)* ❏ *11*

22 How is this information communicated?
Please tick any boxes that apply
Business manual or handbook ❏ *01*
Magazine ❏ *02*
Training video, tape or CD ROM ❏ *03*
Training leaflet/Newsletter ❏ *04*
The Web/Internet ❏ *05*
Training course ❏ *06*
A verbal instruction ❏ *07*
A workmate ❏ *08*
Poster ❏ *09*
Written instruction eg, letter or internal memo ❏ *10*
Other *(please specify)* ❏ *11*

Section 5 – Management

23 What single aspect of your company's food safety and food hygiene management are you most **pleased** with?

24 What single aspect of your company's food safety and food hygiene management causes you most **concern**?

25 Does your business employ any of the following specialist **employees**?
Tick one box only on each line
Yes No Don't know
a Food Safety and Food Hygiene Officer ❑ *01* ❑ *02* ❑ *03*
b Risk Officer or Risk Manager ❑ *01* ❑ *02* ❑ *03*
c External Food Safety and Food Hygiene ❑ *01* ❑ *02* ❑ *03*
Consultants or Advisors
d Other (please specify) ❑ *01*

26 Does your business use any of the following methods to manage food safety and food hygiene standards?
Tick one box only on each line
Yes No Don't know
a Certification Scheme ❑ *01* ❑ *02* ❑ *03*
b Audit ❑ *01* ❑ *02* ❑ *03*
c HACCP/ HACCP-style food safety ❑ *01* ❑ *02* ❑ *03*
management systems
d Inspection ❑ *01* ❑ *02* ❑ *03*
e Sampling ❑ *01* ❑ *02* ❑ *03*
f Traceability ❑ *01* ❑ *02* ❑ *03*
g Other *(please specify)* ❑ *01*

Section 6 – Environmental Health and other Council Officers

27 Do you know of any contact between your business and any council environmental health officers?
Tick one box only
Yes ❑ *01*
No ❑ *02*
(If '**no**' go to question 32)

28 Do you personally have any contact with your local council **environmental health** officers?
Tick one box only
Yes ❑ *01*
No ❑ *02*
Don't know ❑ *03*

29 If **yes**, roughly how frequently are **you** in contact with them?
Please tick any boxes that apply
Daily ❑ *01*
Weekly ❑ *02*
Monthly ❑ *03*
Yearly ❑ *04*
Every few years ❑ *05*
After a food safety and food hygiene incident on the premises ❑ *06*
After a previous failed inspection ❑ *07*
Don't know ❑ *08*

30 Do you remember the last visit or inspection by a local Council **Environmental Health** Officer that you or your site experienced?
Tick one box only
Yes ❑ *01*
No ❑ *02*
Don't know ❑ *03*

31 If **yes**, roughly how long ago was this visit?
Weeks Months Years

32 If you are in contact with the Environmental Health Officer how would you describe this relationship?
Tick one box only
Very Good ❑ *01*
Good ❑ *02*
Neutral ❑ *03*
Bad ❑ *04*
Very Bad ❑ *05*
Don't know ❑ *06*

33 Does your business have any contact with your local Council **Trading Standards** Officers?
Tick one box only
Yes ❑ *01*
No ❑ *02*
Don't know ❑ *03*
34 If **yes**, how frequently are you in contact with them?
Tick one box only
Daily ❑ *01*

Weekly ❏ *02*
Monthly ❏ *03*
Yearly ❏ *04*
Every few years ❏ *05*
Never ❏ *06*

35 If you are in contact with them then how would you describe the relationship of your business with them?
Tick one box only
Very Good ❏ *01*
Good ❏ *02*
Neutral ❏ *03*
Bad ❏ *04*
Very Bad ❏ *05*
Don't know ❏ *06*

36 Are you in contact with any other government or local council officials?
Tick one box only
Yes ❏ *01*
No ❏ *02*
Don't know ❏ *03*

37 If **yes**, please could you name the organisation that the officials represent?

Section 7 – Other Checks

38 Are there any other checks regarding food safety and food hygiene made by your business?
Tick one box only
Yes ❏ *01*
No ❏ *02*
(If **'no'** go to question 41)

39 Who undertakes these checks?
Please tick any boxes that apply
A specialist manager sent by head office ❏ *01*
Your line manager ❏ *02*
An external advisor, consultant or auditor ❏ *03*
A 'mystery shopper' ❏ *04*
An inspector from a Trade Association ❏ *05*

Don't know ❑ *06*
Other *(please specify)* ❑ *07*

40 How frequently are these checks made?
Please tick any boxes that apply
Daily ❑ *01*
Weekly ❑ *02*
Monthly ❑ *03*
Yearly ❑ *04*
Every few years ❑ *05*
After a food safety and food hygiene incident on the premises ❑ *06*
After a previous failed inspection ❑ *07*
Don't know ❑ *08*

41 Does your business belong to any **trade or industry associations**?
Tick one box only
Yes ❑ *01*
No ❑ *02*
Don't know ❑ *03*

42 If **'yes'** which are these?

43 Do these trade or industry associations provide information about food hygiene and food safety?
Tick one box only
Yes ❑ *01*
No ❑ *02*
Don't know ❑ *03*

44 Do they undertake food hygiene and safety checks on your business?
Tick one box only
Yes ❑ *01*
No ❑ *02*
Don't know ❑ *03*

45 How frequently are these checks made?
Please tick any boxes that apply
Daily ❑ *01*
Weekly ❑ *02*
Monthly ❑ *03*

Yearly ❏ *04*
Every few years ❏ *05*
Never ❏ *06*
When we request a visit ❏ *07*

Section 8 – Consultancy and Insurance Checks

46 Does your business engage any **consultancy firms** to help with your management of food safety and food hygiene?
Tick one box only
Yes ❏ *01*
No ❏ *02*
Don't know ❏ *03*
(If **'no'** or **'don't know'** go to question 49)

47 Do they undertake food safety and food hygiene checks on your business?
Tick one box only
Yes ❏ *01*
No ❏ *02*
Don't know ❏ *03*

48 How much contact do you have with them over food safety and food hygiene issues?
Please tick any boxes that apply
Daily ❏ *01*
Weekly ❏ *02*
Monthly ❏ *03*
Yearly ❏ *04*
Every few years ❏ *05*
After a food safety and food hygiene incident on the premises ❏ *06*
After a previous failed inspection ❏ *07*
Don't know ❏ *08*

49 Do you have **insurance** covering food hygiene and food safety risks?
Tick one box only
Yes ❏ *01*
No ❏ *02*
Don't know ❏ *03*

50 If **yes** does your insurance business provide you with information about food hygiene and food safety?
Tick one box only
Yes ❑ *01*
No ❑ *02*
Don't know ❑ *03*

51 Do they undertake food hygiene and safety checks on your business?
Tick one box only
Yes ❑ *01*
No ❑ *02*
Don't know ❑ *03*
52 How much contact do you have with them over food safety and food hygiene issues?
Please tick any boxes that apply
Daily ❑ *01*
Weekly ❑ *02*
Monthly ❑ *03*
Yearly ❑ *04*
Every few years ❑ *05*
Never ❑ *06*

Section 9 – Consumers

53 How important do you think food safety and food hygiene issues are to your consumers?
Tick one box only
Very important ❑ *01*
Important ❑ *02*
Of little importance ❑ *03*
Of no importance ❑ *04*
Don't know/No opinion one way or the other ❑ *05*

54 How concerned do you think your consumers are about the following?
Tick one box only on each line
Very important / Of little importance / Of no importance / Don't know / No opinion one way or the other
Issue

a Price (value for money) ❑ *01* ❑ *02* ❑ *03* ❑ *04* ❑ *05*
b GM (Genetic ❑ *01* ❑ *02* ❑ *03* ❑ *04* ❑ *05*
Modification)
c Food additives ❑ *01* ❑ *02* ❑ *03* ❑ *04* ❑ *05*
d Organic ❑ *01* ❑ *02* ❑ *03* ❑ *04* ❑ *05*
e Labelling and ❑ *01* ❑ *02* ❑ *03* ❑ *04* ❑ *05*
product description
f BSE ❑ *01* ❑ *02* ❑ *03* ❑ *04* ❑ *05*
g The use of pesticides ❑ *01* ❑ *02* ❑ *03* ❑ *04* ❑ *05*
to grow food
h Other *(please specify)*
I ❑ *01* ❑ *02* ❑ *03* ❑ *04* ❑ *05*
II ❑ *01* ❑ *02* ❑ *03* ❑ *04* ❑ *05*

Section 10 – The Food Industry

55 When you are considering food safety and food hygiene risks what is the influence of the following on you?
Tick one box only on each line
Strong influence / Some influence / Slight influence / No influence / Don't know / Not applicable
a Senior management ❑ *01* ❑ *02* ❑ *03* ❑ *04* ❑ *05* ❑ *06*
b Employees ❑ *01* ❑ *02* ❑ *03* ❑ *04* ❑ *05* ❑ *06*
c Shareholders or investors ❑ *01* ❑ *02* ❑ *03* ❑ *04* ❑ *05* ❑ *06*
d Industry association ❑ *01* ❑ *02* ❑ *03* ❑ *04* ❑ *05* ❑ *06*
e Certification scheme ❑ *01* ❑ *02* ❑ *03* ❑ *04* ❑ *05* ❑ *06*
f Insurance company ❑ *01* ❑ *02* ❑ *03* ❑ *04* ❑ *05* ❑ *06*
g Lawyers ❑ *01* ❑ *02* ❑ *03* ❑ *04* ❑ *05* ❑ *06*
h Food Standards Agency ❑ *01* ❑ *02* ❑ *03* ❑ *04* ❑ *05* ❑ *06*
i Environmental ❑ *01* ❑ *02* ❑ *03* ❑ *04* ❑ *05* ❑ *06*
Health Officers
j Trading Standards Officers ❑ *01* ❑ *02* ❑ *03* ❑ *04* ❑ *05* ❑ *06*
k Consumers (ie an ❑ *01* ❑ *02* ❑ *03* ❑ *04* ❑ *05* ❑ *06*
individual that buys
from you)
l Consumers (ie a business ❑ *01* ❑ *02* ❑ *03* ❑ *04* ❑ *05* ❑ *06*
that buys from you)
m Pressure Group/NGO* ❑ *01* ❑ *02* ❑ *03* ❑ *04* ❑ *05* ❑ *06*

n Media ❑ *01* ❑ *02* ❑ *03* ❑ *04* ❑ *05* ❑ *06*
Other *(please specify)*
I ❑ *01* ❑ *02* ❑ *03* ❑ *04* ❑ *05* ❑ *06*
II ❑ *01* ❑ *02* ❑ *03* ❑ *04* ❑ *05* ❑ *06*
* NGO is a Non-Governmental Organisation

56 Do you feel that more could be done to improve food safety and food hygiene in your industry?
Tick one box only
Yes ❑ *01*
No ❑ *02*
Don't know ❑ *03*

57 If **'yes'** what would you suggest?

58 Do you believe it is possible for a food safety and food hygiene risk management strategy to be a tool for creating sustainable competitive advantage over competitors in your industry?
Tick one box only
Yes ❑ *01*
No ❑ *02*
Don't know ❑ *03*

59 What do you think will be the greatest food safety and food hygiene problems facing your industry in the next decade?

END OF QUESTIONNAIRE

Thank you for taking the time to complete this questionnaire.
We may wish to follow up a cross-section of replies. If you are willing to be contacted again then please let us know your personal details below.
Please note that providing this information and agreeing to contact is entirely **voluntary** and any information will be treated as **confidential**.
Title: Ms ❑ Mrs ❑ Mr ❑ Other ❑
Your full name:
Position:
Name of Business:
Business Address:
Contact telephone number or email address:
Date:
Signature:

If you have any questions regarding this questionnaire please contact either:
Bridget M Hutter
Clive Jones
Centre for Analysis of Risk and Regulation (CARR)
The London School of Economics and Political Science
www.lse.ac.uk/collections/carr/

Appendix 3:   Phase 3 interview schedule

Basic facts
1. What is the official title of your job?
2. What does your job involve?
3. How long have you been in your present job?
4. (If applicable) What did you do before?
5. How many people/sites are your responsible for?
6. Are there any food safety/hygiene risks associated with the activities of this workforce?
7. What are the most dangerous food safety/hygiene activities you oversee?

Business's policies for food safety/hygiene
8. Does your business have official policies regarding the food safety/hygiene of staff? [probe: What are they? Where would you find them written down?]
    8.1. Do you know what they are?
9. Are there checks to ensure that you follow this policy [probe: What are they?]
    9.1. If yes – What do you think about these policies?
10. Does anyone in the company have special responsibility for food safety/hygiene?
11. If so, who are they?

Training
12. Have you every received any food safety/hygiene risk management training for your job?
    12.1. IF NO, would you have found it useful if you had?
    12.2. IF YES, when?
13. Who from?
14. Was it helpful when you first started work?
15. Has this training proved to be adequate?
16. If you were worried about any aspect of food safety/hygiene in your workplace who would you talk to?
17. If so, who are they?
18. What do you expect they would do?

Food sector and risk
19. Is the food sector a risky industry to work in?
    19.1. If yes then probe:
20. Is it possible for you to compare it with other industries, to say it is more dangerous than one business sector, or less dangerous than another?
21. Are there many problems with food safety/hygiene in your sector?
22. Are there many food safety/hygiene incidents?
23. Do you know how many food safety/hygiene major/minor incidents there were on this site last year?
    23.1. If yes – What sort of incidents were these? [probe]
24. How do they happen?
25. Whose fault are they usually?
26. Are they often incidents that should not have happened, or are they accidents that could not be prevented?
27. If yes – How could they be prevented?

The Law and Regulations
28. What food safety/hygiene laws do you have to observe?
    28.1. [IF DON'T KNOW, probe: have you heard of the Food Safety Act 1990 or The Food Safety Regulations 1995] IF YES, what do these laws and regulations require you to do?
    28.2. What duties does the law put upon your employers regarding food safety/hygiene? What duties do you have?
    28.3. What do you think about these rules and regulations?
IF NO, continue from here.
29. What are your sources of information re food safety/hygiene risk? [probe]
30. Do you get to hear of changes in the laws or new regulations?
31. Is this information usually written down or does someone tell you?
32. [If written down] How much do you manage to read?

FSA
33. You have told me about the company's checks upon food safety/hygiene, is there anyone else responsible for checking food safety/hygiene?
    33.1. If **YES** What do you know about them?
    33.2. Which organisation are they from?
    33.3. Have you had any direct contact with them?
    33.4. What is your opinion of them?

EHO
34. IF **NO**, have you heard of the FSA?
35. Have you heard of any local council/local authority checks on food safety/hygiene?

35.1. If NO prompt with EHO
35.2. If YES then continue:
36. Do you know the name of your local EHO?
37. Do you know what s/he looks like?
38. Where are the local offices of the EHOs?
39. Would you approach these EHOs for advice on food safety/hygiene matters?
    39.1. IF NO, why not?
    39.2. IF YES, what sort of matters?

EHO Visit

40. Can you recall the last visit of an EHO?
41. Who did s/he speak to during his visit?
42. How long did the EHO stay?
43. What did s/he do during the visit?
44. Do you see the same EHO each time?
45. How long did the EHO stay?
46. What did s/he do during the visit?
47. Do you see the same EHO each time?
48. How frequently do you think businesses should be inspected by an EHO?
    48.1. Should all businesses be subject to the equal levels of inspection?
    48.2. If no - how would you decide on the different levels?
49. How useful do you find EHOs' visits? [Probe: in what sort of ways?]
50. Do you take a lot of notice of EHOs' comments? Which? Always? Why?
51. What sort of things would you ignore if any?
52. Are you asked to do anything which you find irritating or unnecessary?
53. How important do you think EHOs are in bringing about higher standards of food safety/hygiene (a) on your site, (b) generally in your industry?

Enforcement

54. What legal action can EHOs take?
55. Has your firm been
    55.1. served with a notice?
    55.2. prosecuted?
56. Do you know what sort of penalties can be imposed by the courts if someone is taken to court and found guilty?
57. Is legal action something that worries you when an EHO visits?

Personal compliance

I now want to ask you some questions about how food safety/hygiene matters affect you personally.

58. Are you provided with any special food safety/hygiene equipment? [probe]
    58.1. If yes - How often do you use it?
59. Have you ever ignored a food safety/hygiene regulation or company rules?
    59.1. IF NO, can you think of any circumstance when you might ignore a food safety/hygiene rule?
    59.2. IF YES, can you give me an example?
60. How much concern is there amongst your managers about food safety/hygiene risk?
61. What do you think about the company's attitude to food safety/hygiene risk?
62. Do you yourself comply with food safety/hygiene demands, if so why [not]?
63. Do you always comply completely? Why bother?
64. If your managers ignore non-compliance of their staff what do you think would happen eventually?
65. Do you think that people in the industry appreciate the consequences of non compliance with food safety/hygiene rules and regulations?
    65.1. Probe 1: For example, do they understand that not washing their hands before handling food could lead to a customer becoming ill with food poisoning?
    65.2. Probe 2: would they understand the possible consequences of causing food poisoning to a customer on the business?
66. What priority do you give to food safety/hygiene compared to other risks in your business?
67. How important is food safety/hygiene in relation to your other responsibilities?
68. Which aspects of your job take priority over food safety/hygiene matters?
    68.1. And, which take less priority?
69. Do you think that complying with food safety/hygiene demands is costly?
    69.1. IF YES probe: how costly?
    69.2. Do you think that not complying with food safety demands is costly?
    69.3. If yes How?

Customers
70. Do you think your customers appreciate food safety/hygiene issues?
71. Do you think standards of food safety/hygiene influence customer decisions about where to shop/eat?
72. How important do you think food safety/hygiene issues are relative to other customer concerns?

73. How damaging do you think an adverse food hygiene/safety incident would be to your business?
74. Has your store ever been affected by a food recall from a supplier?
    74.1. If yes what effect does that have on you?
    74.2. Is it something customers ever ask about?
75. Do you think customers remember food recalls?

Non-state actors

We've discussed the food safety/hygiene checks carried out by the business and also by Environmental Health Officers.

76. Do any other groups influence the decisions you make regarding how you manage food safety/hygiene risks? Probe.
    Visual prompt with the following list:
    76.1.   Insurance company
    76.2.   Lawyers
    76.3.   Consultancy
    76.4.   Environmental Health Officers
    76.5.   Trading Standards Officers
    76.6.   Food Standards Agency
    76.7.   Pressure Group/NGO
    76.8.   Consumers
    76.9.   Media
    76.10. Other?

Reputation

77. Are you ever concerned about food safety related risks to the reputation of your
    77.1. industry?
    77.2. business?
    77.3. branch?
    77.4. self?
78. If yes probe
79. Have you ever experienced adverse publicity in a branch/outlet?
    79.1. If Yes (a) what was it about?
          What did you do about it?
80. Do you know of anything you or your manager does to specifically manage reputation risks?
    80.1. If yes: What?
81. If no: Why are these risks not managed?
82. Do you agree with displaying inspection scores of an EHO in the window of your outlet?

Thank you very much.

Visual prompt with the following list:

- Insurance company
- Lawyers
- Environmental Health Officers
- Trading Standards Officers
- Food Standards Agency
- Pressure Group/NGO
- Consumers
- Media
- Other?

Bibliography

Adak, G.K. and S.M. Long (2002) 'Trends in indigenous foodborne disease and deaths, England and Wales: 1992 to 2000', *Gut*, **51**, 832–41.

Aldadeff, G. (2003) 'International regulation of NGOs', in European Policy Forum (ed.), *NGOs, Democratisation and the Regulatory State*. London: European Policy Forum, pp. 101–3.

Altman, B. and D. Vidaver-Cohen (2000) 'A framework for understanding corporate citizenship', *Business and Society Review*, **105**(1), 1–7.

Amodu, T. (2008) *The Determinants of Compliance with Laws and Regulations with Special Reference to Health and Safety*. London: HSE Books.

Ayres, I. and J. Braithwaite (1992) *Responsive Regulation*. Oxford: Oxford University Press.

Bailey, C.W. and D. Peterson (1989) 'Using perception surveys to assess safety system effectiveness', *Professional Safety*, February, 22–6.

Bailey, I. and S. Rupp (2004) 'The evolving role of business associations in negotiated environmental agreements: the case of United Kingdom climate change agreements', Climate Policy Research Occasional Paper. Department of Geography, University of Plymouth.

Baldwin R., C. Hood and C. Scott (1998) *Socio-Legal Reader on Regulation*. Oxford: Oxford University Press.

Bardach, E. and R. Kagan (1982) *Going by the Book: The Problem of Regulatory Unreasonableness*. Philadelphia, PA: Temple University Press.

Baron, D.P. (2005) 'Competing for the public through the news media', *Journal of Economics & Management Strategy*, **14**(2), 339–76.

Barton, L. (1993) 'A case study in crisis management: the Perrier recall', *Industrial Management & Data Systems*, **91**(7), 6–8.

Beck, U. (1992) *Risk Society: Towards a New Modernity*. London: Sage Publications.

Beck, U. (2006) 'Living in the world risk society', *Economy and Society*, **35**(3), 329–45.

Better Regulation Executive and National Audit Office (2008) *Effective Inspection and Enforcement: Implementing the Hampton Vision in the Food Standards Agency*, http://www.nao.org.uk/publications/Food SA_ Hampton_report.pdf (accessed 1 September 2010).

Better Regulation Task Force (BRTF) (1999) *Regulation and Small Firms: A Progress Report*. London: Cabinet Office Publications.

Better Regulation Task Force (BRTF) (2004a) *Avoiding Regulatory Creep*. London: Cabinet Office Publications.

Better Regulation Task Force (BRTF) (2004b) *Better Routes to Redress*. London: Cabinet Office Publications.

Black, D. (1976) *The Behavior of Law*. New York: Academic Press.

Black, J. (2002) 'Critical reflections on regulation', CARR Discussion Paper 4, London School of Economics.

Black, J. (2005) 'The emergence of risk based regulation and the new public management in the UK', *Public Law* (Autumn), 512–49.

Blockley, D.I. (1996) 'Hazard engineering', in C. Hood and D.K.C. Jones (eds), *Accident and Design*. London: UCL Press, pp. 31–9.

Booth, S.A. (2000) 'How can organisations prepare for reputational crises?', *Journal of Contingencies and Crisis Management*, **8**(4), 197–207.

Braithwaite, J. (1982) 'Enforced self-regulation: a new strategy for corporate crime control', *Michigan Law Review*, **80**, 1466–507.

Braithwaite, J. (1989) *Crime, Shame and Reintegration*. New York: Cambridge University Press.

Braithwaite, J. (2000) 'The new regulatory state and the transformation of criminology', *British Journal of Criminology*, **40**(2), 222–38.

Braithwaite, J. (2008) *Regulatory Capitalism: How it Works, Ideas for Making it Work Better*. Cheltenham, UK and Northampton, MA, USA: Edward Elgar Publishing.

Braithwaite, J. and P. Drahos (2000) *Global Business Regulation*. Cambridge University Press.

Braithwaite, J. and T. Makkai (1994) 'Trust and compliance', *Policing and Society*, **4**, 1–12.

Brammer, S.J. and S. Pavelin (2006) 'Voluntary environmental disclosures by large UK companies', *Journal of Business Finance and Accounting*, **33**(7–8), 1168–88.

Brunsson, N. and B. Jacobsson (eds) (2000) *A World of Standards*. Oxford: Oxford University Press.

Bruyn, S.T.H. (1999) 'The moral economy', *Review of Social Economy*, **LVII**(1), 25–46.

Buzby, J.C. and P.D. Frenzen (1999) 'Food safety and product liability', *Food Policy*, **24**(6), 637–51.

Cadbury Report (Committee on the Financial Aspects of Corporate Governance) (1992) Report of the Committee on Financial Aspects of Corporate Governance. London: Gee.

Cane, P. and H. Kritzer (eds) (2010) *The Oxford Handbook of Empirical Legal Research*. Oxford: Oxford University Press.

Carroll, C. (2009) 'Defying a reputational crisis – Cadbury's salmonella scare:

why are customers willing to forgive and forget?', *Corporate Reputation Review*, **12**, 64–82.

Cashore B., D. Auld and G. Newsom (2004) *Governing Through Markets: Forest Certification and the Emergence of Non-state Authority*. New Haven, CT: Yale University Press.

Chalmers, D. (2003) 'Food for thought: reconciling European risks and traditional ways of life', *Modern Law Review*, **66**, 532–62.

Charnovitz, S. (1997) 'Two centuries of participation: NGOs and international governance', *Michigan Journal of International Law*, **18**(2), 183–286.

Chartered Institute of Environmental Health (CIEH) (2007) *Food Safety and Standards*. London: CIEH.

Clarke, L.B. (1999) *Mission Improbable: Using Fantasy Documents to Tame Disaster*. Chicago, IL: University of Chicago Press.

Clay, T.R. (1984) *Combating Cancer in the Workplace: Implementation of the California Occupational Carcinogens Control Act*. Irvine, CA: University of California Press.

Clayton, D.A., C.J. Griffith, A.C. Peters and P. Price (2002) 'Food handlers' beliefs and self-reported practices', *International Journal of Environmental Health Research*, **12**(1), 25–39.

Coglianese C. and J. Nash (eds) (2001) *Regulating from the Inside: Can Environmental Management Systems Achieve Policy Goals?* Washington, DC: Resources for the Future.

Coglianese, C. and J. Nash (eds) (2006) *Leveraging the Private Sector: Management-based Strategies for Improving Environmental Performance*. Washington, DC: Resources for the Future.

Cohen, S. (1985) *Visions of Social Control: Crime, Punishment and Classification*. Cambridge: Polity Press.

Coleman, P. and A. Roberts (2005) 'Food hygiene training in the UK: a time for change', *Food Service Technology*, **5**(1), 17–22.

Coleman, P., C. Griffith and D. Botterill (2000) 'Welsh caterers: an exploratory study of attitudes towards safe food handling in the hospitality industry', *Hospitality Management*, **19**, 145–57.

Corneliussen, F. (2004) 'The impact of regulations on firms. A study of the biotech industry', CARR Discussion Paper 19, London School of Economics.

Dawson, S., P. Willman, M. Bamford and A. Clinton (1988) *Safety at Work: The Limits of Self-regulation*. Cambridge: Cambridge University Press.

Dean, B. (2005) *Review of the Food Standards Agency*, http://www.food. gov. uk/aboutus/how_we_work/historyfsa/deanreview (accessed 1 September 2010).

Demortain, D. (2007) 'Standardising through concepts: scientific experts and the international development of the HACCP food safety standard', CARR Discussion Paper 45, London School of Economics.

Department for Environment, Food and Rural Affairs (DEFRA) (2001) *Zoonoses Report 2000*. London: DEFRA.

Department for Environment, Food and Rural Affairs (DEFRA) (2006) *Agriculture in the United Kingdom 2005*. London: HMSO.

Department of Trade and Industry (2006) *Small Business Service*. London: DTI.

Di Mento, J.F. (1986) *Environmental Law and American Business: Dilemmas of Compliance*. New York: Plenum Press.

Doig, A. (1989) 'The resignation of Edwina Currie: a word too far', *Parliamentary Affairs*, **42**, 317–29.

Doner, R.F. and B. Schneider (2000) 'The new institutional economics, business associations and development', International Institute for Labour Studies Discussion Paper 110, International Labour Organization.

Douglas, M. and A. Wildavsky (1982) *Risk and Culture*. Berkeley, CA: University of California Press.

Draper, A. and J. Green (2002) 'Food safety and consumers: constructions of choice and risk', *Journal of Social Policy and Administration*, **36**(6), 610–25.

Dryzek, J.S. (1990) *Discursive Democracy: Politics, Policy, and Science*. Cambridge: Cambridge University Press.

Dunkerly, D. and S. Fudge (2004) 'The role of civil society in European integration', *European Societies*, **6**(2), 237–54.

Ehiri, J., G. Morris and J. McEwen (1995) 'Implementation of HACCP in food businesses: the way ahead', *Food Control*, **6**, 341–5.

Eisner, M.A. (2004) 'Corporate environmentalism, regulatory reform, and industry self-regulation: toward genuine regulatory reinvention in the United States', *Governance*, **17**(2), 145–67.

Elson R., F. Burgess, C.L. Little and R.T. Mitchell (2004) 'Microbiological examination of ready-to-eat cold sliced meats and pate; from catering and retail premises in the UK', *Journal of Applied Microbiology*, **96**(3), 499–509.

Enderle, G. and G. Peters (1998) *A Strange Affair? The Emerging Relationship Between NGOs and Transnational Companies*. Notre Dame, IN: University of Notre Dame.

Ericson R.V., A. Doyle and D. Barry (2003) *Insurance as Governance*. Toronto: University of Toronto Press.

Etienne, J. (2010) 'The impact of regulatory policy on individual behaviour: a goal framing theory approach', CARR Discussion Paper 59, London School of Economics.

Eurobarometer (2006) *Risk Issues*. Brussels: European Commission, http://ec.europa.eu/public_opinion/archives/ebs/ebs_238_en.pdf (accessed 25 August 2010).

European Commission (1996) 'Commission recommendation of 3 April 1996 concerning the definition of small and medium-sized enterprises (96/280/EC)', *Official Journal*, L 107, European Commission, Brussels.

European Union Risk Analysis Information Network (2003) *Catering Food Safety – A Responsibility Ignored?* Budapest: European Union Risk Analysis Information Network.

Fairman, R. and C. Yapp (2004) 'Compliance with food safety legislation in small and micro-businesses: enforcement as a external motivator', *Journal of Environmental Health Research*, **3**(2), 44–8.

Fairman, R. and C. Yapp (2005) 'Enforced self-regulation, prescription, and conceptions of compliance within small businesses: the impact of enforcement', *Law & Policy*, **27**(4), 491–519.

Fearne, A. and D. Hughes (1999) 'Success factors in the fresh produce supply chain: insights from the UK', *Supply Chain Management*, **4**(3), 120–28.

Fennell, D. (1988) *Investigation into the King's Cross Underground Fire*. London: HMSO.

Fielding, L.M., L. Ellis, C. Beveridge and A.C. Peters (2005) 'An evaluation of HACCP implementation status in UK SME's in food manufacturing', *International Journal of Environmental Health Research*, **15**(2), 117–26.

Fisse, B. and J. Braithwaite (1983) *The Impact of Publicity on Corporate Offenders*. Albany, NY: State University of New York Press.

Fisse, B. and J. Braithwaite (1993) *Corporations, Crime and Accountability*. Cambridge: Cambridge University Press.

Fleming, M., R. Flin, K. Mearns and R. Gordon (1998) 'Risk perceptions of offshore workers on UK oil and gas platforms', *Risk Analysis*, **18**(1), 103–10.

Flynn, A., T. Marsden and E. Smith (2003) 'Food regulation and retailing in a new institutional context', *Political Quarterly*, **74**(1), 38–46.

Fombrun, C.J. (1996) *Reputation: Realizing Value from the Corporate Image*. Boston, MA: Harvard Business School Publishing.

Fombrun, C. (2007) 'List of lists: a compilation of international corporate reputation ratings', *Corporate Reputation Review*, **10**(2), 144–53.

Fombrun, C. and V. Rindova (2000) 'The road to transparency: reputation management at Royal Dutch/Shell', in M. Schultz and M.J. Hatch (eds), *The Expressive Organization: Linking Identity, Reputation and the Corporate Brand*. New York: Oxford University Press, pp. 77–96.

Fombrun C.J., N.A. Gardberg and M.L. Barnett (2000) 'Opportunity platforms and safety nets: corporate citizenship and reputational risk', *Business and Society Review*, **105**(1), 85–106.

Food Safety Act (1990) http://www.food.gov.uk/foodindustry/guidancenotes/hygguid/outbreakmanagement (accessed 19 April 2011).

Food Standards Agency (FSA) (2001) *Task Force on the Burdens of Food Regulations on Small Food Businesses*. London: Food Standards Agency.

Food Standards Agency (FSA) (2002) *Catering Workers Hygiene Survey 2002*. London: Food Standards Agency.

Food Standards Agency (FSA) (2003) *Sixth Summary of Progress on the Consolidation and Simplification of Food Hygiene Legislation*. London: Food Standards Agency.

Food Standards Agency (FSA) (2007a) *Annual Report of Incidents 2006*. London: Food Standards Agency.

Food Standards Agency (FSA) (2007b) *Report of the Sudan I Review Panel*. London: Food Standards Agency.

Freeman, P.K. and H. Kunreuther (1997) *Managing Environmental Risk through Insurance*. Boston, MA: Kluwer Academic Publishers.

Frewer L.J., S. Miles and R. Marsh (2002) 'The media and genetically modified foods: evidence in support of social amplification of risk', *Risk Analysis*, **22**(4), 701–11.

Froud, J. (1998) *Controlling the Regulators*. London: Macmillan.

Fulponi, L. (2006) 'Private voluntary standards in the food system: the perspective of major food retailers in OECD countries', *Food Policy*, **31**(1), 1–13.

Gabe, J. (1995) 'Health, medicine and risk: the need for a social approach', in J. Gabe (ed.), *Medicine, Health and Risk: Sociological approaches*. Oxford: Blackwell, pp. 1–18.

Genn, H. (1993) 'Business responses to the regulation of health and safety in England', *Law & Policy*, **15**, 219–33.

Giddens, A. (1990) *The Consequences of Modernity*. Cambridge: Polity Press.

Giddens, A. (1999) 'Risk and responsibility', *Modern Law Review*, **62**(1), 1–10.

Grabosky, P. (1994) 'Green markets: environmental regulation by the private sector', *Law & Policy*, **16**(4), 419–48.

Grabosky, P. (1995) 'Using non-governmental resources to foster regulatory compliance', *Governance*, **8**(4), 527–50.

Grabosky, P. and J. Braithwaite (1986) *Of Manners Gentle: Enforcement Strategies of Australian Business Regulatory Agencies*. Melbourne: Oxford University Press.

Gray, W.B. and J.T. Scholz (1991) 'Analyzing the equity and efficiency of OSHA enforcement', *Law & Policy*, **13**(3), 185–214.

Green, E., A. Draper and E. Dowler (2003) 'Short cuts to safety: risk and "rules of thumb" in accounts of food choice', *Health, Risk & Society*, **5**(1), 33–52.

Gricar, B. (1983) 'A preliminary theory of compliance with OSHA regulation', *Research in Corporate Social Performance and Policy*, **5**, 121–41.

Gunningham, N. (1991) 'Private ordering, self-regulation and futures markets: a comparative study of informal social control', *Law & Policy*, **13**, 297–326.

Gunningham, N. (1995) 'Enforcement, self-regulation, and the chemical industry: assessing responsible care', *Law & Policy*, **17**(1), 57–109.

Gunningham, N. (2002) 'Regulating small and medium sized enterprises', *Journal of Environmental Law*, **14**(1), 3–32.

Gunningham, N. and P. Grabosky (1998) *Smart Regulation: Designing Environmental Policy*. Oxford: Clarendon Press.

Gunningham, N. and J. Rees (1997) 'Industry self-regulation: an institutional perspective', *Law & Policy*, **19**(4), 363–414.

Gunningham, N., R.A. Kagan and D. Thornton (2003) *Shades of Green: Business, Regulation, and Environment*. Stanford, CA: Stanford University Press.

Gunningham, N., R.A. Kagan and D. Thornton (2005) 'Motivating management: corporate compliance in environmental protection', *Law & Policy*, **27**(2), 289–316.

Haines, F. (1997) *Corporate Regulation: Beyond 'Punish or Persuade'*. Oxford: Clarendon Press.

Hampel, R. (1998) *Final Report of the Committee on Corporate Governance*. London: Gee Publishing.

Hampton, P. (2005) *Reducing Administrative Burdens: Effective Inspection and Enforcement*. London: HMSO.

Hancher, L. and M. Moran (1989) *Capitalism, Culture and Regulation*. Oxford: Clarendon Press.

Havinga, T. (2006) 'Private regulation of food safety by supermarkets', *Law & Policy*, **28**, 515–33.

Health Protection Agency (2010) *Food Poisoning Notifications – Annual Totals, England and Wales, 1982 – 2009*, http://www.hpa.org.uk/web/HPAwebFile/HPAweb_C/1251473364446 (accessed 30 November 2010).

Heimer, C.A. (1988) 'Social structure, psychology and the estimation of risk', *Annual Review of Sociology*, **14**, 491–519.

Henson, S. and J. Caswell (1999) 'Food safety regulation: an overview of contemporary issues', *Food Policy*, **24**(6), 589–603.

Henson, S. and M. Heasman (1998) 'Food safety regulations and the firm: understanding the process of compliance', *Food Policy*, **23**(1), 9–24.

Henson, S. and N.H. Hooker (2001) 'Private sector management of food safety: public regulation and the role of private controls', *International Food and Agribusiness Management Review*, **4**(1), 7–17.

Hickman, M. (2006) 'The big question: was Edwina Currie right about salmonella in eggs, after all?', *Independent*, 17 November.

Holleran, E., M.E. Bredahl and L. Zaibet (1999) 'Private incentives for adopting food safety and quality assurance', *Food Policy*, **24**(6), 669–83.

Hood, C. and D.K.C. Jones (1996) *Accident and Design*. London: UCL Press.

Hood, C., H. Rothstein and R. Baldwin (2001) *The Government of Risk*. Oxford: Oxford University Press.

Hornibrook, S.A. and A. Fearne, (2003) 'Managing perceived risk as a marketing strategy for beef in the UK foodservice industry', *International Food and Agribusiness Management Review*, **6**(3), 71–93.

Howard-Grenville J., J. Nash and C. Coglianese (2008) 'Constructing the license to operate: internal factors and their influence on corporate environmental decisions', *Law & Policy*, **30**(1), 73–107.

Hutter, B.M. (1988) *The Reasonable Arm of the Law? The Law Enforcement Procedures of Environmental Health Officers*. Oxford: Clarendon Press.

Hutter, B.M. (1997) *Compliance: Regulation & Environment*. Oxford: Clarendon Press.

Hutter, B.M. (2001) *Regulation and Risk: Occupational Health and Safety on the Railways*. Oxford: Oxford University Press.

Hutter, B.M. (2004) 'Risk management and governance', in P. Eliadis, M.M. Hill and M. Howlett (eds), *Designing Government: From Instruments to Governance*. Montreal: McGill-Queen's University Press, pp. 303–21.

Hutter, B.M. (2005) '"Ways of seeing": understanding risk in organisational settings', in B.M. Hutter and M. Power (eds), *Organizational Encounters with Risk*. Cambridge: Cambridge University Press, pp. 67–91.

Hutter, B.M. (2006a) 'The role of non state actors in regulation', in F. Schuppert (ed.), *Contributions to Governance*. Berlin: Nomos, pp. 63–79.

Hutter, B.M. (2006b) 'Risk, regulation and management', in P. Taylor-Gooby and K.O. Zinn (eds), *Risk in Social Science*. Oxford: Cambridge University Press, pp. 202–27.

Hutter, B.M. (ed.) (2010) *Anticipating Risks and Organising Risk Regulation*. Cambridge: Cambridge University Press.

Hutter, B.M. and T. Amodu (2008) *Risk Regulation and Compliance: Food Safety in the UK*. Report prepared for the Pennington Inquiry into the 2005 South Wales *E. coli* outbreak.

Hutter, B.M. and C. Jones (2006) 'Managing risks: who influences businesses?', *Environmental Health Scotland*, **18**(2), 5–9.

Hutter, B.M. and S. Lloyd-Bostock (1992) 'Field level perceptions of risk in regulatory agencies', in J. Short and L. Clarke (eds), *Organizations, Uncertainties, and Risk*. Boulder, CO: Westview Press, pp. 189–203.

Hutter, B.M. and S. Lloyd-Bostock (1997) 'Law's relationship with social science: the interdependence of theory, empirical work, and social relevance in socio-legal studies', in K. Hawkins (ed.), *The Human Face of the Law*. Oxford: Clarendon Press, pp. 19–43.

Hutter, B.M. and J. O'Mahony (2004) 'Business regulation: reviewing the regulatory potential of civil society organisations', CARR Discussion Paper 26, London School of Economics.

Hutter, B.M. and M.K. Power (2005) *Organizational Encounters with Risk*. Cambridge: Cambridge University Press.

Institute of Grocery Distribution (IGD) (1998) 'Consumer attitudes to British meat and fresh produce', *The Food Project Report Series*. Watford: Institute of Grocery Distribution.

Institute of Grocery Distribution (IGD) (2006a) 'UK foodservice market overview factsheet', http://www.igd.com (accessed 23 April 2007).

Institute of Grocery Distribution (IGD) (2006b) 'UK grocery retailing fact-sheet', http://www.igd.com (accessed 23 April 2007).

James, P. (1997) *Food Standards Agency Report – An Interim Proposal by Professor Philip James*. London: HMSO.

Jasanoff, S. (2005) 'Restoring reason: causal narratives and political culture', in B.M. Hutter and M. Power (eds), *Organizational Encounters with Risk*. Hingham, MA: Cambridge University Press, pp. 67–96.

Jones, S.L., S.M. Parry, S.J. O'Brien and S.R. Palmer (2008) 'Are staff management practices and inspection risk ratings associated with food-borne disease outbreaks in the catering industry in England and Wales?', *Journal of Food Protection*, **71**(3), 550–57.

Jordana, J. and D. Levi-Faur (eds) (2004) *The Politics of Regulation: Institutions and Regulatory Reforms for the Age of Governance*. Cheltenham, UK and Northampton, MA, USA: Edward Elgar Publishing.

Jweeping, E., H. Kunreuther and I. Rosenthal (1998) 'Challenges in utilizing third party inspections for preventing major chemical accidents', *Risk Analysis*, **18**(2), 145–53.

Kagan, R. (2006) 'Environmental management style and corporate environmental performance', in C. Coglianese and J. Nash (eds), *Leveraging the Private Sector: Management-based Strategies for Improving Environmental Performance*. Washington, DC: Resources for the Future, pp. 31–48.

Kagan, R. and J. Scholz (1984) 'The "criminology of the corporation" and regulatory enforcement strategies', in K. Hawkins and J. Thomas (eds), *Enforcing Regulation*. Boston, MA: Kluwer Nijhoff, pp. 69–96.

Kirby, M. and K. Gardiner (1997) 'The effectiveness of hygiene training for food handlers', *International Journal of Environmental Health Research*, **7**(3), 251–8.

Kivimaki, M. and R. Kalimo (1993) 'Risk perception among nuclear power plant personnel: a survey', *Risk Analysis*, **13**(4), 421–4.

Kramer, J. and W.G. Scott (2004) 'Food safety knowledge and practices in ready-to-eat food establishments', *International Journal of Environmental Health Research*, **14**(5), 343–50.

Krimsky, S. (1992) 'The role of theory in risk studies', in S. Krimsky and D. Golding (eds), *Social Theories of Risk*. Westport, CN: Praeger, pp. 3–22.

Kunreuther, H. (2002) 'Risk analysis and risk management in an uncertain world', *Risk Analysis*, **22**(4), 655–64.

Kunreuther, H. and G. Heal (2005) 'Interdependencies within an organization', in B.M. Hutter and M.K. Power, *Organizational Encounters with Risk*. Cambridge: Cambridge University Press, pp. 190–208.

Labour Force Survey (2004–05) Office for National Statistics, Social and Vital Statistics Division and Northern Ireland Statistics and Research Agency. Central Survey Unit, Colchester, Essex: UK Data Archive.

Lang, J.T. and W.K. Hallman (2005) 'Who does the public trust? The case of genetically modified food in the United States', *Risk Analysis*, **25**(5), 1241–52.

Little, C.L., D. Lock, J. Barnes and R.T. Mitchell (2003) 'Microbiological quality of food in relation to hazard analysis systems and food hygiene training in UK catering and retail premises', *Communicable Disease and Public Health*, **6**(3), 250–58.

Lloyd-Bostock, S. (2010) 'Public perceptions of risk and "compensation culture" in the UK', in B.M. Hutter (ed.), *Anticipating Risks and Organising Risk Regulation*. Cambridge: Cambridge University Press, pp. 90–113.

Lloyd-Bostock, S. and B.M. Hutter (2008) 'Reforming regulation of the medical profession: the risks of risk-based approaches', *Health, Risk and Society*, **10**(1), 69–83.

Majone, G. (1990) *Deregulation or Re-regulation: Regulatory Reform in Europe and the United States*. London: Pinter.

Majone, G. (1994) *Regulating Europe*. London: Routledge.

Majone, G. (1996) 'The regulatory state and its legitimacy problems', *West European Politics*, **22**(1), 1–24.

Mason, L. and R. Mason (1992) 'A moral appeal for taxpayer compliance: the case for a mass media campaign', *Law & Policy*, **14**(4), 381–99.

May, P.J. (2004) 'Compliance motivations: affirmative and negative bases', *Law and Society Review*, **38**(1), 41–68.

May, P.J. (2005) 'Regulation and compliance motivations: examining different approaches', *Public Administration Review*, **65**(1), 31–44.

Millstone, E. and P. Zwanenberg (2002) 'The evolution of food safety policy-making institutions in the UK, EU and Codex Alimentarius', *Social Policy & Administration*, **36**(6), 593–609.

Minister for the Cabinet Office (1999) *Modernizing Government* White Paper. London: HMSO.

Mori (2005) 'Europeans vote "no" to poor restaurant hygiene', http://www.ipsos-mori.com/researchpublications/researcharchive/495/Europeans-Vote-No-To-Poor-Restaurant-Hygiene.aspx (accessed 20 April 2011).

Mortlock, M.P., A.C. Peters and C.J. Griffith (1999) 'Food hygiene and hazard analysis critical control point in the United Kingdom food industry: practices, perceptions, and attitudes', *Journal of Food Protection*, **62**(7), 786–92.

Mortlock, M.P., A.C. Peters and C.J. Griffith (2000) 'A national survey of food hygiene training and qualification levels in the UK food industry', *International Journal of Environmental Health Research*, **10**(2), 111–23.

National Audit Office (2000) *Supporting Innovation: Managing Risk in Government Departments*. London: HMSO.

Nayga, R.M. (2003) 'Will consumers accept irradiated food products?', *International Journal of Consumer Studies*, **27**(3), 220.

Nelkin, D. and M.S. Brown (1984) *Workers at Risk: Voices from the Workplace*. Chicago, IL: University of Chicago Press.

Ogus, A. (1994) *Regulation: Legal Form and Economic Theory*. Oxford: Clarendon Press.

Osborne, D. and T. Gaebler (1992) *Reinventing Government: How the Entrepreneurial Spirit is Transforming the Public Sector*. Reading, MA: Addison-Wesley.

Otway, H.J. (1985) 'Regulation and risk analysis', in H. Otway and M. Peltu (eds), *Regulating Industrial Risks – Science, Hazards and Public Protection*. London: Butterworths, pp. 1–19.

Paniselloa, P., C. Quantick and M.J. Knowle (1999) 'Towards the implementation of HACCP: results of a UK regional survey', *Food Control*, **10**(2), 87–98.

Parker, C. (2002) *The Open Corporation: Effective Self-regulation and Democracy*. New York: Cambridge University Press.

Parker, C. and V. Nielsen (2001) *Explaining Compliance: Business Responses to Regulation*.

Parliamentary Office for Science and Technology (2003) 'Postnote food poisoning', http://www.parliament.uk/documents/post/pn193.pdf (accessed 30 November 2010).

Paulus, I. (1974) *The Search for Pure Food: A Sociology of Legislation in Britain*. London: Robertson.

Pennington, H. (1998a) *Report on the Circumstances Leading to the 1996 Outbreak of Infection with E. Coli 0157 in Central Scotland, the Implications for Food Safety and the Lessons to be Learned*. London: HMSO.

Pennington, H. (1998b) 'Factors involved in recent outbreaks of escherichia coli O157:H7 in Scotland and recommendations for its control', *Journal of Food Safety*, **18**(4), 383–91.

Pennington, H. (2009) *Public Inquiry into the September 2005 Outbreak of E.coli O157 in South Wales*. London: HMSO.

Perrow, C. (1999) *Normal Accidents: Living with High-risk Technologies.* Princeton, NJ: Princeton University Press.

Phillips Report into BSE (2000) http://www.bse.inquiry.gov.uk (accessed 1 September 2010).

Pidgeon, N. and M. O'Leary (2000) 'Man-made disasters: why technology and organizations (sometimes) fail', *Safety Science*, **34**(1–3), 15–30.

Pidgeon, N., R.E. Kasperson and P. Slovic (eds) (2003) *The Social Amplification of Risk*. Cambridge: Cambridge University Press.

Plough, A. and S. Krimsky (1987) 'The emergence of risk communication studies: social and political context', *Science, Technology and Human Values*, **12**, 4–10.

Pollak, R.A. (1995) 'Regulating risks', *Journal of Economic Literature*, **33**, 179–91.

Powell, S.C., R.W. Attwell and S.J. Massey (1997) 'The impact of training on knowledge and standards of food hygiene – a pilot study', *International Journal of Environmental Health Research*, **7**(4), 329–34.

Power, M. (1997) *The Audit Society: Rituals of Verification*. Oxford: Oxford University Press.

Power, M. (2005) 'Organisational responses to risk: the rise of the chief risk officer', in B.M. Hutter and M. Power (eds), *Organizational Encounters with Risk*. Cambridge: Cambridge University Press, pp. 132–48.

Power, M. (2007) *Organized Uncertainty. Designing a World of Risk Management*. Oxford: Oxford University Press.

Reason, J. (1990) *Human Error*. New York: Cambridge University Press.

Rees, J. (1994) *Hostages of Each Other: The Transformation of Nuclear Safety Since Three Mile Island*. Chicago, IL: University of Chicago Press.

Rees, J. (1997) 'Development of communitarian regulation in the chemical industry', *Law & Policy*, **19**(4), 477–528.

Renn, O. (1992) 'Concepts of risk: a classification', in S. Krimsky and D. Golding (eds), *The Social Theories of Risk*. Westport, CN: Praeger, pp. 53–79.

Rimmington, J. (1992) 'Overview of risk assessment', Risk Assessment Conference, Queen Elizabeth II Conference Centre, London.

Ronit, K. and V. Schneider (1999) 'Global governance through private organizations', *Governance*, **12**(3), 243–66.

Rose-Ackerman, S. (1992) *Rethinking the Progressive Agenda: The Reform of the American Regulatory State*. New York: Free Press.

Rothstein, H. (2004) 'Precautionary bans or sacrificial lambs? Participative regulation and the reform of the UK food safety regime', *Public Administration*, **82**(4), 857–81.

Rothstein, H. (2005) 'Escaping the regulatory net: why regulatory reform can fail consumers', *Law & Policy*, **27**(4), 520–48.

Royal Society (1992) *Risk: Analysis, Perception and Management*. London: Royal Society.

Saint-Martin, D. (2000) *Building the Managerialist State: Consultants and the Politics of Public Sector Reform in Comparative Perspective*. Oxford: Oxford University Press.

Schofield, R. and J. Shaoul (2000) 'Food safety regulation and the conflict of interest: the case of meat safety and E. coli O157', *Public Administration*, **78**(3), 531–54.

Schultz, M., M.J. Hatch and H.M. Larsen (eds) (2000) *The Expressive Organization: Linking Identity, Reputation and the Corporate Brand*. Oxford: Oxford University Press.

Shaw, A. (1999) 'What are "they" doing to our food? Public concerns about food in the UK', *Sociological Research Online*, **4**(3).

Short, J.F. (1992) 'Defining, explaining, and managing risks', in J.F. Short and L. Clarke (eds), *Organizations, Uncertainties, and Risk*. Oxford: Westview Press, pp. 3–23.

Sigler, J.A. and J.E. Murphy (1988) *Interactive Corporate Compliance: An Alternative to Regulatory Compulsion*. New York: Quorum Books.

Skees, J.R., A. Botts and K.A. Zeuli (2001) 'The potential for recall insurance to improve food safety', *International Food and Agribusiness Management Review*, **4**(1), 99–111.

Slovic, P. (1992) 'Perception of risk: reflections on the psychometric paradigm', in S. Krimsky and D. Golding (eds), *The Social Theories of Risk*. Westport, CN: Praeger, pp. 117–52.

Snider, L. (1987) 'Towards a political economy of reform, regulation and corporate crime', *Law & Policy*, **9**, 37–68.

Southwood, R. (1989) *Report of the Working Party on Bovine Spongiform Encephalopathy*. London: Department of Health.

Stone, C.D. (1975) *Where the Law Ends: The Social Control of Corporate Behaviour*. Prospect Heights, IL: Waveland Press.

Sunstein, C.R. (1990) *After the Rights Revolution: Reconceiving the Regulatory State*. Cambridge, MA: Harvard University Press.

Swinnen, J.F.M., J. McCluskey and N. Francken (2005) 'Food safety, the media, and the information market', *Agricultural Economics*, **32**(1), 175–88.

Taylor, E. (2001) 'HACCP in small companies: benefit or burden?', *Food Control,* **12**, 217–22.

Tierney, K.J. (1999) 'Towards a critical sociology of risk', *Sociological Forum*, **14**(2), 215–42.

Turnbull Report (1999) *Internal Control: Guidance for the Directors of Listed Companies Incorporated in the United Kingdom*. London: Institute of Chartered Accountants in England and Wales.

Turner, B. (1978) *Man-made Disasters*. London: Wykeham.

Turner, B. (1988) 'Connoisseurship in the study of organizational cultures', in A. Bryman (ed.), *Doing Research in Organizations*. London: Routledge, pp. 108–22.

Turner, B. (2001) 'Risks, rights and regulation: an overview', *Health, Risk and Society*, **3**, 9–18.

University of Wales, Institute (UWIC) (2006) *Background Report on Food Law and Food Safety. A Report prepared for the Public enquiry into the September 2005 Outbreak of O157 in South Wales*.

Van Erp, J. (2007) 'Effects of disclosure on business compliance: a framework for the analysis of disclosure regimes', *European Food and Feed Law Review*, **2**(5), 255–63.

Van Erp, J. (2008a) 'The impact of "naming and shaming" on business reputations: an empirical study in the field of financial regulation', http://www.regulation.upf.edu/utrecht-08-papers/verp.pdf (accessed 3 November 2010).

Van Erp, J. (2008b) 'Reputational sanctions in private and public regulation', *Erasmus Law Review*, **1**, 145–61.

Van Erp, J. (2010) 'Regulatory disclosure of offending companies in the Dutch financial market: consumer protection or enforcement publicity?', *Law & Policy*, **32**(4), 407–33.

Vaughan, D. (1982) 'Towards understanding unlawful organizational behavior', *Michigan Law Review*, **80**, 201–26.

Vaughan, D. (1989) 'Regulating risk: implications of the Challenger accident', *Law & Policy*, **11**, 330–49.

Vaughan, D. (1996) *The Challenger Launch Decision: Risky Technology, Culture and Deviance at NASA*. Chicago, IL: University of Chicago Press.

Vaughan, D. (1998) 'Rational choice, situated action, and the social control of organizations', *Law and Society Review*, **32**(1), 23–61.

Vaughan, D. (2005) 'Organizational rituals of risk and error', in B.M. Hutter and M. Power (eds), *Organizational Encounters with Risk*. Cambridge: Cambridge University Press, pp. 33–66.

Vernède, R., F. Verdenius and J. Broeze (2003) 'Traceability in food processing chains – state of the art and future developments', KLICT Position Paper, Wageningen University.

Vickers, I., J. Philip, D. Smallbone and R. Baldock (2005) 'Understanding small firm responses to regulation', *Policy Studies*, **26**(2), 149–69.

Vincent, K. (2004) '"Mad cows" and eurocrats – community responses to the BSE crisis', *European Law Journal*, **10**, 499–517.

Wakefield, S.E.L. and S.J. Elliott (2003) 'Constructing the news: the role of local newspapers in environmental risk communication', *Professional Geographer*, **55**, 216–26.

Walker, E., C. Pritchard and S. Forsythe (2003) 'Food handlers' hygiene knowledge in small food businesses', *Food Control*, **14**(5), 339–43.

Williams, R. and D. Barrett (2000) 'Corporate philanthropy, criminal activity, and firm reputation: is there a link?', *Journal of Business Ethics*, **26**(4), 341–50.

Wilthagen, T. (1993) 'Reflexive rationality in the regulation of occupational health and safety', in R. Rogowski and T. Wilthagen (eds), *Reflexive Labour Law*. Boston, MA: Kluwer-Nijhoff, pp. 345–76.

Winter, M. (2003) 'Responding to the crisis: the policy impact of the foot-and-mouth epidemic', *Political Quarterly*, **74**(1), 47–56.

Worsfold, D. (2001) 'Food safety behaviour in butchers' shops', *Nutrition & Food Science*, **31**, 1–13.

Worsfold, D. (2005) 'A survey of food safety training in small food manufacturers', *International Journal of Environmental Health Research*, **15**(4), 281–8.

Worsfold, D. and C.J. Griffith (2003) 'Widening HACCP implementation in the catering industry', *Food Service Technology*, **3**(3–4), 113–22.

Wright, C. and A. Rwabizambuga (2006) 'Institutional pressures, corporate reputation, and voluntary codes of conduct: an examination of the equator principles', *Business and Society Review*, **111**(1), 89–117.

Yeager, P. (1991) *The Limits of Law: The Public Regulation of Private Pollution*. Cambridge: Cambridge University Press.

Index